Privatization, Thatcherism, and the British State

ANDREW GAMBLE*

THE CRISIS OF SOCIAL DEMOCRACY

The Conservative victory in the 1979 General Election brought into office a government that was determined to end British decline and the crisis of state authority by making an ideological and political break with social democracy. This project has taken its name from the Conservative Prime Minister, Margaret Thatcher. But 'Thatcherism' has always been a highly controversial term. Opinion is divided as to whether the election of the Thatcher Government marked a major watershed in British politics, comparable to 1945. Many have argued that Thatcherism is more noteworthy for its rhetoric than for its achievements. They have been opposed by those who, while admitting that Thatcherism has often been incoherent and contradictory, nevertheless insist that what distinguishes the Thatcher Government from most of its predecessors is its strategic purpose.[1] Thatcherism projects a vision of a new social and economic order, which carries with it major implications for political and legal relationships.[2]

Thatcherism has appeared most clearly as a radical force through its challenge to many features of the existing state. Its main target has been social democracy. During the 1970s it came under strong attack in many countries, both as a form of government and as a governing doctrine. In Britain many of the assumptions and the priorities that had been established in the 1940s and the years of prosperity that followed were questioned and discarded. As the balance of forces between classes and nations shifted, so a new politics began to emerge, giving opportunities for both left and right. Old orthodoxies were swept away.

The 1940s settlement in Britain had created a framework for policy which proved durable. It was based on a series of compromises from which emerged a new understanding about the constraints within which government operated and a new conception about the relationship between the public and private sectors.

At the heart of this settlement was an enlargement of the functions and responsibilities of the state. The public enterprise sector was substantially

*Department of Politics, University of Sheffield, Sheffield, South Yorkshire S10 2TN, England.

1

increased through the nationalization of major public utilities such as gas, electricity, coal, and the railways. Collective welfare provision was extended through implementation of the Beveridge report on social security and the establishment of the National Health Service; public housing programmes were expanded, state education was restructured; and the Government accepted new responsibilities for planning the economy and the environment.

After 1951 with the return of the Conservatives into government the collectivist advance of the 1940s was stemmed but not reversed. The high levels of public spending and taxation remained; so did the bulk of industries taken into public ownership. The prosperity and relative harmony of the 1950s made the 'mixed economy' and the 'Welfare State' seem permanent fixtures of a modern capitalist economy. These reforms appeared to have succeeded in overcoming the defects of capitalism and so blunting the social challenge to it. Many socialists regarded the achievements of the 1940s as compromises – liberal rather than socialist solutions to the problems which capitalism created. But a growing number began to argue that a capitalism reformed by the policies of Keynes and Beveridge was a capitalism within which all the key objectives of socialism could be achieved.[3] Public ownership of the means of production, distribution, and exchange was no longer necessary as a general principle. Public ownership could be decided pragmatically in particular circumstances.

Conservatives came to a similar conclusion. For many in the party the question of public or private ownership has always been a question of expediency not principle. There was a ritual battle over the steel industry, but even here its eventual inclusion in the public sector in 1967 was accepted. As long as the private sector remained vigorous and competitive the existence of a large public sector did not trouble Conservatives.

There was a similar acceptance by the Conservatives of the programmes which made up the Welfare State. Collective funding of education, housing, health, and social security was regarded as a necessary responsibility for government in a modern industrial society. There was argument over how universal some benefits and services should be. Conservatives favoured using selectivity wherever possible in order to reduce the costs of welfare. But there was little questioning of the need for the bulk of welfare services to be provided by the state.

While the economy boomed and prosperity spread the permanence of the 1940s settlement seemed assured. Yet the experience of the boom itself was to sow the seeds for the destruction of the settlement. The failure of the British economy to match the performance of its rivals brought criticism of policies and institutions. Ambitious plans to modernize the British economy and British society were launched in the 1960s. When these only partially achieved their objectives and the high hopes which had been raised were disappointed, there developed more fundamental questioning and a growing polarization of political opinion at first within the two major political parties, and later between them.

The 1940s settlement broke down during the 1970s. Many of its institutions were later dismantled by the Thatcher Government in the 1980s. The policies

THATCHER'S LAW

Edited by

ANDREW GAMBLE

and

CELIA WELLS

GPC
BOOKS

GPC Books is an imprint of the University of Wales Press, 6 Gwennyth Street, Cardiff CF2 4YD

The contents of this book were first published in Journal of Law and Society Vol. 16 No. 1 (1989), and are reprinted with the permission of Basil Blackwell Ltd, 108 Cowley Road, Oxford OX4 1JF

British Library Cataloguing in Publication Data

Thatcher's Law.
  1. Great Britain. Politics, 1979–1989
  I. Gamble, Andrew   II. Wells, C.   III. Journal of law
and society
  320.941

ISBN 0-7083-1053-2

Typeset in Wales by Megaron, Cardiff
Printed in Great Britain by Whitstable Litho Ltd, Whitstable, Kent

Contents

of the Thatcher Government were possible because by the time it took office so many of the policies and the ideas associated with the 1940s had been discredited, and British politics and government had clearly reached an impasse. Political science in the 1970s was dominated by analyses which diagnosed a crisis of state authority both in terms of effectiveness and legitimacy. Notions of 'overload', adversary politics, legitimation crisis, and fiscal crisis were developed to explain what was happening, employing a variety of political and theoretical perspectives.[4]

There was widespread agreement that the framework of post-war politics was no longer facilitating solutions to the problems confronting governments. Managing the economy so as to secure stable prices, full employment, rising living standards, and balanced trade had become much harder by the end of the 1960s and became still more so after the first oil shock and the world recession in 1973-5. Britain fared less well than most similar economies because of earlier failure to remedy the serious weaknesses in British economic performance. In a period of world economic slow-down these weaknesses were fully exposed. The political issue became how to distribute the costs of coping with the recession and creating the conditions to expedite recovery.

The British economy would have faced a difficult period of adjustment in any case at the end of the long boom. It was magnified, however, by the scale of the changes which took place in the world economy during the 1970s. The decline in the ability of the United States of America to perform a hegemonic role in the world economy; the exhaustion of old technological systems and the emergence of new ones; changes in the pattern of the world division of labour; the growing internationalization and interdependence of the world economy; and the development of different occupational and work structures forced a new policy agenda onto all states.[5]

In countries such as Britain this process was accelerated because of the desperate need to find more effective policies to reverse the country's relative economic decline and to restore to its political institutions the legitimacy which had been badly tarnished during the repeated crises of the previous decade.

PRIVATIZATION AND THE THATCHER GOVERNMENT

In Britain crucial steps which repudiated the 1940s settlement and recognized the new agenda were taken by the Labour Government from 1975 onwards. But the political initiative was captured by the Conservatives. Under Margaret Thatcher, who ousted Edward Heath from the party leadership in 1975, the Conservatives successfully identified themselves with the new policy agenda by repudiating many aspects of the 1940s settlement and developed a programme influenced by the radical ideas of the New Right.

Thatcher's pronounced ideological stance was unusual for a Conservative Party leader. So, too, was her rejection of the politics of consensus and compromise and her embrace of conviction politics. This rhetoric, however, was always much more radical than the policies which were adopted in opposition or pursued in government.[6] Nevertheless, the change in style and direction was pronounced enough to justify talk of 1979 as a watershed election and to credit the Conservative Government of the 1980s as having launched the 'Thatcher Revolution'. Conservative supporters of Margaret Thatcher were not backward in making claims for the scope and importance of the changes she was introducing.[7]

One of the most distinctive new policies which came to symbolize the determination of the Thatcher Government to reverse the 1940s settlement was privatization. Selling nationalized industries back into private ownership was visible proof that collectivism could be turned back. Yet although privatization figured within private discussions on policy within the Conservative Party before 1979, and was an explicit premise in the kind of thinking enshrined in the secret Ridley Report of 1978,[8] there was no public commitment to denationalization either before the election or in the 1979 manifesto. The Conservatives were committed to reforming industrial relations, and to running nationalized industries as commercial concerns, but not to selling them off. The Government seems to have stumbled into the policy. Having successfully piloted the sale of a few small publicly-owned industries and assets, ministers began to realize that the principle could be extended. It was not until 1983 and 1984 that ministers began to set out the principles behind privatization and to justify the measures that had already been taken as part of a coherent programme.

From the beginning privatization was always wider than simple denationalization – the reversal of earlier measures of nationalization. It has come to be the term used for all withdrawals from direct state involvement in the provision of goods and services. Privatization is best considered not as a single doctrine, still less as a blueprint, but as a set of rather disparate and often uncoordinated initiatives, which taken together have far-reaching implications. The privatization programme raises some key questions for analysis, in particular the legal and constitutional implications of such major changes in the relationship between state and the economy and the wider civil society. These implications are explored in the essays that follow which focus on particular aspects of privatization.

THE PROGRAMME AND IDEOLOGY OF THE NEW RIGHT

One of the sources of inspiration for the privatization programme was the ideas of the New Right. The New Right is not a unified movement or a single body of doctrine. The term itself is a contentious one and it is important to distinguish between the liberal and conservative strands of the New Right. What unites all its strands, however, and justifies the use of the term 'New Right' for this strange amalgam of individuals, pressure groups, and research institutes, is their common rejection and criticism of the ideas, institutions, and policies of social democracy, of corporatism, and of the 1940s settlement.[9]

What the New Right seeks is the redefinition of the relationship between the state and the economy. But except among the anarcho-capitalist fringe of the New Right there is no disposition to do away with the state altogether. Rather, the emphasis is upon stripping from the state the extended roles and additional functions which have been placed upon it during the social democratic era in order to restore its authority and make the state strong again.

The New Right seeks to create a free economy and a strong state; only if the economy is free can the state be strong; and only if the state is strong can the economy be free. For the New Right the remorseless growth of the modern state, measured by its spending programmes and the range of its interventions, has been a disaster and must be reversed if a free and prosperous society is to survive.

One of the greatest evils identified in New Right literature is the way in which the expanding state leads to the replacement of market exchange by political bargaining. This politicization of decision-making is the consequence of state intervention and has to be reversed.

The faith in market co-ordination as superior to any form of political or administrative co-ordination is fundamental to the thinking of the liberal New Right, and provides the ideological underpinning for the notion of privatization. Four particular arguments can be found in New Right literature as to why markets are superior:[10] (i) state intervention does not work; (ii) all alternatives to markets are deeply flawed; (iii) government failure is more prevalent than market failure; (iv) anything beyond the minimal state violates individual rights.

The first argument concentrates on empirical demonstrations that state intervention produces inefficiency and waste, because it leads to decisions which ignore or override factors which markets would recognize. This is a restatement of the classic free market case, applied to the analysis of the working of contemporary policies – ranging from macro-economic management to micro-controls and regulations.[11]

The other three arguments are theoretical arguments that assert the inherent drawbacks of state activity beyond a certain minimum. The New Right draws on work by the Austrian school to claim that there exists no alternative to markets for co-ordinating activity in an economy with a developed division of labour. The dispersed character of information makes a centralized system of co-ordination extremely inefficient in allocating resources and providing incentives.[12]

The nature of public sector decision-making has been analysed with the aid of economic models. New Right authors argue that for too long the imperfect real-world market has been compared with the perfect idealized state. The idea of an omniscient and omnipotent state dedicated to realizing the public interest is rejected in favour of a model that treats the state as peopled by individual politicians and officials. Like all individuals they are assumed to maximize utility in pursuing their interests. Where they differ from the individuals in private markets is that they are not subject to budget constraints or to competition in doing so. The outcomes of public decision-making

5

processes reflect the nature of bureaucratic and political organization and the calculation of the individuals within them as to how best to advance their interests. The strength of the New Right critique is that individuals cannot be blamed for acting as they do; they are acting rationally. What is wrong is the politicization of decision-making which allows so many decisions to be taken by politicians and officials instead of by producers and consumers.[13]

This theoretical assault has been further buttressed by philosophical arguments that defend the concept of a minimal state and seek to show that any concept of an extended state which involves redistribution of income and wealth violates individual rights. Taxation and public spending programmes, except where these are directed to supporting the basic functions of the state – the preservation of law, order, and a stable currency, involve coercion and hence are illegitimate.[14] The detailed arguments for this position and the objections to them do not concern us here. What such arguments demonstrate is the root and branch rejection of the case for collectivism and the new optimism and confidence of the defenders of the liberal case.

New Right ideas became increasingly influential during the 1970s. They were seized upon by the groups around Thatcher, and played a part in the development of the new Conservative programme. That programme initially was characterized as monetarist, because such emphasis was placed upon the macro-economic policies for reducing inflation. But the commitment to making sound money the priority for macro-economic stabilization and the abandonment of any direct government responsibility for full employment and rising living standards obscured the more long-term supply-side policies to which the Government was also committed but which took longer to become established.

The central objective of the Thatcher Government has been to roll back the state by reducing the level and range of government interventions in the economy. This was to be achieved by restoring sound money, by reducing public expenditure both in absolute terms and as a proportion of Gross Domestic Product, and by removing all obstacles to the working of free markets.

The Thatcher Government aims to restore both the effectiveness and the legitimacy of government. It has had no detailed blueprint for policy. Like all administrations, many of its policies have been improvised, dictated by immediate circumstances and pressures. In some cases this has meant the Government achieving the opposite of that intended. The most celebrated example of this was when public expenditure and taxation rose rather than fell during the first phase of the Thatcher Government.

The record of the Thatcher Government, far from being the smooth planned application of Conservative principles to the problems of the economy, has been a series of blunders. The Government made some major misjudgements during its first two years. Its monetary targets led to a rapid rise in interest rates and coincided with the second oil shock. As a result, sterling rose to very high levels. The combination of an overvalued pound sterling and excessive interest rates put enormous pressure on British industry at the very moment that the world economy was moving back into recession. The result was a severe shake-out of labour and widespread bankruptcies. Unemployment climbed sharply, eventually peaking at over three million.[15]

There is little doubt that the great shake-out was not intended by government ministers. Their intention had been to squeeze inflation gradually out of the economy. What they managed to engineer was a very rapid deflation which administered a very severe shock to the manufacturing sector, wiping out a large part of it. From this low base at the end of 1981 the economy began to recover.

The monetarist experiment lasted only two years. Its high water mark was reached in the 1981 budget when the Chancellor of the Exchequer increased taxation and deflated the economy further in the midst of the recession. But after that point, with inflation falling rapidly, monetarism was quietly abandoned, the monetary targets were revised or ignored, and the Government began to practise discretionary economic management once again. The focus switched to the supply-side aspects of policy – how a capitalist economy might be reinvigorated.

The Government was determined from the outset to break with the assumptions and priorities of the 1940s settlement, and this meant trying out a range of policies which experimented with reducing the role of the state. They included the dismantling of corporatism, the encouragement of popular capitalism through schemes to widen property ownership, and measures to reduce trade union political and bargaining strength. But the programme which achieved the greatest momentum of all was privatization.

THE PRIVATIZATION PROGRAMME

By 1987 privatization had become one of the most distinctive policies and themes of the Thatcher Government. It had not always been so. There was no mention of privatization in the 1979 manifesto. The policy developed not from any blueprint or comprehensive plan developed in opposition, but from a series of *ad hoc* decisions and experiments. The scope of the policy was broadened considerably during the early years of the Thatcher Government, and was given retrospective justification and coherence by government ministers, particularly John Moore MP.

However, the policy did have important antecedents. There was no doubting the hostility of the New Right to all forms of public enterprise and to the delivery of services through the public sector. There had been much analysis and discussion through the 1970s concerning the desirability of returning nationalized industries to the private sector and dismantling the public provision of welfare.

What had previously acted as a break on policy in this area was firstly an estimate of what was politically practicable, and secondly a judgement of how important a principle was at stake. Conservatives had in the past had few difficulties in accepting a nationalized sector of industry, particularly in the area of public utilities, or in endorsing the Welfare State. Conservative Governments had been instrumental in the development of both. The traditional piecemeal, pragmatic attitude of Conservatives to change ruled out a crusade against the state sector. Mistrusting simple ideological solutions to questions of public policy, Conservatives had favoured minor adjustments to the role of the public sector rather than radical reorganization.[16]

There had always been those in the Conservative Party, however, who thought differently, and who argued that the Conservatives had betrayed their traditions by accepting such a large change in the relationship between state and civil society which the reforms of the 1945 Labour Government required. In the 1960s Enoch Powell MP had breathed new life into the party's libertarian tradition through his speeches in favour of market liberalism. He specifically called amongst other things for the denationalization of all the major state industries:

> It is . . . widely regarded, even among those who most desire it, as impracticable to denationalize a wide range of the nationalized industries. . . . Therefore everyone settles down into a sort of glazed hopelessness . . . concluding that whenever the Socialists are in, nationalization always advances, and whenever the Conservatives are in, nationalization always retreats. So they accept that they are regrettably fated to live in a country increasingly under State control. Thus every Conservative feels a growing sense of contradiction: he proclaims capitalism, but acquiesces in socialism.[17]

Powell asserted that so long as a Conservative Government had the will to do it, there was nothing impracticable about denationalizing all the nationalized industries.

In this area as in so many others Powell anticipated ideas that were to become influential in the formation of Thatcherism in the 1970s. In proposing denationalization he was not so much out of step with his party as appeared at the time. The far-reaching policy review which Edward Heath had initiated in the 1960s had explored the feasibility of denationalization and a switch from universal to selective welfare benefits.[18] Key aspects of the new agenda with which Thatcher was later to become identified were already being discussed in the 1960s. It influenced the strategy of disengagement which the Heath Government launched in its first eighteen months in office. But, as Powell correctly saw, it would require exceptional political will, as well as favourable political circumstances, to initiate and carry through such a substantial change in policy.

The idea that Conservatives should stop simply trying to administer the existing state, and reverse what Keith Joseph MP – in similar vein to Powell – called the ratchet of socialism, grew in force after the shipwreck of the Heath Government in 1974. Nevertheless, the precariousness of the Conservatives' position dictated caution. The new leadership knew the broad direction in which it wanted to move, but it did not wish to excite opposition unnecessarily by including in its manifesto policies which it might be unable to deliver.

One major clue, however, to the longer-term strategic thinking of the leadership was the Ridley Report on nationalized industries, leaked in 1978 to *The Economist*. This report identified the political problems which the nationalized industries and their unions would create for a Conservative Government and suggested ways in which the problem could be handled. Along with the suggestions as to how to provoke and break strikes, which attracted most attention, the Ridley report also clearly signalled the long-term aim of moving nationalized industries out of the public sector once they had been reconstructed and the battle against their workforces won.[19]

The cautious, non-committal statements about the nationalized industries in 1979 contrast sharply with the claims that were being made for privatization by 1983 and still more by 1987. After the shock of the monetarist slump in the first two years of the Thatcher Government, privatization emerged as one of the major themes of the economic recovery and of the Government's plans for the economy.

Denationalization was an important part of privatization, with the great flotations of British Telecom and British Gas. But privatization came to signify much more than this. It became the term used to describe the new relationship which the Government wished to see between the state and civil society.

The new doctrine of privatization – invention of the term is claimed by David Howell MP, one of the veterans of the policy reviews in the 1960s – was forcefully set out in relation to nationalized industries by John Moore MP, Financial Secretary to the Treasury in 1983:

> Privatization is a key element of the government's economic strategy. It will lead to a fundamental shift in the balance between the public and private sectors. It is already bringing about a profound change in attitudes within state industries. And it opens up exciting possibilities for the consumer; better pay, conditions and employment opportunities for the employees; and new freedom for the managers of the industries concerned.[20]

Moore considerably overstressed the coherence of the policy. He also oversimplified its rationale when he stated in the same speech that the main objective of privatization was to promote competition and improve efficiency. This objective was the one to which the Government usually gave least attention. What his speech indicated, however, was how potent a symbol privatization had become.

THE DIFFERENT KINDS OF PRIVATIZATION

Privatization refers to a number of different policy initiatives launched under the Thatcher Government.[21] The most basic distinction is between the privatization of assets and the privatization of services. The former includes the sale of nationalized industries and government shareholdings in private companies, government land and property, and council houses. This is where the shift in the balance between public and private sectors has been most marked. The transfer from public to private ownership of so many state assets will be seen as a distinguishing feature of the Thatcher years. It is discussed in detail by James Foreman-Peck in relation to the nationalized industries, and by Roger Burridge and Ann Stewart in relation to housing.

The second sense in which privatization is used – the privatization of services – is less dramatic and more complex, but no less important for an understanding of the overall thrust of the strategy to create a free economy. Privatization in this area is often much less clear-cut than in the case of denationalization. It involves the reorganization of the state sector, and changes in the responsibilities and tasks of different agencies. In the essays that follow, Martin Loughlin provides an overall account of the implications of these changes for the relationship between central and sub-central government; Geoff Whitty and Ian Menter analyse the different strategies employed in education; Pete Alcock investigates the impact on social security and the erosion of the notion of rights to state welfare; Jane Lewis analyses the additional burdens placed on women by the contraction of state support for community care.

Four important ways of privatizing public services have been employed. They are charging, contracting out, liberalization, and withdrawal.

Charging involves making users pay for services, although the provision of the service remains in public hands. The main change lies in how the service is financed. Individual contributions replace central or local taxation. Sometimes charges are imposed for the first time; sometimes they are raised to what are considered 'market levels'. In either case an attempt is made to transfer the burden of providing the service from the individual as taxpayer to the individual as consumer. Examples of this type of privatization include education, health, pensions, and housing.

Contracting out is more radical than charging because it means that the service is provided by the private sector. The state gives up its role in service delivery, and instead retreats to an enabling role. It remains the client for the service and invites bids from private companies – and if necessary from its own employees, for example, in the case of direct labour organizations. It chooses the best bid and contracts out the service. If it is not satisfied by the performance it need not renew the contract. The public body is therefore able to select the contractor who offers to provide the required service at the lowest possible cost and the highest possible quality. Contracting out implies a very large reduction in the number of people directly employed by the state and other public bodies, and the curtailment of the role of public sector managers, so that they become concerned primarily with assessing rival tenders rather than with the direct provision of services. Instances of contracting out strategies are discussed by Whitty and Menter and by Burridge and Stewart in relation to education and housing.

Liberalization means the introduction of competition in order to break up monopoly power, whether this is exercised by a company, an agency, or a profession. In principle liberalization could permit competition to be between different agencies within the public sector, but in practice it is more likely to involve the injection of competition by the licensing of private sector companies. As a policy, liberalization goes beyond the confines of the public sector. Many groups in the past succeeded in establishing monopoly positions, often with state support. By withdrawing its protection and legislating to enforce competition the state obliges all institutions to submit to market criteria. Examples of sectors where attempts have been made to promote liberalization include telecommunications, broadcasting, transport, and the optician service. The issues involved in public regulation are discussed by Foreman-Peck.

Withdrawal is a form of privatization which involves the state abandoning its responsibility for the provision of a particular service. The responsibility is shifted to the private sector, either to voluntary organizations in civil society or more often to families. Government policies towards social security and community care analysed by Alcock and Lewis describe two instances of this process.

By removing community care from the formal to the informal sector the Government assumes that there is a strong informal sector capable of taking up the burden. This burden falls largely on women, and therefore contributes to the feminization of poverty. Privatization in this sense means imprisonment of some individuals, mainly women, in a private sphere because of the withdrawal of state support which would allow them the same access to the public sphere of civil society as other citizens.

THE POLITICAL CALCULUS OF PRIVATIZATION

If the term 'privatization' has a wide range of meanings, it also has been pursued by the Government for a wide range of reasons. There has never been one single coherent privatization programme. Each measure of privatization needs to be analysed to see what particular set of aims and circumstances prompted it.

At least six principal objectives of the privatization programme have been identified: the extension of freedom of choice; efficiency and the elimination of waste; the reduction of the Public Sector Borrowing Requirement; the control of public sector pay and weakening of the power of public sector unions; the removal of many decisions from the political process altogether; the widening of share ownership both among citizens and employees; the promotion of liberalization and competition; and the enlargement of active citizenship and the contraction of state dependency.[22]

These objectives are not all compatible, and there have been many instances when the Government has been forced to make trade-offs between its different objectives. Cento Veljanovski defends the Government by arguing that critics of the proposals for selling state assets fail to understand the political context in which privatization has to take place, and judge the programme by the inappropriate standard of whether it has promoted greater liberalization and competition.

This standard may be inappropriate, although since it was the main objective of privatization proclaimed by John Moore MP, it would seem to be the criterion by which the Government would wish to be judged. But Veljanovski's approach has much to commend it. Indeed, the actions of the

Government only become explicable when there is some understanding of how it calculated the trade-offs between its different goals.

The priority the Government gave to its different objectives helped determine the timing of the disposal of state assets, and the kind of industries that were established in the private sector. The Government in general did not seek to break up major state monopolies like British Telecom and British Gas, but instead preferred to sell them relatively intact, with only limited attention given to allowing new competitors into the industry and setting up appropriate regulatory machinery.

Critics argued that in this way a great opportunity was lost, and that the performance of a private monopoly was likely to be as inefficient as the public sector monopoly it replaced. The Government was charged with being more interested in maximizing the revenue for the Treasury than in establishing a genuinely competitive regime for the new industry.

Maximizing revenue from the sale and making as large a contribution as possible to the reduction of the Public Sector Borrowing Requirement were certainly important subsidiary aims. Another important goal, however, in many of the big sales was to widen share ownership among employees of the former nationalized industry and the general public. The size of the sales made the Government anxious to secure a transfer that was as smooth as possible. This requirement was difficult to realize without the willing co-operation of the management of the nationalized industry, and inevitably the management opposed the breaking up of their industry. In order to placate public sector managers, therefore, the Government gave less priority to the achievement of liberalization, and concentrated on the goals of raising money for the Exchequer and widening share ownership.

Just as the Labour Government after 1945 had compromised on the terms in which it had introduced nationalization in order to ensure the smoothest possible political transfer to ownership, so the Thatcher Government compromised in the way in which it introduced privatization. To their critics both Labour and Conservative Governments failed to realize the full potential that a change of ownership could create. But supporters argued that such compromises were necessary in order to win a wider strategic battle. The sale of particular nationalized industries was regarded as making an important contribution to the wider programme of privatization – to shift attitudes and criteria, and to make the market once more the arbiter of public policy. Government was to have in future a supportive enabling role in the economy, rather than a controlling and interventionist role. Any measure which increased choice, reduced dependency on the state, and reduced the range of decisions which were subject to the political process, was regarded as beneficial.

The Thatcher Government was playing for high stakes. To advance its wider political goals it had to be sure to do nothing to weaken its political position. It was therefore normally prepared to be cautious and flexible, aiming to outstay its enemies rather than necessarily confront them, although at times it was prepared to do this as well. As the initial privatizations of assets proved successful the Government grew bolder and more confident and began to plan larger and larger privatizations. But the accidental and circumstantial nature of the process should not be overlooked.

The first privatizations of assets were all small affairs – like the sale of the shareholdings of the National Enterprise Board. Apart from Britoil in 1982 the first really major privatization was British Telecom in 1984. At first there was no intention to sell it off. All the planning was devoted to how to introduce competition into the industry while maintaining British Telecom in the public sector. But when government ministers were faced with the problem of financing British Telecom's investment plans without significantly adding to the Public Sector Borrowing Requirement, privatization suddenly became an attractive option. Once in the private sector British Telecom's management would be free to raise whatever they needed through the money markets.

LAW AND THATCHERISM

A common response to the Thatcher Government has been to contrast its radical rhetoric with its rather meagre accomplishments. But although this is a necessary corrective to some of the more romantic interpretations of Thatcherism it is easily overdone. The radicalism of the Thatcher Government has not consisted in the implementation of detailed blueprints. Nevertheless, the cumulative impact of the actions and policies of the Thatcher Government has challenged established institutions, shifted the priorities governing policy, and re-defined the limits of the politically practicable.

One key aspect of this challenge to the old consensus is constitutional. The Thatcher Government, while not espousing any new constitutional doctrine, has encouraged a new relationship between state and civil society. A state tradition in the European sense never developed in Britain, and there has always been reluctance to develop a body of public law for the regulation of civil society. The British state preferred to rule through public bodies and informal networks.[23]

The resistance in Britain to developing a coherent legal conception of the state and its relationship to civil society posed obvious difficulties during the rise of the extended collectivist state in the twentieth century. The operations of this state and its agents could be reconciled only with difficulty with the character of British public law. In the theory of the constitution there remained a clear separation between the public and private sectors, although in practice the line became increasingly blurred.

The reconciliation between the expanding functions of the state and the liberal bias of the constitution was achieved through the erection of a dense network of public agencies with varying degrees of autonomy from the centre, and the gradual accumulation of precedents and guidelines which helped define a consensus on the objectives and the implementation of policy between the different actors involved.

In Britain new functions and roles for government tended to be accommodated within existing constitutional forms. Institutional continuity and the formal character of the British state were preserved even while the substance and reach of government were altering substantially.

This contrast between the form and substance of British government has been much analysed. Keith Middlemass has pointed to the trend towards corporate bias in British government since the 1920s, and the decline of Parliament. In his account it was necessary for the major producer interests to emerge as governing institutions in order to make possible the economic and political management of an increasingly complex society.[25]

The success with which interests were accommodated, consensus maintained, and the state extended, while the old constitutional doctrines of parliamentary sovereignty and the new separation of powers remained intact, was often hailed as a triumph of British political genius. But amidst the economic and political turbulence of the 1970s the defects of these arrangements were more often noted than their merits. One influential interpretation of the causes of Britain's relative economic decline ascribes it to the failure of the many attempts to construct a developmental state in Britain. The lack of a strong executive with the powers to implement policy is perceived as the cause of many policy failures.

In David Marquand's recent forceful statement of this thesis social democracy has never had a proper trial in Britain because the institutional and constitutional conditions for its success have never been present. The liberal ethos of the British state and public institutions has been strong enough to prevent the reorganization of the state and the reform of major institutions that were required for the establishment of a successful social democratic regime.[26]

As Loughlin argues below, social democratic regimes have been legitimated through their success in delivering economic growth and prosperity. What unhinged social democracy in Britain was the relative failure of the regime to deliver prosperity and growth, not as measured by its own previous performance, but in comparison with the performance of its main trading partners. This failure destroyed the domestic consensus on collectivist welfare, Keynesian demand management, and the status of the trade unions as a governing institution.

It is against this background that the Thatcherite project has to be assessed. There are elements of radicalism and conservatism in the project. The project has been radical in so far as it has challenged so many of the institutions of post-war social democracy and even the very idea that consensus is required for good government. The ideas and practices of institutions throughout the public sector have been shaken up by the skilful deployment of not one but a range of policies. At the same time, the project has been conservative because the ideal that has guided the various challenges has been the hope of returning to a much simpler relationship between state and civil society, the recreation of a liberal regime, in which government's role is once more only regulatory and enabling, not interventionist and executive.

The Thatcherite project in its intentions – although much more haltingly in its practice – repudiates post-war social democracy and, indeed, most of twentieth-century collectivism. It seeks to strip away the encroachments of the state on market exchanges between individuals, and restore the tarnished character of the British liberal polity. It wants to close the gap between the theory and the practice of the British constitution, and bring back limited politics by drastically restricting the scope and number of the decisions that are made by public bodies.

As the contributors to this special issue of the *Journal of Law and Society* make clear, however, the Government's consistency in pursuit of this goal has been very uneven. This introduction has concentrated on the programme of privatization, and the political calculus that has determined the Government's moves in this area. The Government has constantly had to make trade-offs between its different objectives. If this is true for privatization it is still more true for the whole Thatcherite project, where the liberal and conservative strands of the New Right have often been in conflict.

The Thatcher Government has sought to promote a free economy and a strong state, but these terms and the relationship between them are understood differently by the groups that have rallied around Thatcher. The market liberals on the New Right make the achievement of a free economy the main priority. The state has to be strong to police the market order and overcome the resistance of any organized interests to the application of its rules. It also has to be limited so that it does not encroach on the sphere of individual market exchange. As Foreman-Peck shows, these ideas have guided the Government's thinking in its approach to the nationalized industries.

For the conservative strand of the New Right the emphasis is reversed. The priority is to establish and maintain state authority. A free economy in the sense of a private domain in which individuals own and enjoy property is an important bulwark of state authority, but it is not an end in itself. It is part of a wider system of institutions which makes social order possible and finds its highest expression in the state. These institutions had been understood in the past to include education, public housing, social security, and community care. Privatization, as interpreted by some of its more radical advocates, threatens to pull down all these institutions.

The gulf between market liberal and conservative conceptions runs deep. It accounts for some of the hesitancy and inconsistency that has been observed in the actual implementation of the programme. Deregulation, for example, is an essential part of the programme for a free economy, but the Thatcher Government at the same time baulks at many of the consequences – such as the free choice of life styles. The Government would prefer to impose a solidaristic national culture with a restricted set of approved life styles, but this nostalgic and reactionary notion is constantly undermined by the individualism which the free market sedulously fosters. Similarly, the Government advocates increasing censorship of the content of television programmes, picking up demands long urged by campaigners against permissiveness, but at the same time it undermines its own position by pushing ahead with deregulation of television which will make control of programme content more difficult. It wants to strengthen the institution of the family, by encouraging women to stay at home and discouraging divorce and family break-up, while at the same time its policies on the labour market enable and require more women than ever to seek employment and become independent agents in civil society rather than dependants within families. It wishes to restore the traditional character and authority of major public institutions like universities, but in applying free market criteria and subordinating these institutions to consumer demand it threatens to destroy what conservatives regard as most precious about them – their ability to safeguard and transmit a particular tradition of learning.

A single-minded bid to promote a free economy as libertarian groups on the New Right propose would lead the Government into a much more radical reshaping of the British state than anything which has appeared so far. The conservative strand of the New Right has had greater influence in the formulation and development of the Thatcherite project. Market liberal ideas have been employed in a number of fields, most notably in the various experiments of privatization, but their use has always been subordinated to the calculation of the political interest of the Conservative Party. Restoring the authority of the British state and the dominance of the Conservatives within it has generally been the most important consideration in the development of policy, rather than any abstract commitment to a free economy as such.

The Thatcherite project, as a result, has often appeared uncertain and unfinished, as several of the contributions to this special issue – in particular those on education and housing – make plain. The Government has been most decisive in pressing home its attack upon those institutions in British society which lend support to the Labour Party and to the regime of social democracy. The weakening of the influence of trade unions and the severe legal restrictions placed on their activities, the curtailment of the functions and the finance of local authorities, the reduction in employment in the public sector, the privatization of nationalized industries, and the sale of council houses have all been pushed through because they brought important strategic gains to the Conservatives, and helped consolidate their dominant electoral position. But in other areas the Conservatives have moved much more cautiously. Taxes have been cut but the tax base has been broadened only slightly, and the Government has so far maintained collective provision in the fields of health and education.

The Government's radicalism has therefore been restrained both by calculation of its political and electoral interests and by tension between the divergent ideological strands of the New Right. But it is also heavily constrained by the institutional character of the state over which it presides. Dispensing with the long-established consensual understandings of the relationship between central government and other public agencies as well as groupings in civil society has not been costless. A further meaning of the free economy and the strong state is that the effect of seeking to create a free economy creates resistance and opposition which in turn requires that the state become more coercive and more repressive. As Alcock and Lewis argue, the full effects of this are experienced by those groups who have been most dependent on state support.

As Norrie and Adelman demonstrate, however, the turn to a strong state in this sense began long before the advent of the Thatcher Government. The balance between coercion and consent has often shifted, but neither is ever entirely eclipsed. What has to be analysed for the Thatcher Government is the precise nature of its turn to more coercive measures. For Norrie and Adelman the Thatcher Government is distinctive because it has been able to draw on a strong vein of popular support for its authoritarianism. The further moves towards a strong state under the Thatcher Government have been precipitated by the conflicts which the pursuit of the free economy have aroused, but they have been facilitated because the Government has been able to mobilize and articulate an authoritarian consensus for many of its measures.

The Thatcher Government has therefore been noteworthy for policies that have promoted a free economy and destroyed many of the pillars of the social democratic regime, but also at the same time for measures that have increased the central powers of the state. The Government has sometimes justified the taking of additional powers as centralizing in order to decentralize. But in many cases, such as the imposition of a national curriculum, or the setting up of new national bodies to replace local government bodies, the prospect of decentralization looks remote. What the Government is apparently intent on doing is to weaken the autonomy and legitimacy of all intermediate institutions, so removing the institutional basis for any opposition to policies determined at the centre. The old collaborative and consensual approaches with local government and trade unions have been rejected. In the new regime legitimate authority is to be concentrated at the centre. There is to be an end to weak government, which is interpreted as the need for the centre to seek consensus for its policies and rely on collaborators among the organized interests of civil society and at local and regional levels of the state.

There are some obvious difficulties with this scenario, however. For it to be successful government needs to be genuinely limited to a few minimal functions, and civil society reorganized so that those forces which support limited government gain an unassailable position, while those forces in favour of extended government are permanently subordinated. But it is not so easy to dismantle the extended state of social democracy. The effect of destroying its political supports while only partially disengaging from its functions makes the implementation of national policy very much more difficult, as Loughlin argues. The Thatcher Government proclaims a limited state but runs an extended state, while denying to itself the assistance of the policy networks that are required to implement its policies.

The result is curious. The Thatcher Government has only partially restored state authority in the sense it understands it because it has only made small steps towards restoring the minimal state. It has continued to preside over the

17

same vast swollen public sector of its predecessors. It has restructured public spending but has not substantially reduced it. It has freed itself from the clutches of some lobbies and special interests, but by no means from all. Rather it has become beholden to a different set of organized interests and lobbies. Like its predecessors, too, it finds itself obliged to manage its empire and to promise superior performance and effective delivery of services.

In this sense there is not much difference between it and its predecessors. Legitimacy is still more determined by economic performance than by a wholesale change in the relationship between state and civil society. The electoral success of the Thatcher Government has been chiefly due to its economic success between 1982 and 1988. Its policies appeared to pay off through a marked improvement in economic performance. This effect was reinforced by carefully targeted policies to reinforce the material well-being of key electoral groups and help dispose them to vote Conservative. Political calculations such as these helped determine several key parts of the privatization programme, including the council house sales and the share offers in nationalized industries.

The big question mark over the Thatcher years, however, is how durable the changes will prove when circumstances change. The success of the Thatcher Government owes much to the dominating personality of Margaret Thatcher herself and to the improved performance of the economy. How will it fare when Margaret Thatcher leaves office and when the economy turns down? Will the new regime be strong enough to withstand the pressure for new extensions of the state?

One of the ironies of Thatcherism is that from a New Right perspective, utilizing the arguments of public choice theory, there is no reason to think that the Thatcher Revolution will be durable. The minimal state is still a distant dream. The Thatcher Government has changed the character of the distributional coalitions in British politics, but it has not managed to abolish distributional coalitions. The Government and Margaret Thatcher herself have been very adept practitioners of what the New Right calls political activism. Ministers have often displayed great skill in highlighting a particular issue, promising action, and obtaining maximum media coverage for it. They have succeeded in mobilizing support, the life-blood of politics. But the follow-through has often been much less impressive. The original objectives of the policy have often been thwarted by the manner in which the policy has been implemented.

There are similar problems with many other aspects of the Thatcher Government from a public choice perspective. The Government has been at its least radical in contemplating changes to the constitution or the organization of government. The power of the bureaucracy is central to the public choice account of why and how the state expands. One of the most important weapons the bureaucracy has is secrecy. Yet it is the secrecy of the governmental process and the traditional relationship between ministers and civil servants which the Thatcher Government has been so keen to defend, when necessary across four continents. There has been no attempt to place legal limits on central government. Instead, the position of the central executive civil service has been strengthened. The power of every organ of government has been reduced and circumscribed with the exception of the power of the central government itself. It is difficult to see how a government which sees no need to limit its own activities but claims an absolute and binding electoral mandate for whatever it does is a credible vehicle for the consolidation of a new limited state.

Rather than the dawning of a new era for the limited state it is far more likely that we are witnessing a change in the way the extended state is organized. Some of its activities are being contracted, others are being expanded. But the overall range of governmental responsibilities and the intrusiveness of government throughout civil society is unlikely to diminish very much. What has changed is the autonomy and legitimacy of most intermediate institutions. Only the central state and the institutions of market exchange are to enjoy legitimacy. The Conservatives would like to see the change in the balance of forces in civil society become permanent, because this would maintain the present pattern of state policy, and freeze out alternatives. But this achievement has no secure popular base behind it, and depends on the economic recovery continuing.

NOTES AND REFERENCES

1 For the debate on Thatcherism see D. Kavanagh, *Thatcherism and British Politics* (1987); R. Jessop et al., *Thatcherism* (1988); A. Gamble, *The Free Economy and the Strong State* (1988).
2 See C. Graham and T. Prosser, *Waiving the Rules* (1988).
3 The most influential book was Anthony Crosland's *The Future of Socialism* published in 1956.
4 For general reviews of this literature see A. H. Birch, 'Overload, Ungovernability, and Delegitimation: The Theories and the British Case' (1984) 14 *Brit. J. Political Science* 135-60; D. Held, 'Power and Legitimacy in Contemporary Britain' in *State and Society in Contemporary Britain*, ed. G. McLennan (1984).
5 See E. A Brett, *The World Economy Since the War* (1985); S. Gill and D. Law, *The Global Political Economy* (1988).
6 P. Riddell, *The Thatcher Government* (1985).
7 See P. Cosgrave, *Thatcher: The First Term* (1985).
8 Details of the Ridley Report appeared in *The Economist*, 27 May 1978.
9 Among many books which survey the New Right are D. King, *The New Right* (1987); N. Barry, *The New Right* (1987); D. Green, *The New Right* (1987); and N. Bosanquet, *After the New Right* (1983).
10 I have explored this argument in greater detail in 'The Political Economy of Freedom' in *The Ideology of the New Right*, ed. R. Levitas (1984).
11 See M. Friedman, *Capitalism and Freedom* (1962).
12 See F. Hayek, *Law, Legislation, and Liberty* (1982).
13 See D. C. Mueller, *Public Choice* (1979).
14 See R. Nozick, *Anarchy, State, and Utopia* (1974).
15 Different interpretations of this record are offered by W. Keegan, *Mrs Thatcher's Economic Experiment* (1984) and G. Maynard, *The Economy under Mrs Thatcher* (1988).
16 See I. Gilmour, *Inside Right* (1977).
17 E. Powell, *Income Tax at 4/3d in the £* (1970) 56-7.

18 The Heath policy review is discussed in J. Ramsden, *The Making of Conservative Party Policy* (1980) ch. 9.
19 Ridley Report, op. cit., n. 8.
20 Parts of John Moore's speeches are reproduced in *Privatization and Regulation – the UK Experience*, ed. J. Kay (1986).
21 Writing on privatization includes Kay, op. cit., n. 20; D. Heald, *Public Expenditure: Its Defence and Reform* (1983); C. Veljanovski, *Selling the State* (1987); M. Pirie, *Privatisation in Theory and Practice* (1985); T. Prosser, *The Nationalized Industries and Public Control – Legal, Constitutional and Political Issues* (1986); D. R. Steele and D. Heald, 'The Privatization of Public Enterprises 1979-83' in *Implementing Government Policy Initiatives – The Thatcher Administration 1979-83*, ed. P. M. Jackson(1985).
22 See the discussion in Veljanovski, op. cit., n. 21; and Steele and Heald, op. cit., n. 21.
23 A point argued strongly by J. Kay and D. Thompson in 'Privatization: A Policy in Search of a Rationale' (1986) 96 *Economic J.* 18.
24 See Prosser (op. cit., n. 21) for a clear statement of this argument.
25 K. Middlemass, *Politics in Industrial Society* (1979).
26 D. Marquand, *The Unprincipled Society* (1988).

Law, Ideologies, and the Political-Administrative System

MARTIN LOUGHLIN*

The modern state is highly differentiated and highly complex. Its complexity is such that it is not easily captured in the languages we use to conceptualize this set of authority-structures. We may perhaps recognize the difficulty most clearly in the orthodox distinctions that are made between state and society, public and private, and planning and the market. But this problem may be seen not only in attempts to conceptualize the role of the state in modern society; it also exists in our characterizations of the internal complexity of the political-administrative system. The separation of powers doctrine, for example, does not accurately grasp the contemporary functions of our institutions of legislature, executive, and courts; the policy-administration distinction is an inadequate expression of the allocation of political and official tasks; and the vision of centralized, hierarchical authority conjured up by the concept of legal sovereignty is belied by any examination of the processes of public policy formation. We live in a world of disjuncture between social and political reality and the public languages through which we try to picture it.

Perhaps the most important of these public languages are those of politics and law. And in both of these languages we can identify the strains arising from the changes of the twentieth century. During this century the rhetoric of political languages has certainly registered a collectivist note – one thinks here of 'One Nation' Toryism, the articulation of conceptions of 'positive liberty' by Liberals, or Labour's vision of 'the Parliamentary road to Socialism'.[1] These collectivist political ideologies, however, have generally been expressed within the language of the authority-structures of the nineteenth century. Furthermore, not only have these ideologies been articulated within the framework of a traditional distinction between state and society, but they have also absorbed the traditional view of the nature of the internal arrangements of the state. That is, these collectivist ideologies have been expressed within terms of a formal separation of powers, a distinction between policy and administration, and the near-exclusive view of a hierarchical, centrally-directed political will. The languages of law are similarly – and, indeed, more

*Faculty of Law and Financial Studies, University of Glasgow, Glasgow G12 8QQ, Scotland.

I am grateful to Tim Murphy for comments on an earlier draft.

rigorously – spoken through that traditional framework. However, because of the dogmatic form of legal discourse, together with the fact that the shift to collectivism has not easily been accommodated in legal discourse, the tension between socio-political realities and law has been particularly acute.

To the extent that there has been a reconciliation of the tensions between these political and legal languages and modern social and political realities, this has taken place within the relatively closed and informal world of the political-administrative system. One consequence for political languages is that they have taken on an increasingly formal character. For law, however, the reconciliation has meant nothing short of its displacement as a means of expressing the constitution of society.

One important question which arises from this analysis concerns the legitimacy of the political-administrative system. How can this system be legitimated if it does not operate in accordance with our traditional languages of legitimation? The answer, it would seem, is that its legitimacy is a function of success. That is, the political-administrative system is legitimated by its achievement in bringing about substantial improvements in material conditions. It delivered the goods. Consequently, throughout much of the twentieth century, when living standards for the majority were improving, the nature of the political-administrative system was not called into question. But by the 1970s the strains were noticeable.

The reasons for these strains are very complex and it is not for us to try to analyse them here. Nevertheless, we may note that most accounts focus on the relationships between state and society. At this level commentators highlight the relationships between the economic crisis and fiscal strain and point to the fact that, in so far as similar sorts of strains have been felt throughout advanced societies, they seem to have a structural dimension.[2] However, it would appear that, whatever the nature of the crisis at the level of state and society, there has also been a crisis *within* the political-administrative system – a calling into question of the structure of the system. Recently the political science literature has abounded with analyses of this crisis; whether in terms of 'institutional sclerosis',[3] 'pluralistic stagnation',[4] 'overload in government',[5] 'the Wenceslas myth',[6] or 'the rationality crisis'.[7]

One apparent consequence of the crisis of understanding in the relationship between state and society has been a paradigmatic shift in the language of political discourse. This shift may be understood crudely as a shift from a collectivistic to an individualistic language. The early recognition of this shift seems to have contributed to the electoral success of the Conservative Party. But – and this is to get closer to the heart of our concerns – this shift from collectivistic to individualistic political discourse has not been accompanied by a more sophisticated characterization of the nature of the modern state. That is, at the state/society level it simply involves a shift from a public to privatistic ethos; from the language of planning to the language of markets. And in terms of the internal arrangements of the political-administrative system, the vision of a hierarchical, one-way flow from policy to administration within the formal language of constitutional discourse has been promoted.

This shift in the language of politics, then, is a shift within an established (and inadequate) framework. This new language, resting on an atomistic view of individuals and an idealized view of markets, is no better able to grasp the complexities of the relationships between state and society. It also fails to provide a more sophisticated view of the internal complexity of the political-administrative system. Nevertheless, because of the political successes of the Conservative Party, the Government has been able to promote ever more radical reforms based on this political outlook.

It would appear that, by failing to acknowledge the complexities of modern realities, many of the policy initiatives will fail to achieve their objectives. This belief is entailed in the stance which is adopted in this paper. However, the paper is not primarily concerned with the success or otherwise of the substantive policies of the Conservative Government. Rather, it will be concerned to explore the impact which the promotion of reforms based on this political ideology has had on our understanding of the role of law in the political-administrative system.

At this point I should enter one caveat. I do not propose to examine reforms to the entire political-administrative system and will be concerned only with the changes in the relationships between central departments and local authorities. I do so not simply on grounds of competence and manageability but also because, whatever the policy importance of developments in other spheres, it is in the field of central-local government relations that we see most clearly the consequences of the switch from collectivist to individualist policies in the context of a highly complex administrative system.

THE ROLE OF LAW IN THE TRADITIONAL FRAMEWORK OF CENTRAL-LOCAL GOVERNMENT RELATIONS

When examining the role of law in the political-administrative system we should bear in mind the fact that we are concerned with a set of relations between institutions which are, in a basic sense, *constituted* by law. If we are to understand these relations we must get to grips with the nature of these constitutive rules. This is a task for which traditional legal theory ill equips us. If, for example, we were to follow the modern trend in viewing law as a species of game, it is clear that bilateral games such as chess are inappropriate models[8] and even more complex games such as cricket are unsatisfactory examples in so far as the objective is primarily to explain the expression 'He is out'.[9] We need to consider models of much more complex games; games which need not be competitive, may not make provision for an authoritative umpire/adjudicator, and do not necessarily prescribe the conditions of success and failure.[10] The model I have in mind is of a system which is more dynamic and fluid and less value-laden than traditional models of legal systems. But it is one that more accurately reflects the relationships between law and the political-administrative system than those presented in traditional legal theory.

In the post-war period, the basic function of law in the sphere of central-local government relations has been to establish a general and flexible framework through which the complex business of government could be conducted. The main business was carried out through administrative processes and in accordance with administrative norms which evolved in the course of practice. While the procedures through which administrative decisions were made were often the subject of statutory regulation, the law did not attempt normative regulation of the objectives of these systems. Whatever was achieved through this framework was the result of bargaining by politicians and administrators. These actors were obviously subject to a range of constraints, including those of inertia, lack of clarity of goals, and limited perceptions as well as obvious resource constraints. But legal constraints were not prominent in this catalogue. The nature of this traditional legal framework may be seen by examining the role of law in relation to local authorities, central departments, and the relations between these two types of agencies.

First, in relation to local authorities, the primary legal objective has been to vest a broad enabling power in authorities. This has permitted authorities to respond to new problems as they have emerged without being unduly constrained by the *ultra vires* doctrine. Local housing authorities, for example, while under a duty 'to *consider* the housing conditions of their district with respect to the provision of further housing accommodation' are simply empowered to provide housing accommodation through the processes of building, converting, acquiring, or repairing.[11] Even when duties have been imposed on local authorities to provide services, the nature of the obligation is ambiguous. Thus, the basic duty of the local education authority is 'to contribute towards the spiritual, moral, mental, and physical development of the community by securing that efficient education . . . shall be available to meet the needs of the population of their area'.[12] It is difficult to construe provisions of this nature as 'Hohfeldian' duties;[13] 'efficiency' in educational provision is not easily determinable through formal court proceedings, particularly when it is loosely tied to such broad and general objectives and when the local authority itself seems best placed to determine the needs of the constituent population. And when we examine the regulatory activities of local authorities we generally find that, although formal procedures have been established, the statutory framework is constructed without any indication of the objectives which the regulatory system is designed to achieve. By so doing, it is possible for the nature of the regulatory system to be radically changed without the need for statutory reform.

In relation to central departments, the pattern is broadly similar. That is, the enabling statutes provide central departments with very broad powers to supervise the activities of local authorities. Central departments are given a variety of supervisory powers, including powers of inspection, inquiry, appeal, approval, and default. In the field of education, for example, the administrative powers of the Secretary of State for Education include the power to establish a local inquiry and to give directions to local authorities if they have failed to discharge any duty imposed on them or if they have acted, or are proposing to act, unreasonably.[14] Furthermore, given the inadequacy of the local tax base, local authorities are financially dependent on central government. In this context central government's power to provide grants in aid of local expenditure is potentially a very important control mechanism. As a result, even the essentially advisory functions of central government take on greater normative force when located within a hierarchical framework or a structure of financial dependency. It was largely in recognition of the possible consequences of financial dependency that during the post-war period the principle was established that the vast bulk of grant-aid would take the form of a general or block grant, unhypothecated to specific services.

The role of law in the post-war system of central-local government relations has, therefore, been to establish a structure which would maximize the ability of local authorities to act and central departments to regulate. Consequently, this legal framework did not aim to establish a normative structure which demarcated matters local from matters central. Nor was this legal framework indicative of the reality of relations within the political-administrative system. Central departments may have possessed very broad supervisory powers, but many of them were rarely used.[15] Local authorities may occasionally have found that the *ultra vires* doctrine frustrated their actions, but often they would simply seek, and obtain, these new powers.[16] In general, the legal structure provided a rather distorted picture of the operational administrative system.[17] The legal constitutive structure was designed not so much to establish the rules of the game but rather to establish a structure in which the rules of the game were internal to the system.

Thus, in order to understand central-local government relations an understanding of 'administrative rules' which had evolved through networks of administrative practices was much more important than a knowledge of the legal formalities. The more important of these administrative networks may be viewed as a 'national world of local government'.[18] Key actors in this national world include professional organizations, whose specialization, national organization, and common technical language facilitates a two-way transmission of accessible knowledge;[19] party political organizations, through which, for example, the centre may make appeals for loyalty in order to try to realize their objectives;[20] and representative associations of the various units of local government, which provide a more formal input/output link between the 'village of Whitehall' and the local government system.[21] This elaborate administrative network operates with virtually no formal statutory recognition.

Law has therefore not been a particularly active force in the shaping of the political-administrative system. Certainly the broad structure was legally constituted and detailed legal procedures were often laid down. But when we come to view these structures dynamically – in terms of what was provided and how – legal matters were of marginal importance. The primary guidance, control, and evaluation mechanisms were informal and were internal to the system.

The Conservative administrations of the 1980s have brought about a fundamental reorganization of this system of central-local government relations. A variety of stories about these changes could be told. The changes may be viewed primarily in terms of a political struggle between Conservative central government and Labour local authorities representing the ideologies of individualism and collectivism.[22] Alternatively one could take what might be termed a structuralist approach. From this perspective, we could focus on the determined pursuit by the Conservative Government of a particular strategy for local government, a strategy drawn essentially from the school of public choice. This is the story of a government seeking to eliminate the redistributive dimension to local government functions; converting all services into trading services or local public goods; and then, by strengthening the mechanisms of exit and voice, trying to privatize as many local authority services as seems feasible.[23]

There is, however, another story to be told. This is not about struggle or structure but primarily about process. It concerns a radical administration with high hopes but short vision or, to put it another way, an administration whose intended reach is greater than its grasp. It is about a government infected by 'hyperactivism' which, Conservatives tell us, 'is a morbid condition . . . because it tends to induce activity before experience has generated enough understanding of our situation to allow us to act wisely'.[24] It is about a government that has reappropriated an individualistic political language but has been unable or unwilling to grasp the complexities of either the state/society relationship or the internal complexity of the political-administrative system.

These different stories obviously are interwoven. The structuralist approach, when viewed as part of a grand depoliticization strategy – an attempt to reduce the political power of local government – blends with the vision of central-local relations as essentially one of struggle. The politic-ization of the central-local relationship challenges the authority of traditional administrative networks and may therefore be seen as a key factor in the process of reconstituting the relationship along hierarchical lines. The structuralist approach seems at least in part based on the view that the political-administrative system which has emerged in post-war Britain is overly bureaucratic, is unresponsive to new challenges, and has become a self-serving set of institutions.

Nevertheless, the main focus I shall adopt in this paper is that of process. This is not only because I have already made some attempt at examining developments from the other perspectives. It is also because, from this perspective, the issue about the functions of law in the political-administrative system is highlighted. It was mentioned in the introductory section that many had identified a growing crisis in the political-administrative system caused not simply as a reverberation of economic crisis but by a belief in the existence of widespread policy failure. The Conservative Government's reforms, then, must not only be seen as a response to a crisis in the state/society relationship but also to this apparent crisis in the political-administrative system. Again, as we have seen, the Government has viewed that system as part of the problem. The apparent solution has been to shake up the system and challenge the conventional practices. In so doing it has undermined the traditional system of central-local government relations, founded on bargaining through administrative networks, and sought to reconstitute the relationship in a different form. In the process of reconstitution, the nature of the legal relationship between central departments and local authorities has been transformed. In fact, it can be argued that the Government's reforms have led to what may be termed a 'juridification' of central-local government relations.

THE JURIDIFICATION OF CENTRAL-LOCAL GOVERNMENT RELATIONS

The juridification of central-local government relations has its roots in two related, though distinct, processes. First, there is legalization of the central-local relationship which arises simply because the Government, in challenging the traditional networks, undermines the authority of those administrative arrangements. To the extent that conventional practices lose their authority, the institutions of central and local government inevitably, and in many cases for the first time, turn to the legal framework in order to determine their rights, duties, powers, and liabilities. Thus, there is a sense in which juridification of the relationship is essentially the result of the existence of the 'normative gap'. However, juridification of the central-local relationship is also a consequence of a particular form of restructuring of the relationship promoted by the Government. This form of restructuring envisages that local authorities will be rule-bound agencies subject, to a much greater degree, to judicial control and that the central-local relationship will be reconstructed in an authoritative, hierarchical form. We will examine each of these processes in turn.

1. *Juridification as a Product of the Normative Gap*

This form of juridification is the one which has been most immediately felt in the 1980s. The signs can be seen in the heightened legal consciousness of actors in the system, the increased importance of lawyers in policy-making processes, and the extent to which basic disputes between agencies within the system are being dealt with by the courts. The clearest example of juridification of relations which results from the disintegration of the traditional framework is to be seen through developments in the field of local government finance in England. In order to examine the nature of juridification which results from the normative gap, we shall therefore focus on this experience.

On assuming office in 1979, the Conservatives felt that the financial mechanisms within the system lay at the heart of many of the problems which they had identified. Considerable effort was put into reforming these mechanisms to provide incentives to reduce expenditure and to restore local financial accountability. The system of grant distribution was comprehensively reformed in 1980 and a new system of capital expenditure controls was introduced.[25] When the new block grant mechanism did not yield the desired economies the Government moved swiftly to amend the system by engrafting on to the block grant mechanism a new set of expenditure targets.[26]

From the outset the Government displayed great political will and was prepared to use to the full the available (including retrospective) legislative powers. But did they succeed in realizing their aims? Hardly. By 1984 local government revenue expenditure was nine per cent higher in real terms than when the Conservatives took office.[27] Furthermore, the consensus of official and academic opinion suggests that responsibility for this state of affairs lay firmly at the Government's door.[28] Consequently, it was 'more out of exasperation than with a conscious sense of direction'[29] that the Rates Act 1984, enabling central government to control the amount of rates which local authorities could raise, was enacted. This measure constituted an unprecedented centralization of political power and threatened 'to undermine what remain[ed] of financial accountability in local government'.[30]

In short, the Government entirely lost control over local government expenditure. There were two main reasons. First, the Government tried to use the grant system to achieve too many conflicting objectives; they did not fully understand the complexity of the system they sought to influence and did not appreciate the limitations of the instruments they had chosen to achieve their objectives. Secondly, the Government's formal directive strategy resulted in the shaking up, if not breaking up, of the informal policy network. But what the Government failed to recognize was the importance of that network to the successful implementation of their objectives. That is, the rejection by the Government of the strategy of incorporation – of using the policy network as a device of policy implementation – had a significant effect on normative control mechanisms. As the Audit Commission stated in 1984, local authorities, recognizing that the nature of the game was changing, 'responded to the uncertainties inherent in the present grant distribution arrangements in an entirely understandable and predictable way'.[31] And a major part of this response was to explore – and use – their formal legal autonomy in financial matters.

This form of legalization of central-local relations placed the Government in great difficulties. It was seeking to establish a 'command and control' regime in a complex financial system that had been established on an informal, consensual, and bargaining foundation. This the Government fully realized only in 1983 when drafting the Rates Bill. The Rates Act 1984 marks a turning point in the drafting of legislation on local government finance. It is drafted like Finance Act legislation; that is, on the assumption that those to whom it is directed will act as utility-maximizers and will explore all available avoidance routes. The Government, having examined the potential avoidance mechanisms, then drafts the legislation in such a manner as to try to ensure that these routes cannot successfully be taken.

As such, the Rates Act 1984 is a very competent piece of drafting, and local authorities have not been able to elicit the support of the courts in throwing spanners in the works.[32] Nevertheless, it has not solved the Government's problems. This is because, when one views the overall system, rate-capping is of marginal importance as a control mechanism. Furthermore, the basic statutory framework laid down in the Local Government, Planning and Land Act 1980 was constructed on the traditional foundations. This means that local authorities can use the discretionary techniques *within the basic framework* rather than within the rate-capping process to try to ensure that they never enter the sphere of rate-capping. Consequently, during the 1980s a major 'creative accounting' industry has emerged to exploit the flexibility within the basic framework, particularly to switch expenditure between revenue and capital accounts and to devise schemes to avoid capital expenditure controls. While the Government has gradually attempted to close down various methods of avoidance[33] it has often been a matter of closing the door after the horse has bolted.[34]

The discretion available to local authorities in the framework of the Local Government, Planning and Land Act 1980 has not been the only problem for the Government in seeking to establish a command and control regime. As we have seen, discretion is one basic feature of the traditional structure of central-local government relations. Other relevant features include both the lack of legal consciousness in the traditional arrangements and also the fact that the traditional legislation had not been drafted with the possibility of adjudication in mind.

This lack of legal consciousness in traditional arrangements has also created problems for the Government in the politicized and legalized environment of the 1980s. Liverpool City Council, for example, in 1984 exploited the fact that there was no statutory requirement to set the general rate by a particular date in order to highlight grievances about grant entitlement.[35] This tactic was then taken up by a number of rate-capped local authorities in 1985, albeit without much success.[36] Once again the Government subsequently acted to formalize the position.[37] The general point here is that so much of the traditional structure of central-local government relations was not reflected in statutory form precisely because the real business was conducted through conventional administrative channels. Furthermore, the traditional arrangements were built on the foundation of partnership and it was never envisaged that authorities would exploit their formal freedoms in this manner. But when the authority of that conventional world is undermined by the termination of the partnership, the conventional authority structure crumbles and the entire system is destabilized.

The related point about the nature of traditional legislation, however, is even more important. If we are required, as a result of the breaking up of the traditional administrative network, to look to the statutory framework in order to reconstruct an authority structure we are placed in certain difficulties. This is not simply because of the problem of lacunae, caused by the lack of legal consciousness when drafting traditional legislation, but also with the fundamental point about the inherent opacity of the legislation. This may be illustrated by example. I defy any lawyer, however skilful, to study Part VI of the Local Government, Planning and Land Act 1980 (establishing the mechanisms for payment of rate support grants) and discern its meaning. It is not simply dense or complicated; it is impenetrable. The reason for this reflects a basic, though neglected, feature of modern regulatory law. What has happened is that the highly complex process of devising systems for distributing grant is carried out through the established policy networks. Once the system has been formed Parliamentary Counsel is required to provide a legal foundation for it. The foundation must not be too specific, because the Government needs the flexibility to adjust it in the light of new circumstances. But it must not be too flexible, because local authorities need certain protections against gross manipulation which could undermine the relative freedoms that lie at the heart of local government. The result is a facilitative, but impenetrable, legal framework which, since it seeks to legitimate a technical economic model, simply cannot be understood *unless* one first understands the model on which it is based.[38]

In the traditional world of central-local government relations this point was of primarily academic interest.[39] In the legalized world of the 1980s, however, it became a matter of the utmost practical importance. Initially, the focus of legal attention was on the use of multipliers to impose grant penalties on local authorities which exceeded the Government's expenditure targets. This matter came to a head when a small group of authorities which felt aggrieved by the way in which they were penalized by the 1985-6 targets challenged the legality of their construction. They succeeded in the Court of Appeal, only to find that the decision was unanimously reversed by the House of Lords. This case, *Nottinghamshire County Council* v. *Secretary of State for the Environment*,[40] is generally referred to by public lawyers as being concerned with the constitutional limits of judicial review and Lord Templeman's comments, reminding agencies that judicial review 'is not just a move in an interminable game of chess' and that in future local authorities should 'bite on the bullet and not seek to persuade the courts to absolve them from compliance with the Secretary of State's guidance',[41] have been widely quoted.

One commentator has suggested that the case shows the Law Lords 'displaying a fine understanding of the legislative, political, and constitutional contexts in which judicial review operates'.[42] A more accurate analysis is that it shows the court displaying complete bewilderment with the material with which it was presented. Further, since the court was faced with the fact that the application of common sense to the issue would render unlawful the Government's entire system of expenditure targets, the case shows the extent to which the courts stand in a particular relationship to the political-administrative system. Nevertheless, in one sense Lord Templeman's use of the game analogy is both insightful and revealing. His speech on this issue is in effect an articulation of the sense of the traditional framework in which law did not establish a normative framework and which was therefore designed to be an internal rule game.

The Government abandoned the system of expenditure targets in 1986 and thereafter sought to control local authority expenditure through the block grant distribution mechanism reinforced by the power of rate capping. This change, however, did not cause local authorities to heed Lord Templeman's advice. Local authorities simply adjusted their legal focus towards the general statutory framework governing grant distribution. The first challenge came from Birmingham City Council which was caught by the Secretary of State's use of multipliers in 1986-7 to prevent local authorities making windfall gains as a result of the decision to dispense with expenditure targets. This challenge, based on the argument that the Secretary of State for the Environment had misconstrued his power to use multipliers, succeeded in the Divisional Court.[43] Before the judgment was delivered, however, the Minister, no doubt having been advised that the Government would lose the case, made a statement in the House of Commons to the effect that Birmingham City Council's interpretation of the provision rendered the entire system unworkable and cast doubts not only on the legality of the current year's settlement but also on all grant determinations since 1981-2. The solution took the form of the Rate Support Grants Act 1986, which provided for the retrospective validation of all determinations under section 59 of the Local Government Planning and Land Act 1980 and made certain changes to the framework of Part VI of the Act in order to minimize the possibility of further legal challenge.

Nevertheless, as the Government itself probably realized, matters were not quite so simple. Less than two months after the Rate Support Grants Act 1986 received the Royal Assent the Secretary of State for the Environment reported to the House of Commons that a discrepancy had been discovered in the conventions followed by local authorities in compiling their expenditure accounts and in the construction of 'relevant expenditure'[44] and 'total expenditure',[45] two key concepts in the block grant mechanism. What is particularly interesting about this difficulty is that in 1981, when it was still not clear that a new regime of central-local relations was emerging, this ambiguity had been discovered and had been resolved by the issuance of administrative guidance. Nevertheless, the Government, having in 1986 obtained the Attorney-General's advice to the effect that their conventional accounting practices were legally incorrect, decided that clarificatory legislation was required. However, this was not simply a matter of clarification. The Government was under some legal pressure. Thus, on the day following the Secretary of State's statement the London Borough of Greenwich obtained by consent a declaration that, so far as it related to them, the Rates Limitation Order 1986 was *ultra vires* since an unlawful expenditure calculation had been used as the basis for designation.

These events had a profound significance. Their effect was to put in doubt the legality of all rate support grants settlements since the introduction of the block grant mechanism. It also meant that, until the matter was rectified, the Secretary of State could not continue with either the rate support grant process or complete the rate-capping process for 1987-8. The proposed

31

solution, once again, was to bring forward, as a matter of urgency, legislation 'to validate . . . all past decisions involving the use of relevant or total expenditure and allow decisions to be properly taken for the remainder of the present rate support grant system'.[46] This was done in the Local Government Finance Act 1987, although the Government also used the opportunity to formalize further the grant regime and adjust it to the command and control regime. Furthermore, concern was expressed in the legislation at the nature of the retrospective validation:

> 4.-(1) Anything done by the Secretary of State before the passing of this Act for the purposes of the relevant provisions [i.e. Part VI of the 1980 Act] . . . shall be deemed to have been done in compliance with those provisions.

> (6) Subsection (1) above shall have effect notwithstanding any decision of a court (whether before or after the passing of this Act) purporting to have a contrary effect.

These provisions are extraordinarily wide. Attempts were made during the parliamentary proceedings to limit retrospection to the calculations made by the Secretary of State for the Environment concerning relevant or total expenditure, but these were unsuccessful. It seems that, by this stage, the Government wished to ensure once and for all that local authorities would in fact have no choice but to bite on the bullet in matters of grant allocation decisions.[47]

Developments affecting the English system of local government finance thus highlight in an acute fashion the processes of juridification consequential upon the disintegration of the traditional framework of central-local government relations. To the extent that a normative gulf has emerged in the system, agencies have turned to law as the final determinant of the structure of authority. This has been an uncertain and unsatisfactory process. First, the Government, in switching to law as the primary normative control mechanism, seemed to underestimate the importance of the policy network to the successful implementation of policy. Secondly, the traditional legal framework was never designed as a normative structure governing central-local relations and therefore contained major gaps and obscurities.

Law has retained a very simple structure in the British system of government. The paradigmatic form of law as a means of resolving bi-polar problems through tripartite procedures has dominated the consciousness of lawyers with the result that great areas of the political-administrative system, although legally constituted, have grown up free from active legal regulation. Regulation and co-ordination of the system was achieved through administrative networks. In challenging these networks and seeking to control from the centre the Government fell victim to two failures. First, it did not appreciate that complex systems often react in counter-intuitive ways. From the first moment, then, the Government was forced to react in a crisis manner, through directive law, in relation to a system that was threatening to get out of control primarily as a result of the Government's own initiatives. Secondly, as more issues went to the courts for resolution, the dominance of this simple legal structure meant that the courts were placed in the situation of having to choose between placing a forced simplicity on the issues or abnegating their responsibilities for adjudicating legal questions.[48] Whichever way they chose, the situation seemed unsatisfactory. Consequently, this aspect of the process of juridification has been associated with uncertainty, confusion, and failure.

2. *Juridification as a Product of Restructuring*

There is also a second form of juridification which must be examined. This process is a consequence of the form of restructuring of the political-administrative system being promoted by the Government. We have seen that in the traditional framework of central-local government relations local authorities were vested with very broad enabling powers which maximized their discretionary powers of action. This feature of the traditional framework has been significantly modified by the Government. The Government's objective has been to limit the discretionary power of local government by imposing procedural constraints on authorities' powers, by imposing new duties on authorities, and by seeking fundamentally to reorganize the institutional framework through which local authorities provide services. These changes have the effect of making legal norms of much greater importance to the exercise of local government functions than has traditionally been the case.

Reforms along these lines have had an impact on almost every aspect of local government functions. The effect has been to impose formal structures on discretionary processes. A few examples might help us to focus on their effects. Thus, although traditionally local authorities have been free to establish their own budgetary processes, since 1984 they have been required by statute to consult with representative bodies of industrial and commercial ratepayers about their expenditure proposals.[49] Again, although the traditional framework of local government does not recognize the existence of party politics, under the Local Government Act 1985 local authorities were placed under a duty to make appointments to joint boards in such a manner as to reflect 'the balance of the parties for the time being prevailing in the council'.[50] And finally, it has recently been made explicit that it is the duty of the local authority, in exercising its contracting power relating to supplies or works, to disregard non-commercial considerations.[51] These types of formalization of local government decision-making processes should be seen not simply as restrictions on traditional autonomies but as particular forms of constraint in which a much more important supervisory role will be played by lawyers and courts.

General reforms of this type have certainly been an important aspect of this form of juridification. Nevertheless, the most significant reforms which have contributed to the legalization of this system have resulted from structural changes in the institutional arrangements through which local authorities provide services. Take, for example, the field of urban public transport provision. The flexible and enabling framework of the 1960s has, during the 1980s, been radically reformed in the wake of disagreements between the

33

centre and the localities over the means of ensuring efficient urban transport systems. Initially the Government sought to achieve its policy objectives through the formalization of the efficiency criterion, by requiring authorities to justify the levels of revenue support to public transport operators through a statutory cost-benefit exercise.[52] It was hoped that this exercise, in the context of the uncertainties caused by the resurrection of the concept of fiduciary duty,[53] would transform these basic duties into justiciable constraints. When this exercise failed,[54] more radical solutions followed. This has taken a number of forms: deregulation of the bus licensing system; the reorganization of public transport companies along commercial lines; a new duty on local authorities not to inhibit competition in the provision of transport services; the power of local authorities to provide service subsidies to transport providers only in accordance with a strict tendering system; and the modification of the local authority's basic duty from that of providing an *integrated* and efficient public transport system to meet the *needs* of the area to that of formulating policies to cater for any appropriate public transport requirements that would not otherwise be met.[55] The overall effect has been to challenge the authority's traditional discretion in respect of the planning, financing, and provision of service. This is achieved by imposing distinct formal structures on each function and by asserting the primacy of the market in matters of service provision, modifying the planning function to the residual one of planning only for services that the market cannot provide, and ensuring that service subsidies are provided only in accordance with a system of competitive tendering.

Developments of this nature have occurred over a broad range of local authority services. However, while the Government's objective has been to achieve a specific form of restructuring of local government, it is necessary in order to appreciate the significance of this goal from the perspective of legalization to examine the impact on relationships between central departments, local authorities, consumers, and agencies of review. That is, while the primary objective has been to structure and limit the discretionary power of local authorities, this has been achieved by radically altering the nature of legal relationships within this sphere of the political-administrative system.

In the field of public sector housing, for example, the legal relationship between local authorities and consumers has been transformed during the 1980s by giving tenants security of tenure and then building on to the concept of the secure tenancy a range of rights – the right to buy, the right to a mortgage, rights of exchange and succession, rights to make improvements and carry out repairs, and rights to be consulted about housing management issues.[56] Furthermore, because many local authorities could be expected not to agree with the Government's objectives, broad supervisory powers were required. The Secretary of State's powers to supervise the processing of council house sales in England and Wales[57] provides a good illustration. The power to intervene arises where it appears that tenants 'have or may have difficulty in exercising the right to buy effectively and expeditiously'.[58] Under this provision 'the Secretary of State may do all such things as appear to him

34

necessary or expedient to enable secure tenants . . . to exercise the right to buy'. This power, it was felt by the courts, 'may well be without precedent in legislation of this nature' and that 'short of seeking to exclude altogether any power of review by the courts, the wording . . . has clearly been framed by Parliament in such a way as to maximize the power of the Secretary of State and to minimize any power of review by the court'.[59] Nevertheless, since broad supervisory powers have also been a feature of the traditional framework, it is worth emphasizing that equally important as the nature of the power is the fact that these powers are designed to be used actively, since conventional notions of partnership have in many areas broken down. And central departments have been very active in their monitoring of the process of council house sales. Finally, in 1984 a power was given for assistance, including the giving of advice and arranging for legal representation, to any person who is exercising the right to buy and is raising a question of principle.

In the housing field, therefore, we see a strengthening of the mechanisms of 'voice' and 'exit' in circumstances in which the financial and institutional pressures[60] are on the local authority to withdraw from the business of directly providing housing for its local population. The overall effect is a very significant reduction in the discretionary power of local authorities. Similar trends may also be seen in education. Voice mechanisms were bolstered in parental choice provisions of the early 1980s[61] and, more recently, with the powers for greatly strengthening the parents' role on school governing bodies and greatly strengthening the power of such bodies.[62] Exit mechanisms were set in motion with the assisted places scheme in 1980[63] and are potentially to be greatly expanded by the recent 'opt out' provisions.[64]

The overall goal of the Government's strategy is to establish strict guidance, control, and review mechanisms in local government. Guidance is set clearly in a market framework. Control may be primarily the responsibility of central government but the Government has also put in place many procedures to enable consumers of services, ratepayers, or 'potential contractors'[65] to use the courts as agencies of control. And the administrative review mechanisms of audit and the Local Commissions of Administration have been attuned for market guidance – through 'economy, efficiency, and effectiveness' audit[66] – and strengthened.[67] The guidance, control, and review mechanisms established by the Government will considerably formalize this sphere of the political-administrative system. This process of formalization is in itself a process of juridification since the normative framework will be an explicitly legal framework.

It is obviously more difficult to evaluate this form of juridification, since many of the reforms have only recently been set in motion. Nevertheless, at this stage two points can be made. First, we may return to the point mentioned in the previous section about the simplistic jurisprudential basis of British public law. If the legalization of the political-administrative system is to be viewed as part of a strategy of attempting to establish a more effective structure of government, however, we must ask whether the courts have the necessary cognitive, organizational, or power resources to enable them to respond effectively to the control tasks assigned. Secondly, and more generally, we might note that it is ironical that, at a time when the problem of the policy effectiveness of the political-administrative system has been widely recognized in advanced societies, we seem to be proposing the solution of legalization at precisely the time when most societies have identified over-legalization as a major problem.[68]

CONCLUSIONS

The reforms to the political-administrative system promoted over the last decade of Conservative administration have had a significant effect on its structure. In this essay I have examined, in particular, the impact which these changes have had for our understanding of the functions of law within the political-administrative system. I have argued that the overall impact has been the juridification of central-local government relations. I have also tried to show that the effects of legalization have not been wholly positive. It is not difficult to show that those aspects of the process of juridification which have resulted from the disintegration of the traditional framework of central-local government relations have been nothing short of disastrous for the Government. However, when one considers juridification resulting from the particular form of restructuring which is promoted by the Government, the picture, of necessity, is not so clear cut. It is at this point that the issue of ideology comes in.

My general argument is that many of the failures, both actual and potential, are attributable to the promotion of reforms based on an anachronistic ideology. The policy failures consequential upon the disintegration of the traditional framework, for example, are founded on the failure of the Government to appreciate the internal complexity of the political-adminis-trative system. This complexity cannot be entirely attributable to the self-serving ends of the dominant participants, as is implied by public choice theory. Nevertheless, it could be argued that such policy failures are an inevitable part of any scheme for radical reorganization. There is undoubtedly an element of truth in this. But the catalogue of initatives which have failed to achieve the objectives set for them by the Government is such as to suggest that a primary reason lies with the shackles imposed by the ideological perspective of the Government.

By analogy we might argue that the difficulties which have been, and will be, experienced by the Government in implementing its programme of re-structuring the central-local relationship are similarly rooted in a limited ideological world view. In considering this aspect of the process of juridi-fication we are concerned not so much with the hierarchical or 'rational central rule'[69] approach to the issue of government but rather with the public/private issue in the guise of the relationship between state and society. Here the Government's reforms have been founded on an ideological belief in the efficiency of markets, the virtues of competition, and the beneficent effect of

36

increased consumer and taxpayer influence. This is not to say that such devices are of no value as guidance, control, and evaluation mechanisms. But these reforms – whether we are considering the use of enterprise zones in the planning system, increased parental influence in the running of schools, or the introduction of the community charge as the solution to the problem of accountability in local government finance – have been promoted without detailed examination of the impact which these reforms may have on the fields they affect.

The problem here is that we cannot solve problems based on the complexity of the modern world by legislating them out of existence. To put the issue crudely, we cannot find the solution to the problem of hierarchies in a shift to markets unless we also confront the issue of hierarchies *in* markets. And in terms of the political-administrative system, it is generally felt that its complexity is a function of the fact that it is expected to have regard to many different goals – economy, efficiency, effectiveness, equity, procedural propriety, responsiveness – which cannot easily be hierarchically ordered.[70] If we accept that these are all relevant goals in dynamic administrative programmes we do not resolve the problem of social choice by legislating a hierarchy.

The question of whether these ideologically-based reforms will ultimately produce a more enlightened or effective system of government is obviously very contentious. It is, however, an issue of secondary importance in this essay. Here our main concern has been to examine the impact which such reforms have had on the functions of law in central-local government relations. Nevertheless, the questions are directly linked when we consider one especially important matter. This is what many would term the constitutional issue, although it could also be viewed functionally as the structural conditions for evolutionary development. This problem may be highlighted by considering two central themes of Conservative constitutional thought: the fear of centralized power and the need to delimit the proper sphere of government. With the Thatcher Government these two themes, which Conservatives felt were in harmony, have directly clashed. The Thatcher administrations have taken an ideological stance on the latter theme, but in seeking to reform and delimit the power of government (and local government in particular) they have used to the full the legal authority of the central state.

It is worth reflecting on this question of the use of legal authority. The pace of legislative change in this area has been such that virtually all notion of conventional restraint has dissolved. Major changes in the institutional arrangements of local government, including the abolition of the county councils in London and the metropolitan areas, have taken place without any independent review of proposals.[71] Statutory consultation requirements have been flouted[72] and mechanisms such as the Consultative Council on Local Government Finance have been used simply as channels for informing affected parties of firm proposals. The volume and complexity of new legislation has caused the Government to use parliamentary procedures mainly as an opportunity to tidy up the rough drafts submitted for ratification.[73] And whenever the timetable seemed not to fit in with the Government's plans, the guillotine has been applied.[74]

This lack of conventional restraint can also be seen in the form of law used by the Government. Powers have been given to government ministers in forms which seem designed deliberately to avoid the possibility of judicial review.[75] Duties have been imposed on local authorities which seem designed deliberately, although through the medium of ambiguity, to destabilize existing programmes.[76] Retrospective legislation has been used, not only to restore existing but unfounded expectations but also to maximize the manoeuvrability of the Secretary of State for the Environment,[77] to nullify the effects of inconvenient judicial decisions,[78] to prevent local authorities from using accounting devices to increase their entitlement to grant,[79] and ultimately to try to remove the entire rate support grant system from the supervision of the courts.[80]

This is a dangerous strategy. If, as seems possible, the apparent attempt to return to some golden age of limited government is not realized, the constitutional legacy of the Thatcher years may well be the destruction of the checks of countervailing structures which, since Magna Carta, have been a primary characteristic of British governmental arrangements and the entrenchment of the centralized, hierarchical, and authoritarian power.

NOTES AND REFERENCES

1 On this point see W. H. Greenleaf, *The British Political Tradition. Volume 2. The Ideological Heritage* (1983).
2 See, for example, J. O'Connor, *The Fiscal Crisis of the State* (1973); R. Bacon and W. Eltis, *Britain's Economic Problem: Too Few Producers* (1976); I. Gough, *The Political Economy of the Welfare State* (1979); K. Newton, *Balancing the Books: Financial Problems of Local Government in West Europe* (1979).
3 M. Olson, *The Rise and Decline of Nations: Economic Growth, Stagflation, and Social Rigidities* (1982) 78.
4 S. H. Beer, *Britain Against Itself: The Political Contradictions of Collectivism* (1982) Part One.
5 A. King, 'Overload: Problems of Governing in the 1970s' (1975) 23 *Pol. Studies* 283; J. Douglas, 'The Overloaded Crown' (1976) 6 *Brit. J. Pol. Sci.* 483; C. Offe, 'Ungovernability: The Renaissance of Conservative Theories of Crisis' in C. Offe *Contradictions of the Welfare State* (1984).
6 S. Brittan, *The Role and Limits of Government: Essays in Political Economy* (1983) ch. 1.
7 J. Habermas, *Legitimation Crisis* (1975) Part II, ch. 5.
8 Compare R. Dworkin, *Taking Rights Seriously* (1977) ch. 4.
9 H. L. A. Hart, 'Definition and Theory Jurisprudence' (1954) 70 *Law Q. Rev.* 37.
10 See A. Febbrajo, 'The Rules of the Game in the Welfare State' in *Dilemmas of Law in the Welfare State*, ed. G. Teubner (1985); M. Shubik, 'The Games within the Game: Modelling Politico-Economic Structures' in *Guidance, Control, and Evaluation in the Public Sector*, ed. F.-X. Kaufmann (1986) ch. 28.
11 Housing Act 1985 ss. 8, 9; Housing (Scotland) Act 1987 ss. 1, 2.
12 Education Act 1944 s. 7; compare Education (Scotland) Act 1980 s. 1.
13 W. H. Hohfeld, *Fundamental Legal Conceptions as Applied in Judicial Reasoning* (1964).

14   Education Act 1944 ss. 93, 99, 68 respectively; Education (Scotland) Act 1980 ss. 67, 70 (there is no direct equivalent of the power in section 68 of the Education Act 1944).

15   Compare *Secretary of State for Education and Science* v. *Tameside Metropolitan Borough Council* [1977] A.C. 1014. This is a good example of a rare use of the directive power in the context of education.

16   Examples that come to mind include concessionary fares schemes on municipal transport undertakings (see *Prescott* v. *Birmingham Corporation* [1955] Ch. 120; Public Service Vehicles (Travel Concessions) Act 1955) and the use of agreements by local planning authorities to negotiate infrastructure arrangements with developers on major development projects (see J. Jowell, 'Bargaining in Development Control' (1977) *J. Planning and Environmental Law* 414 at 415-8.

17   A good example is provided by the Education Act 1944, a strict reading of which might cause one to believe that the primary agents in the education system were parents and the Secretary of State for Education. This is far from being accurate: see M. Loughlin, *Local Governments in the Modern State* (1986) 119-21.

18   R. A. W. Rhodes, *The National World of Local Government* (1986); and see, on this subject generally, Rhodes's *Beyond Westminster and Whitehall* (1988).

19   M. Laffin, 'Professional Communities and Policy Communities in Central-Local Relations' in *New Research in Central-Local Relations*, ed. M. Goldsmith (1985).

20   J. Gyford and M. James, *National Parties and Local Politics* (1983).

21   K. Isaac-Henry, 'Local Authority Associations and Local Government Reform' (1975) 1 *Local Government Studies* 1; 'Taking Stock of the Local Authority Associations' (1984) 62 *Public Administration* 129.

22   I consider aspects of this approach in 'Municipal Socialism in a Unitary State' in *Law, Legitimacy, and the Constitution*, eds. P. McAuslan and J. McEldowney (1985) ch. 4.

23   This structuralist approach is the basic framework I use in *Local Government in the Modern State* (1986).

24   K. Minogue, 'On Hyperactivism in Modern British Politics' in *Conservative Essays*, ed. M. Cowling (1978) 177 at 120-1.

25   Local Government Planning and Land Act 1980 Parts VI and VIII.

26   Local Government Finance Act 1982 s. 8.

27   R. Rhodes, 'The Changing Relationships of the National Community of Local Government 1970-83' in *New Research in Central-Local Relations*, ed. M. Goldsmith (1986) 122 at p. 132.

28   Audit Commission, *The Impact on Local Authorities' Economy,. Efficiency, and Effectiveness of the Block Grant Distribution System* (1984); National Audit Office, *Report by the Comptroller and Auditor General. Department of the Environment: Operation of the Rate Support Grant System* (1985); House of Commons, Seventh Report from the Committee of Public Accounts, Session 1985-6, *Operation of the Rate Support Grant System* (H. C. 47); J. Gibson, 'Local "Overspending": Why the Government Have Only Themselves to Blame' (1983) 3 *Public Money* 19; R. Jackman, 'The Rates Bill – A Measure of Desperation' (1984) 55 *Pol. Q.* 161.

29   R. Jackman, op. cit., n. 28, p. 170.

30   id.

31   Audit Commission, op. cit., n. 28, p. 27.

32   See *R.* v. *Secretary of State for the Environment, ex parte Greater London Council* [1985] Divisional Court, 3 April (unreported); *London Borough of Greenwich* v. *Secretary of State for the Environment* [1985] *The Times*, 19 December; *R.* v. *Secretary of State for the Environment, ex parte London Borough of Islington* [1986] Divisional Court, 26 March (unreported); *R.* v. *Secretary of State for the Environment, ex parte West Yorkshire Police Authority* [1986] Divisional Court, 1 July (unreported).

33   See, for example, Local Government Act 1987 s. 1 and sched. 1; Local Government Finance Act 1988 ss 130-2.

34   See P. Smith, 'The Potential Gains from Creative Accounting in English Local Government' (1988) 6 *Government and Policy* 173. Smith estimates that grant gains of up to fifty per cent could have been achieved by local authorities during the period 1982-6 by the use of creative accounting techniques.

35 See General Rate Act 1967 s. 2 (compare s. 12(6)).

36 See *R. v. London Borough of Hackney, ex parte Fleming* [1987] 85 L.G.R. 626; *Lloyd v. MacMahon* [1987] 2 W.L.R. 821.

37 Local Government Act 1986 s. 1.

38 A similar point can be made about the public transport statutes of the 1960s. They were not drafted with the idea of adjudication in mind. This goes some way towards explaining the difficulties experienced by the courts in determining whether the revenue support policies of the 1980s were lawful: see *Bromley London Borough Council* v. *Greater London Council* [1983] 1 A.C. 768; *R. v. Merseyside County Council, ex parte Great Universal Stores Ltd.* [1982] 80 L.G.R. 639.

39 This is not to say that it was unimportant. It raises a fundamental point, which has never properly been taken on board by mainstream jurisprudence, about what we think we are talking about when we use the term 'law'. And see the point above on the use of the analogy of games (n. 8, n. 9, n. 10).

40 *Nottinghamshire County Council* v. *Secretary of State for the Environment* [1986] 2 W.L.R. 1.

41 id., p. 23.

42 S. Lee, 'Understanding Judicial Review as a Game of Chess' (1986) 102 *Law Q. Rev.* 493 at 496.

43 *R. v. Secretary of State for the Environment, ex parte Birmingham City Council* [1986] Divisional Court, 15 April (unreported).

44 Local Government Planning and Land Act 1980 s. 54(5).

45 Local Government Planning and Land Act 1980 s. 56(8).

46 107 *H.C. Debs.*, col. 1053 (16 December 1986).

47 In order to ensure that this was indeed the end of the matter similar forms of retrospective and ouster clauses were incorporated into the Scottish system of local government finance: Local Government Finance Act 1987 Part II. Compare the legal framework for the distribution of grants established by the Local Government Finance Act 1988 Part V.

48 In case this should seem too crude a distinction, consider the differences between the Court of Appeal and the House of Lords in *Nottinghamshire County Council* v. *Secretary of State for the Environment*, op. cit., n. 40, and *Wheeler* v. *Leicester City Council* [1985] 1 A.C. 1054. And also consider the difference between the Divisional Court and the higher courts in *Bromley London Borough Council* v. *Greater London Council*, op. cit., n. 38.

49 Rates Act 1984 s. 13; Rating and Valuation (Amendment) (Scotland) Act 1984 s. 4; Local Government Finance Act 1988 s. 134.

50 Local Government Act 1985 s. 33.

51 Local Government Act 1988 ss. 17, 18.

52 Transport Act 1983.

53 *Bromley London Borough Council* v. *Greater London Council*, op. cit., n. 38.

54 See M. Loughlin, 'Lawyers, Economists, and the Urban Public Transport Policy Process' in *Transport Subsidy*, ed. S. Glaister (1987).

55 Transport Act 1985.

56 Housing Act 1985 Parts IV and V; Housing (Scotland) Act 1987 Part III.

57 Compare the procedures in Scotland where there were no similar powers and the Secretary of State had to rely on the general default power under Local Government (Scotland) Act 1973 s. 211. This power was nevertheless invoked in the context of the processing of council house sales: see C. Himsworth, *Public Sector Housing Law in Scotland* (1985) 77.

58 Housing Act 1980 s. 23; see now Housing Act 1985 s. 164.

59 *Norwich City Council* v. *Secretary of State for the Environment* [1982] 1 All E.R. 737, 748-9.

60 Financial pressures have been applied not only through the general expenditure controls on local authorities but also through the manner in which the housing subsidy systems have been used. The primary institutional pressures can be seen in the Housing Act 1985 Part XIII and Housing (Scotland) Act 1987 Parts IX and X.

61 Education Act 1980 ss. 6-9; Education (Scotland) Act 1980 ss. 28-28H.

62 Education (No. 2) Act 1986, Education Reform Act 1988 Part I, c. III and IV; proposals for introducing similar reforms in Scotland are likely to materialize in a Bill to be introduced in

the 1988-9 parliamentary session.

63 Education Act 1980 s. 17; Education (Scotland) Act 1980 ss. 75A, 75B.

64 Education Reform Act 1988 Part I, c. IV; Scottish reforms along such lines are likely to be included in the 1988-9 Bill.

65 Local Government Act 1988 s. 19(7).

66 Local Government Finance Act 1982 Part III (England and Wales), Local Government Act 1988 s. 35 (Scotland).

67 Local Government Act 1988 s. 30, sched. 4 (giving powers to the auditor to issue prohibition orders and seek judicial review). See also the Government's proposals in *The Conduct of Local Authority Business* (1988; Cm. 433) ch. VI. And see Local Government and Housing Bill, Session 1988-9, H.C. Bill 53, especially Part II.

68 See, for example, M. Galanter, 'Legality and Its Discontents: A Preliminary Assessment of Current Theories of Legalization and Delegalization' in *Alternative Rechtsformen und Alternativen zum Recht*, eds. E. Blankenburg et al. (1980) 11; G. Teubner, 'After Legal Instrumentalism? Strategic Models of Post-Regulatory Law' in *Dilemmas of Law in the Welfare State*, ed. G. Teubner (1985) 299; R. Stewart, 'The Discontents of Legalism: Interest Group Relations in Administrative Regulation' (1985) *Wisconsin Law Rev.* 655.

69 See H. van Gunsteren, *The Quest for Control* (1976).

70 D. Grunow, 'The Development of the Public Sector' in *Guidance, Control, and Evaluation in the Public Sector*, op. cit., n. 10, p. 44.

71 This point raises the question of why the Government chose to establish the Widdicombe Committee of Inquiry (1986; Cmnd. 9797) into the conduct of local authority business. On this question see M. Loughlin, 'The Conduct of Local Authority Business' (1987) 50 *Modern Law Rev.* 64.

72 See, for example, *R. v. Secretary of State for Social Services, ex parte Association of Metropolitan Authorities* [1986] 1 W.L.R. 1.

73 A good example is provided by the Local Government Finance Act 1988. The Bill entered the House of Commons 100 pages in length, with 131 clauses and twelve schedules, and as a result of over 200 Government amendments, left it as a Bill of 151 pages, 150 clauses, and sixteen schedules. It then went to the House of Lords and returned to the House of Commons with a further 417 amendments by the Government. Consideration of the Lords' amendments was subject to a guillotine. (See 137 *H.C. Debs.*, col. 1100; Michael Howard MP, Minister for Local Government.) The Act consists of 179 pages, 152 sections, and thirteen schedules.

74 Most of the major local government Bills of the 1980s have been subject to an allocation of time motion: Education (No. 2) Bill 1979-80 (twice); Housing Bill 1979-80 (twice); Transport Bill 1982-3; Housing and Building Control Bill 1982-3; Rates Bill 1983-4; Rating and Valuation (Amendment) (Scotland) Bill 1983-4; Local Government Bill 1984-5 (twice); Transport Bill 1984-5 (twice); Local Government Finance Bill 1986-7 (twice); Abolition of Domestic Rates etc. (Scotland) Bill 1986-7 (twice); Education Reform Bill 1987-8 (twice); Local Government Finance Bill 1987-8 (twice); Housing Bill 1987-8.

75 op. cit., n. 52, n. 57, n. 58.

76 Examples can be seen in the Transport Act 1983 ss. 4(3)(5), 5(2) (see also Department of Transport, *Public Transport Subsidy in Cities* (1982; Cmnd. 8735) para. 13) and in the Local Government Act 1988 s. 28.

77 Local Government Finance Act 1982 s. 8(10).

78 See, for example, London Regional Transport (Amendment) Act 1985.

79 See, for example, Rate Support Grants Act 1986; Local Government Act 1987; Local Government and Housing Bill, Session 1988–9, H.C. Bill 53 Part IV.

80 Local Government Finance Act 1987 s. 4 and Part II.

Lessons of Thatcherism: Education Policy in England and Wales 1979–88

GEOFF WHITTY* AND IAN MENTER*

INTRODUCTION

Twelve years after it was announced by James Callaghan, the Great Education Debate is happening. Indeed, it may already have happened. Or seen from another perspective, it may not have been a debate at all.

The educational manifestation of the crisis in social democracy was marked most clearly by Labour Prime Minister James Callaghan's speech at Ruskin College, Oxford, in October 1976. His expression of concern about progressive tendencies in education and of education's poor performance in meeting the needs of industry represented the first major landmark in the move towards the dismantling of the education system created by the Education Act 1944. It represented an acceptance, if not a total endorsement, of the critique of state education which had been offered by a number of right-wing educationists in the 'Black Papers', the first of which was published in 1969.[1] The main themes of Callaghan's initiative were talk of a national core curriculum and a desire for education to become more responsive to the demands of industry. A third theme was highlighted at this time by the crisis at William Tyndale Junior School in Islington, London, when a group of parents and governors lost confidence in the progressive teaching approaches employed by the staff. This affair received massive press coverage and led to a quasi-judicial inquiry which together had the effect of legitimating the notion that teachers had too much autonomy and were pursuing disruptive if not subversive ends.[2] Overarching these three themes was a concern, again much promoted in the tabloid press, about supposed 'falling standards' in education.[3]

*Department of Education, Bristol Polytechnic, Redland Hill, Bristol BS6 6UZ, England.

We would like to thank our colleagues in the Bristol Polytechnic Education Study Group – Nick Clough, Veronica Lee, and Tony Trodd – for their help in preparing this paper. The paper also draws on work carried out with Tony Edwards and John Fitz on an ESRC-funded research project on the state and private education, and with Arthur Keefe and Anne Chappell on a Bristol Polytechnic research project on privatization in health, welfare, and education.

Although there were attempts to stimulate a nationwide discussion around such issues, led by Shirley Williams MP, then Secretary of State for Education, the general level of debate was low-key and indecisive. The official Great Debate was closed not with a major Education Bill being presented to Parliament, as one might have expected, but with a consultation paper published in 1977.[4] Nevertheless, although few major changes were immediately discernible in the organization or practice of education, a significant ideological shift had been achieved. There was a new kind of consensus in political discussion about education, a consensus of concern which spanned conventional left-right divisions. For professionals, too, working in the system at the time, clear changes started to take place. A stream of documents, particularly on curriculum matters, started to emerge from Her Majesty's Inspectorate of Schools and from the Department of Education and Science.[5] Talk of more assessment of children's attainment developed, and the Assessment of Performance Unit was set up and started to test national samples of children in primary and secondary schools. Concern moved away from the organization of schooling to the content and outcomes. The 1960s and early 1970s had seen a steady growth in the number of comprehensive schools, and the last significant structural change made by a Labour Government to the system was the abolition of direct grant schools in 1976. But by 1979, while there was still considerable debate about the effectiveness of comprehensive schools, the focus of debate within the state education system was much more on the educational process.

Against this background we consider in this paper how the Thatcher Government has developed and implemented education policy. In so doing we attempt to assess the extent to which education policy has been an integral part of a broader government strategy. While it is obvious that the most massive upheavals in education since 1944 will result from the Education Reform Act 1988, there are nevertheless important and revealing precursors to these proposals in earlier Conservative policies. We trace these through the 1980s, in particular looking at how appropriate it is to describe the changes in terms of privatization. In then drawing out some of the ideological justifications for these policies as well as their origins, we consider whether there is consistency between the changes that relate to the structure of the education system and those relating to the curriculum. We then discuss the nature of the process by which the Government has sought to secure all of these so-called reforms, both structural and curricular, and the extent to which they have been resisted. In conclusion, we outline the state of development of viable alternative policies on the political left and consider some of the lessons that can be learnt from the Thatcherite project.

THATCHERITE EDUCATION – THE FIRST PHASE

When the Thatcher Government came to power in 1979, there was nothing to suggest that it would seek significantly to alter the structure of the education system. Its education policy responded to that range of concerns and interests that have traditionally influenced the Conservative Party in Britain, even if the balance between the different strands had shifted somewhat since the days of the Heath Government.[6] Although one of the more contentious items in the new Government's policy, the Assisted Places Scheme, did involve providing opportunities for pupils to move out of state schools into the private sector, this was hardly a radical departure, especially when seen in the context of education policy as a whole.[7] Indeed, the scheme was conceived more as a restoration of a style of education increasingly unavailable within the maintained sector as a result of comprehensivization than as an encouragement of the private sector *per se*. Indeed, Mark Carlisle MP, the Secretary of State for Education responsible for the scheme, argued that it could be 'fairly looked upon as an extension of the maintained sector'.[8]

Although that scheme was developed for the Conservative Party in opposition by Stuart Sexton, a policy adviser who has subsequently become linked with some of the favourite policies of the New Right, its origins came from a proposal by direct grant school members of the Headmasters' Conference. It was thus closely tied to that segment of the private sector whose links with the Conservative Party are more with the 'Old Tories' than with the privatizers of the New Right. The Centre for Policy Studies appears not to have had any part in its evolution and leading members of the Institute of Economic Affairs have regarded it with some suspicion.[9] It was only after it had been in operation for some time that the scheme came to be regarded by some commentators as a harbinger of the more radical proposals of the New Right, for which in retrospect it can certainly be seen as preparing the ground.[10] However, even when Rhodes Boyson MP and Sir Keith Joseph MP were at the Department of Education and Science together, the ideas of the New Right on using education vouchers to create an education market were dismissed as impractical despite their philosophical attractions. This was partly because Department of Education and Science officials persuaded ministers of the bureaucratic enormity of organizing such a system, but also because in the context of compulsory education the introduction of vouchers for every child of school age would actually increase state expenditure on education in the short term. Thus, even had government ministers been committed to such a course of action, they would have come into conflict with the Treasury priority of reducing the Public Sector Borrowing Requirement and preventing the introduction of major new spending programmes. In any event, some of Joseph's other policies, such as those on vocational education involving the Manpower Services Commission, had strong corporatist elements within them even if they were more market-oriented than the equivalent policies of Labour Governments.[11]

There has therefore been no major expansion of private provision within education, at least during its compulsory phase, yet some commentators have increasingly identified privatization as a feature of the education service under Thatcherism.[12] This is because there has been in the field of education 'creeping privatization' in a variety of senses and emanating from a variety of sources.[13] Thus, in absolute terms, and as conventionally understood, the private sector's share of mainstream educational provision has remained small even under the Thatcher Government. Its share is larger than it was in the 1960s and 1970s, but still somewhat smaller than in the immediate post-war period. Nevertheless, the 1980s have seen a small increase in intakes to independent schools and this has constituted a rather larger increase in their share of the market as it has been accompanied by an overall fall in the size of the age cohort. These schools currently account for about seven per cent of the overall school population in England and Wales, somewhat less than this in Scotland, and rather more in Northern Ireland. The proportion increases steadily throughout the compulsory years of schooling, but it rises dramatically in the post-compulsory phase. Over a quarter of school-leavers with three passes at A-level, the main qualification for entry to higher education, come from the private sector.[14] Higher education itself has not been significantly privatized in the narrow sense, though the University of Buckingham received its full university status under the Thatcher regime. Nevertheless, the changes made to the funding and management of universities, polytechnics, and colleges in the Education Reform Act 1988 are only the legislative culmination of a succession of attempts to increase private sector influence in the system and make it more responsive to market forces. In the area of training, where government-sponsored training schemes expanded rapidly under the aegis of the Manpower Services Commission, the policies of the Thatcher Government have brought about a progressive increase in the amount of off-the-job training offered by private providers (including private colleges such as Sight and Sound) forcing colleges of further education, maintained by local education authorities, to compete in the market.

This last example neatly encapsulates two of the general trends that have characterized education policy under the Thatcher Government and which, in different senses, have contributed to a degree of privatization of the system. These are, first, the use (and in some cases diversion) of public money to support education and training by private providers and, secondly, the attempt to make the public sector behave more like the private sector. These have – so far, at least – been more significant features of privatization in education than the wholesale transfer of public provision into the private sector, but they have also contributed to a blurring of the distinction between public and private provision and possibly to a preparation of the ground for a more fully privatized system in the future. We can now see that some of the promises made in the Conservative Party's 1979 General Election manifesto, which became policy commitments immediately after the election and were translated into legislation in the Education Act 1980, have contributed to this process, even if they were originally more modest in their intent. In terms of the concerns of this paper, the two most significant elements of this legislation were the establishment of the Assisted Places Scheme (the origins of which we discussed above), which offered financial support to parents of limits means who wished to send academically able children to certain prestigious independent schools, and the provisions which increased parental rights in the allocation of children to maintained schools.

The Assisted Places Scheme, particularly after Sexton's ambitious plans had been pruned in the context of the 1979-80 public expenditure review, was a fairly modest instance of the use of public money to buy privately provided services and, as indicated earlier, it was not primarily conceived as a privatization measure. In 1987–8 there were about 27,000 pupils holding assisted places in England and Wales, at annual cost to the Exchequer of about £47 million. Nevertheless, despite official claims to the contrary, there is some evidence that even this limited input of money has assisted independent schools themselves rather than just their pupils, particularly by providing them with a continuing supply of just those pupils whose academic success will ensure that the schools retain their market attraction in the future. Conversely, it is often argued that the removal of those pupils from the maintained sector has reduced the capacity of schools in that sector to compete. Yet much more significant than any actual creaming effect has been the symbolic importance of the scheme as signifying on the part of the Government a massive vote of no confidence in the capacity of state schools to provide for academically able pupils, which through a 'moral panic' on the part of parents could become a self-fulfilling prophecy.[15] The contrary argument that the scheme will act as a spur to poor state schools to improve is somewhat belied by the fact that its first pupils have been drawn from 'good' state schools rather than from the so-called 'sink' schools of the inner city to which government ministers had frequently referred in legitimating the scheme.[16] Yet, though the scheme was in essence only a variant of the traditional scholarship ladder for individuals, the fact that it has not self-evidently brought about the desired systemic effects in the maintained sector – that is, 'pulling up' poor quality schools and restoring traditional approaches in secondary education – is now being used as a justification for proposing more radical measures of privatization.

Similarly, there is little evidence that the provisions of the Education Act 1980 to increase parental choice by limiting the rights of local education authorities to allocate pupils to certain schools and introducing an appeals mechanism have had the beneficial systemic effects that were used to justify them. Yet, here again, it is the weakness of the concept of parental choice employed in the provisions of the Act and the rights retained by local education authorities to continue certain long-standing practices in the school allocation policies that are now being invoked to explain the continuing existence of poor schools and to justify more radical measures. The claim is that the right of local education authorities to set planned admission limits for their schools has allowed vested interests to protect the existing system from the real rigours of market forces and that still more needs to be done to make schools more accountable to their clients, who are simultaneously seen as parents and employers (but rarely pupils). For these reasons, the thrust of subsequent policy, particularly as enshrined in the Education (No. 2) Act 1986 and the Education Reform Act 1988, has been to increase yet further the rights of parents and

46

school governing bodies and to diminish the powers of local education authorities. Meanwhile, governing bodies themselves are being opened to greater parental and industrial influence at the expense of governors from local education authority, teacher, and pupil sectors. Even with these reforms, though, a state education system dominated by local education authorities is seen by the Government as suspect and incapable of meeting its requirements.

PHASE TWO – A NEW APPROACH?

The decision to create new types of schools, termed by the Secretary of State for Education as 'half-way houses' between the private and public sectors, is now at the centre of the Government's strategy for reducing local education authority powers and making schools more directly responsive to consumers.[17] In legal terms, the recent blurring of the boundary between the two sectors marks a change in policy, since there had been a conscious decision at the time of the making of the Assisted Places Scheme not to change the status of independent schools receiving state funds, even to the extent of reintroducing the direct grant regulations. The theory was that it was pupils not institutions who were in receipt of state aid. The announcement by the Secretary of State for Education, Kenneth Baker MP, at the 1986 Conservative Party Conference of the proposed establishment of up to twenty city technology colleges was developed into a policy that heralded 'a new choice of school', described in the official prospectus as 'independent schools' that will not charge fees, with initial capital costs met by charitable trusts financed by industrial sponsors and baseline recurrent expenditure met by central government. Particularly when the Government subsequently agreed to make a substantial contribution towards these colleges' initial capital costs, this offered the private sector something akin to the maintained sector's voluntary aided schools, where only fifteen per cent of capital costs have to be met by their sponsoring foundations – usually the churches – while recurrent expenditure is entirely met by the local education authorities.

In 1987, during the General Election campaign, the boundary was further blurred by the announcement that some maintained schools (both county and voluntary) were to be allowed to 'opt out' of local education authority control; this proposal was firmed up in the Education Reform Act 1988 under the title of grant maintained schools, which are to be maintained schools funded directly by central government rather than the local education authorities. As originally drafted in the Bill, the opting out proposals would have allowed any secondary school and primary schools of over 300 pupils to opt out of local education authority control and become centrally-funded grant maintained schools after a simple majority vote of parents in favour of opting out. Following a defeat in the House of Lords, the Government has amended the relevant clause so that a second vote will need to take place if less than fifty per cent of those eligible to vote (which may be up to four parents per child) do so in the first ballot.

47

When the clauses dealing with opting out and with the creation of city technology colleges are seen alongside others that permit open enrolment to local education authority schools, at least to their physical limits, and allocate funds to such schools via a formula largely driven by pupil numbers, it is clear that the Education Reform Act 1988 could radically alter the shape and function of the state education system in the coming years.[18] In so far as these proposals involve aiding schools rather than individuals, they might appear to be out of step with the central tenets of Friedmanite economics. However, it should be noted that, unlike social democratic universalistic policies or policies of positive discrimination, they only reward schools which can demonstrate their capacity to compete successfully for individual clients in the market. One of the ideas behind all such proposals is to allow the market (or, strictly, a quasi-market) to discipline poor schools by putting them out of business. Unlike the planned admissions limits used since the Education Act 1980, which recognized a need to temper market forces with a modicum of planning, these proposals effectively give 'parental choice' its head.

While administrative chaos is likely in the short term, the longer-term outcome (particularly of the opting out provisions) is likely to be one in which many of the positive benefits of the old partnership between central government, local government, and the teaching profession are lost along with its shortcomings, especially if Mrs Thatcher is right about the number of schools that will eventually opt out.[19] Certainly a resegmentation of the system and a return to selection will become real possibilities. Whether this is a result of conscious policy or merely the outcome of a series of apparently unrelated decisions, critics of current government proposals have discerned a possible future scenario in which a clear hierarchy of schools will re-emerge. This might run from independent schools at the pinnacle through city technology colleges and grant maintained schools to local education authority maintained schools, possibly with an internal hierarchy between voluntary and council schools.[20] This danger will be increased if grant maintained schools exercise their right, as enshrined in the Education Reform Act 1988, to apply to the Secretary of State for Education to change their status and thereby become overtly selective. In the longer term, it could even be that city technology colleges and grant maintained schools will increasingly move into the private sector, thus making possible a largely privatized system based on education vouchers, which are still by no means off the agenda of the New Right.[21]

In that situation local education authority or 'council' schools could again become the poor relations of the system and the preserve of those unable or unwilling to compete in the market. As such, they might well become straightforward institutions of social control for the inner cities, where the primary concern of the staff will be the social welfare of young people rather than their education. There is, of course, an apparent paradox here in the fact that these are the schools over which central government will have least control but where the local education authority will have most responsibility. The Government itself has chosen not to deny that one outcome of its policies may be to increase racial segregation between schools. In the House of Commons on 1 December 1987 the Labour Party spokesperson, Jack Straw MP, said of the open enrolment proposals that they would 'lead to educational apartheid and racially segregated schools'. When the Bill was being debated in the House of Lords in May 1988, the opposition lost an amendment which would have allowed an education authority to reduce pupil numbers 'if they caused an undesirable imbalance in racial composition which might prejudice racial harmony within the school or community'. Baroness Hooper, the Government's education spokesperson in the House of Lords, argued that racial prejudice was impossible to legislate against, saying 'Segregation is no part of this Bill. We underline the fact that in giving parents choice, we do not wish to circumscribe that choice in any way.'[22]

THE ATOMIZATION OF EDUCATION

However, even with the blatant inequalities of provision that are likely to emerge from the virtually unfettered exercise of parental choice in the coming years, the legitimacy of the system and the notion of an open society can still be maintained by devices such as the Assisted Places Scheme, which ostensibly offer opportunities to worthy disadvantaged children to 'escape' from their backgrounds, while actually (on the evidence available so far) attracting middle-class children and helping to increase the market appeal of the independent sector.[23] As a leading Conservative critic of the Government's initiatives has pointed out, they 'all help most those children with parents best able to play the system to escape from poor schools. They do nothing for the quality of education of the majority who remain behind.'[24] Furthermore, those in the inner cities may increasingly become the only groups in society receiving only the basic state provision. They may thereby become further divided even from the rest of the working class and its political movements. In the current – virtually universalistic – system of state provision, it is at least possible to conceive of groups opposed to the injustices of the system combining to fight for gains that individually they could never hope to win. The atomization of decision-making which is a feature of current government policy threatens not only the negative conception of collectivism associated with inhuman state bureaucracies; it also constitutes an attack on the very notion that collective action, rather than the individual exercise of supposedly free choice in an unequal society, is a legitimate way of struggling for social justice.

Clearly, a great deal of the broad Thatcherite argument for privatization is tied up with the principles of monetarism. However, in spite of this and in view of the Government's continuing major commitment to public expenditure on education at least in the medium term, one might argue that the privatization of education has so far occurred more in an ideological than in a budgetary sense, in contrast to some other sectors. In other words, much of it has been about giving private individuals a sense of control over their own lives. Thus, the 'private' in privatization signals not only the favouring of private rather than public enterprises, but also (and arguably more significantly) a commitment to restore decisions that have hitherto been made by professional experts (in this case the 'liberal educational establishment') to those individuals whose lives are actually involved. It is this latter 'populist' strand that has been exploited by the media, especially through the spectre of left-wing teachers and local education authorities, to win support for many of the Government's policies.

As we implied earlier, the clauses in the Education Reform Act 1988 on financial delegation and devolved management in local education authority schools, which are often presented as relatively uncontentious, will help to undermine the role of local education authorities and make rational planning of educational provision extraordinarily difficult.[25] They are justified by an appeal to principles of devolution and democracy and to the efficiency of making decisions 'on the ground'. Moreover, as in other parts of the Welfare State, the allocation of cash-limited budgets to cost centres is seen as both a way of keeping expenditure within set limits and introducing financial discipline into the public sector. However, when taken together with the opting out and open enrolment proposals, even these aspects of the Act can also be seen as part of the broader attempt to atomize decision making in education and to ensure that educational policy develops through the exercise of market preferences rather than collective struggle.

The combination of the various measures to devolve decision making to individual headteachers and governing bodies will particularly limit opportunities for collective trade union struggles over education, especially in the broader context of the Government's repeated moves to restrict the operations of all trade unions. Even before the Education Reform Act 1988, the Government had imposed in 1987 a new structure for the pay and conditions of schoolteachers, which led to the abolition of the Burnham Committee which for some forty years had been the body responsible for negotiating such matters. Additionally, new regulations introduced the notion of 'directed hours', the 1,265 hours during a year when every teacher is now directly responsible for her or his work to the headteacher. Now, within the Education Reform Act 1988 itself, there are various features which will change teachers' relationships with their employers and, in doing so, possibly undermine the capacity of teacher trade unions to organize collectively to defend teachers' employment and conditions of service. These include the increased power of governing bodies to hire and fire and to vary staffing levels, and the lack of obligation on a local education authority to retain the services of a teacher who expresses opposition to working in a grant maintained school, if that teacher's school chooses to 'opt out'. Either *de jure* in the case of grant maintained schools, or *de facto* in the case of local authority maintained schools with delegated financial management, there will be many more 'employers' for trade unions to deal with. A further straw in the wind perhaps is the plan by Nottingham City Technology College not to recognize the main unions and instead enter into a no-strike agreement with a staff association or with the non-TUC-affiliated Professional Association of Teachers.[26]

At the same time, the unions are having to confront potential 'dilution' of the profession. In May 1988, while the debate on the Education Reform Bill was still progressing, the Secretary of State for Education launched yet another consultative paper, a Green Paper entitled *Qualified Teacher Status*.[27] Kenneth Baker MP put this document forward partly to tidy up anomalies in existing non-standard routes to qualified teacher status, but also with the intention of addressing the shortage of teachers in certain subjects which is expected to worsen during the 1990s. Another example of 'bringing in market forces', this time through deregulation, the plan is to create a new route into teaching through 'licensing' which does not entail a specific period of pre-service training. This route would be open to people with appropriate alternative qualifications or experience. Despite the widespread concern about the proposals within the profession and without waiting for the end of its own consultation period, the Government decided to introduce a late and largely unnoticed amendment to the Education Reform Bill, which amongst other things granted the Secretary of State for Education powers to make regulations relating to licensed teachers.

While being presented as a specific measure to address a particular short-term problem, the teaching unions are concerned that it may well represent the thin end of the wedge in the deprofessionalization of teaching. Increasingly during the 1980s teaching had been moving towards becoming an all-graduate profession. However, with the increased power of governors under the Education Reform Act 1988 – especially in the new grant maintained schools – there will be some temptation to employ licensed teachers as a matter of course, either because they prove cheaper to employ than trained graduates or perhaps also because they have a less critical perspective on the education system than those who have experienced initial teacher education. Furthermore, it could be attractive to the Government that some trade unions might be unwilling to admit as members teachers who have entered the profession through the licensing route and some of the new-style governing bodies might well share the Government's view. Significantly, the initiative on qualified teacher status followed closely from the pronouncements of Oliver Letwin on the subject in his regular column in the *Times Educational Supplement* owned by Rupert Murdoch.[28] There he proposed the complete removal of professional training as a requirement for teachers, whether pre-service or 'on-the-job'. Although it is possible, therefore, to read the Green Paper as a pre-emptive move by the education bureaucracy against the even worse excesses that might follow the adoption of the views of Letwin and his associates, it also demonstrates at least a degree of ambivalence about Sir Keith Joseph's earlier strategy to improve teaching quality through the control of the curriculum of initial teacher education.[29] However, intervention in the curriculum at all levels remains an important part of government policy, and it is to that which we now turn.

New Right ideology is based on a blend of moral and economic doctrines. They are sometimes complementary but sometimes in tension. So on the one hand, the ideology is based on the economic libertarianism of thinkers such as Friedman and Hayek, but on the other it is based on social and moral authoritarianism.[30] These twin strands characteristically lead to increased central intervention in social provision but often in the form of deregulation and privatization as can be seen in health, housing, and social services.[31] At the same time increased powers are given to the police, immigration laws become increasingly repressive, and 'alternative' lifestyles – especially those which challenge conventional family life – are characterized as abnormal and as a threat to society (for example, the Local Government Act 1988 section 28, and the treatment of the 'New Age Travellers').

With regard to education, the espousal of the twin economic goods of individual freedom and market forces is presented by the Government as offering the best chance of serving long-term national interests. Schools which are responsive to choices made by parents in the market are believed to be more likely than those administered by state bureaucrats to produce high levels of scholastic achievement, to the benefit of both individuals and the nation. The strength of the state therefore has to be used to remove anything that interferes with this process or with the development of an appropriate sense of self and nation on the part of citizens. Thus, not only do the powers of local education authorities and the teachers' trade unions over the structures of education need to be reduced, it also becomes imperative to police the curriculum to ensure that the pervasive collectivist and universalistic welfare ideology of the post-war era is restrained so that support for the market, enterprise, and self-help can be constructed. The suggestion by junior minister Bob Dunn MP, in an address to the Institute of Economic Affairs, that 'a study of the life and teachings of Adam Smith should be compulsory in all schools' is perhaps only an extreme version of the sort of thinking that underlies many of the Government's curricular initiatives.[32]

As in other aspects of New Right policy, espousal of this economic doctrine is linked with support for a particular notion of the 'responsible' family and an insistence on the maintenance of a common 'national identity'. If we take just one of these themes, 'national identity', and examine it in more detail, the role of education in the New Right project becomes clearer. 'Race' and 'nation' are themselves crucial interconnected concepts in New Right ideology.[33] During the last two decades the concern of liberal and progressive educationists about criticisms of educational provision made by black students, parents, and their organizations,[34] as well as by black academics and educationists,[35] has given rise to the development of what Mullard has called 'racial forms' of education – most recently, 'multicultural' and 'anti-racist' education. Such forms of education seek variously to address the 'underachievement' of black pupils, to 'promote racial harmony' and intercultural understanding, or to eliminate racism from education. It is these forms of education which have come in for the most vehement attack from the educational ideologues of the New Right in a spate of papers, speeches, pamphlets, and books as well as in the Right's *causes célèbres* of Honeyford, Savery, McGoldrick, Brent, and Dewsbury.[36] At the centre of these polemics has been a notion of 'British' education and culture, based on Christian and English traditions.

The influence of such New Right views can be detected in the Education Reform Act 1988 in a number of manifestations.[37] Examples of this include the very emphasis on 'national' in the proposed national curriculum, the centrality of a notion of national testing with all the cultural bias which that implies, the failure to recognize languages other than Welsh and English as pupils' first languages, and the omission in any of the consultation papers, let alone in the legislation itself, of any reference to the 1985 report of Lord Swann's Committee of Inquiry into the Education of Children from Ethnic Minority Groups, entitled *Education for All*.[38] These examples demonstrate just one aspect of the influence of New Right thinking on curriculum policy and of the way in which curriculum policy supports a particular view of society and citizen.[39] As Anne Sofer of the Social and Liberal Democrats recently put it, the 'draconian control' now to be exercised over the curriculum by the Secretary of State for Education as a result of the Education Reform Act 1988 has to be seen in a context where:

> The prevailing philosophy is one that does get excited about Christianity being absolutely predominant in RE, about the need to make sure British history prevails over other sorts of history and to stamp on anything that has the label anti-racism attached to it.[40]

It is important to recognize, then, that although there are numerous and often contradictory influences at work in the Government's curriculum policies, they are not as incompatible with its policies on the structure of the education system as is sometimes suggested by critics who detect a fundamental inconsistency between the notion of a devolved system of school management and a national curriculum imposed by legislation. In the first period of the Thatcher Government, from 1979 to 1983, the preferred strategy on the control of the curriculum was to continue the 'opinion moulding' approach started by Callaghan with his 1976 speech at Ruskin College, but aided by media attacks on 'trendy left-wing teachers' and 'loony-left councils' and some rather more direct intervention from government ministers than had been evident in the past. Thus, as one radical teachers' magazine put it in 1983:

> All Tory ministers seem to have been enlisted to the fight. Keith Joseph has tried to muzzle science teachers; Tebbit to restrict Youth Training Schemes; Heseltine to intervene in the content of classroom resources [for peace education]. All are concerned about the social *content* of the curriculum and are trying to ensure that it never raises questions about the *status quo*.[41]

The attempt to influence the nature of the school curriculum without direct legislative intervention was strengthened in 1983 by the carrot of money from the Manpower Services Commission for the Technical and Vocational Education Initiative. However, despite some success with these measures, the Government has more recently decided to enshrine curriculum policy in legislation. In their different ways, the provisions on sex education in the Education (No. 2) Act 1986, the notorious section 28 of the Local Government Act 1988, and the proposals for a national curriculum in the Education Reform Act 1988 all represent a clear attempt to reduce the professional autonomy of teachers and the independent role of local education authorities in the 'secret garden' of the school curriculum. The remarkable oversight which has led to section 28 of the Local Government Act 1988 failing to have direct relevance to schools, given the removal of sex education from local education authorities' remit in the Education (No. 2) Act 1986, is an indication more of the haste of policy making than any lack of homophobic zeal on the part of the Government! Curricular policies such as these again demonstrate the strategy of combining the taking of powers at the centre with a devolution of decision-making to parents and governors, thus making teachers more accountable for what they teach to those outside the liberal educational establishment.

The Government's approach does, however, reflect a certain amount of tension between the various groups associated with the New Right about the appropriate balance between central powers and market forces in determining the nature of the school curriculum. The influential New Right pressure group on education, the so-called Hillgate Group, seems to take the view that, although market forces should ultimately be seen as the most effective way of determining a school's curriculum, central government intervention is necessary as an interim strategy to undermine the power of vested interests that threaten educational standards and traditional values.[42] In the longer term, though, the notion of a curriculum established by parental demand in the market may well prevail. This view is most forcefully argued by Stuart Sexton, now Director of the Education Unit at the Institute of Economic Affairs, and it was his view that informed Sir Keith (now Lord) Joseph's unsuccessful amendment to the curriculum provisions of the Education Reform Bill in the House of Lords.[43] Although the Government resisted that amendment, it is nevertheless consistent with a long-term preference for market forces that the Government has felt it appropriate not to impose its national curriculum and the associated attainment targets and testing arrangements on independent schools (including those in receipt of public funds through the Assisted Places Scheme) and only in broad terms on the new city technology colleges. The inclusion of grant maintained schools in the arrangements presumably implies that they will take some time to throw off their local education authority origins and develop the responsive new working practices that the Government would like to see emerge.

The way in which the school curriculum has been conceptualized in the Government's proposals itself reveals a significant shift of power within the education bureaucracy. The language of the consultative document on the national curriculum is very different from that of the stream of curriculum documents which preceded it and which were explicitly penned by members of Her Majesty's Schools Inspectorate.[44] Indeed, the consultative document largely ignores developments in curriculum theory during this century. The close similarity between the selection of 'foundation subjects' in that document and the secondary school syllabus laid down by the Board of Education in 1904 demonstrates this.[45] From a situation where some ten years ago Her Majesty's Inspectors were regarded as stalwart conservative members of the establishment they are now apparently seen by the Government as part of the liberal professional lobby within education and as something of a threat.[46] It is apparent that they were not to be entrusted with the writing of the national curriculum document. It must be deduced that the authors of this document were civil servants unfamiliar with educational theory or practice, other than perhaps their own experience as pupils, mostly in rather different settings than those experienced by the majority of school pupils in Britain. Yet, if the national curriculum is partly about building a consensus around a new and profoundly inegalitarian social order, then it is scarcely surprising that all those who have been associated with the development of liberal, let alone socialist, educational practice in the post-war period should be progressively marginalized by the Government in its construction.

THE GREAT NON-DEBATE

Even though commentators sometimes assume that the new consensus has already been successfully constructed, there has been ample evidence of considerable popular and professional opposition to the proposals for the future of education. Much has been said about the volume of response to the Government's consultation papers and about Kenneth Baker's refusal to publish these responses or indeed to pay significant heed to them in the Education Reform Bill as published. Now that others have started to publish the responses it is quite clear that the real support for the package of proposals as a whole is limited to a group of right-wing Conservatives.[47] The churches, parents' and governors' organizations, trades unions, local authorities and their organizations, educationists, and academics were almost at one in their rejection of key aspects of the Bill. Edward Heath MP argued forcefully against major aspects of the Bill in the House of Commons, as did two former Conservative Secretaries of State for Education, Mark Carlisle and Keith Joseph, in the House of Lords. What is perplexing and disturbing is that the Bill went forward with its major provisions virtually unchanged, in spite of this opposition, and that much of the debate now is about 'damage limitation' rather than about seeking out real alternatives. For example, the debate on testing is no longer about whether there should be national testing at seven, eleven, fourteen, and sixteen years of age, but is now limited to a discussion of what would be the best or perhaps the least deleterious form of testing at these ages. Those public opinion polls which have been conducted indicate that a minority of parents are seriously dissatisfied with their children's school and that the majority of parents are opposed to the creation of grant maintained schools.[48] There is, however, consistently distorted reporting of such polls in sections of the popular media.[49]

The minimal effect on the proposals of the responses from political and professional quarters can be attributed not only to the successful accumulation of power by the Thatcher Government but also to its successful political and ideological offensive against teachers and local authorities, especially those which are controlled by the Labour Party. This has been an increasingly important aspect of the Conservative Government's policy since 1979. The portrayal of the Greater London Council and the metropolitan authorities as an inefficient and unnecessary layer of government had been sustained effectively enough for their demise to be achieved in 1986-7. During the second term of the Thatcher Government, and especially in the run up to the 1987 General Election, the portrayal of certain authorities as 'loony left' and extremist was also successfully achieved. The tabloid press has undoubtedly been extremely influential and helpful to the Government in this area, particularly through the use of largely fabricated stories about Brent, Haringey, and the Inner London Education Authority.[50] Several such stories were linked to education, as demonstrated first by a Conservative Party poster for the 1987 General Election which suggested that Labour would 'get police out of schools' and give schoolchildren lessons in 'homosexuality', and secondly by Mrs Thatcher's speech to the 1987 Conservative Party Conference when she referred to anti-racist mathematics as an absurdity. However, the Government has also been prepared to ignore public opinion when it has proved incapable of moulding it, as in the case of the long-running pay dispute with the teachers' union and with its proposals for the abolition of the Inner London Education Authority.

Nevertheless, two groups outside of government did have a notable influence on particular aspects of the Education Reform Bill 1987 as it made its way through the parliamentary process. The first was the university lobby. We noted earlier the limited steps towards privatization in higher education that had been made during the first phase of the Conservative Government's education policy. Major restructuring of funding of all higher education institutions was proposed ahead of other aspects of the Bill, but subsequently included in it. As a result, the University Grants Committee is to be replaced by a University Funding Council while polytechnics and colleges of higher education are to be removed from the responsibility of local education authorities and given corporate status, similar to that already enjoyed by universities but funded by a separate body, the Polytechnic and Colleges Funding Council. Underlying these proposals is a move towards contract funding. Higher education institutions will have increasingly to tender not only for research funding but also for the funding of courses. In the House of Lords the voice of universities was very clearly raised, not only concerning these funding changes but particularly on the issue of academic freedom (where contract funding is indeed seen as a major threat) and on the question of tenure of academic staff, where the universities have traditionally held privileged status. By contrast, the voice of the polytechnics was barely audible.

The second influential lobby, again manifested most clearly in the House of Lords, was the Church of England. From the outset church organizations had expressed extreme anxiety about many aspects of the Bill. It has to be said that their success in amending it has been very limited but nevertheless significant. During June and July 1988 a somewhat surprising coalition emerged in the House of Lords between Baroness Cox, a leading acolyte of the New Right, and Dr Leonard, the Bishop of London. Their common concern was the matter of religious education and collective worship in schools. When the foundation subjects of the national curriculum had been announced in the summer of 1987, and subsequently confirmed in the Bill in November of that year, it was certainly surprising that a Conservative Government had not seen fit to include religious education. This was particularly strange given the fact that under the Education Act 1944 religious education had been the only mandatory subject in the school curriculum. Initially the reaction to this omission concerned simply the status of religious education and the Government responded by specifying more clearly that, along with the components of the national curriculum, it was to be part of the 'basic curriculum' of all maintained schools. However, during 1988 the most vocal concerns expressed by Conservatives and leading churchpeople were about the centrality of Christianity in schooling. The result of much hurried drafting and redrafting within the House of Lords was an amendment supported by the Government but moved by the Bishop of London, which affirmed not only the place of religious education and a daily act of collective worship but asserted in a more explicit way than before the primacy of Christianity. Many religious organizations, teachers' organizations, and political groups expressed opposition to it, but the strength of the alliance between the established church and the Conservative Party secured the amendment (with significant cross-party support). The Conservative Member of Parliament, Timothy Raison, who currently chairs the House of Commons Select Committee on Education, was quoted as saying in favour of the amendment: 'You do not know about civilization unless you know about Christianity and you do not know about English literature unless you know about the Bible and prayer book.'[51]

While the Establishment thus modified Kenneth Baker's Bill in the House of Lords, there was also significant debate about the provisions of the Bill within the Thatcher Government itself. Most notable have been the recurrent tensions between Kenneth Baker and Margaret Thatcher over certain key features of the proposals. Starting with the well-publicized pre-election differences over their predictions of the number of schools which would choose to opt out, differences over the potential for such schools to select their pupils and charge fees, through to more recent tensions over the nature of attainment testing as part of the national curriculum plans, there are clearly important disagreements between the two. The extent to which this Prime Minister has fulfilled a personal political mission has been a subject of considerable interest for political commentators. (And her excursion into the realm of theology in May 1988 illustrates how 'mission' is a very appropriate word.)

The role of various individuals and groups in influencing the Secretary of State for Education and the Prime Minister respectively must to some extent be a matter of speculation. However, the fact that each appears to have different advisers does explain some of the tensions between them. The individuals who seem to have had most influence on Margaret Thatcher include Oliver Letwin, Baroness Cox (a member of the Hillgate Group), and Brian Griffiths. Griffiths is said to be behind the vetoing of certain appointments to the new quangoes to be set up under the Education Reform Act 1988.[52] Kenneth Baker, on the other hand, while listening to the views of such right-wing ideologues, also has to listen much more than Margaret Thatcher to the professionals – civil servants, Her Majesty's Inspectors, educationists, and (occasionally) teachers. As we have noted, there are certainly differences in perspectives between these groups and also to some extent within them. In the overall shaping of policy what has emerged more and more clearly over recent months is the effectiveness of small but well-organized right-wing pressure groups. Some, such as the Institute for Economic Affairs and the Social Affairs Unit, have been active across a wide spectrum of political issues, particularly with regard to privatization. Indeed, in their pronouncements on education their main concern has been with structural issues such as opting out, though we noted earlier their associated suspicion of a curriculum set by legislation rather than market forces. Other groups, such as the Council for Educational Standards and the Hillgate Group, have been more directly concerned with the content of education and the effects of comprehensive schooling and examination reform. The Centre for Policy Studies, which was largely the brainchild of Sir Keith Joseph, has produced pamphlets on both aspects (for example, on opting out and on the English curriculum).[53]

A SOCIALIST ALTERNATIVE?

Despite the growing influence over government policy of the ideologues on the New Right, the universities and the Church of England have demonstrated that it is still possible for other groups to have some effect on Conservative legislation. Yet the influence of the official parliamentary opposition has been minimal. In education, as in other aspects of social policy, this failure to resist the worst excesses and distortions of Thatcherism to some extent reflects the broader disarray within the left and the labour movement. A very serious disjunction has arisen within the left over recent years. This may be characterized in two ways. There has been a failure to develop a modern form of socialism which builds on and unites new social movements, such as those of women, ecology, peace, and black people.[54] This in particular has been the cry of the Eurocommunists and to some extent of Labour Party activists.[55] But the second theme, which is somewhat contradictory with the first, is the failure of the left actually to mobilize around the very deeply divisive tendencies within Thatcher's Britain. This critique argues that the policies of this Government are fundamentally class-based, that Thatcher's rhetoric of classlessness is precisely designed to obscure this fact and consequently that the 'traditional' class analysis of the left must be what guides effective opposition.[56] What is agreed by both camps, however, is that the absence of well-developed and popular alternative policies has been disastrous.[57]

What are the implications of this last point for educationists and socialists (feminists, anti-racists, and so on) when considering education? The lessons of contemporary Thatcherism include an acknowledgement of the importance of 'fringe group' or 'think tank' activities. The effective implementation ten years on of radical policies developed during a period of opposition is all too obvious. Progressive educationists have a critical role to play here, both in informing debate in political arenas and in ensuring that teachers and other educationists understand the implications of proposals and developments as they arise.[58] There are many problems of strategy arising from the confusions discussed in the previous paragraph and it may well be difficult to decide on the most significant points of intervention at any one time or on the particular style of intervention. The creation of broad alliances must also be considered, but experience – for example, over the popular cause of the National Health Service – shows that this in itself is not enough.[59]

Within the Labour Party a number of groups already exist which are concerned primarily with education, although they have different relationships with the Labour Party and apparently different views of what a socialist education policy should comprise. The education front bench team (apart from claiming to have thought of the national curriculum first!) appears largely to have adopted the language of parental rights and accepted an increasingly consumerist view of state education.[60] There is little evidence of a meaningful dialogue between this team and the teachers' organizations, however. During 1988 an 'Education Forum' was set up, comprising a broad range of interests that the Labour Party would wish to involve in education policy making.[61] The long-standing education group within the party, the Socialist Education Association, has by and large been remarkably quiet during the last few months. A number of Labour Party educationists are members of the non-party Education Reform Group, set up in response to Kenneth Baker's Bill. This group consists of education professionals and is publishing a series of 'Ginger Papers'.[62] In July 1988 a new think tank was established with the explicit purpose of doing for the left what the Centre for Policy Studies and similar bodies had so successfully done for the right. It is chaired by Baroness Blackstone (an educationist) and includes several other notable public figures. This group is concerned with a whole range of policy issues rather than just education and is formally independent of the Labour Party.[63] On the left of the Labour Party another group appears to be attempting to make connections with other aspects of debate within the party. This is the Socialist Teachers' Alliance, a long-standing group of left-wingers, which in the past has concentrated on influencing the policy of the National Union of Teachers. Its focus now is increasingly within the Labour Party, aligning itself clearly with the left of the party and currently working on the production of an 'Education Charter'. The draft of this charter avoids adopting consumerist language in the Tory sense and it points to the possibility of addressing genuine popular concerns about education without adopting Conservative solutions and claiming them as its own. The charter therefore talks in terms of pupils', parents', and teachers' democratic rights within education and is particularly concerned to attack inequalities. In contrast with official Labour Party pronouncements to date, this amounts to one of the most comprehensive statements yet available from the left on a popular alternative to the Conservative Government's education policy.[64]

CONCLUSION: WHITHER STATE EDUCATION?

The extent to which this Government has changed the nature of law-making is well revealed in the field of education policy. First, it is only with the third term of the Thatcher Government that legislation has been the main tool of educational policy. Previously, the emphasis was very much on opinion moulding, albeit heavily influenced by financial controls.[65] But secondly, a comparison with the last Education Act of similar magnitude, Butler's Education Act 1944, reveals fully the extent of the Thatcherite project. As befitted a parliamentary Act which enshrined the social democratic settlement in education, there was a period of consultation lasting approximately two years before the legislation was published and major amendments were made to the Bill as it progressed through Parliament, in response to criticism from professional, political, and popular quarters. The major proposals within Kenneth Baker's Education Reform Bill, on the other hand, were the subject of consultation typically over a period of two months and the vast majority of the amendments which have been made have had the purpose of making the legislation more effective rather than changing its intentions. It is true that some important defeats occurred in the House of Lords – for example, on opting out, academic freedom in universities, and religious education – but the Government did not accept all of these amendments in their entirety.

In moving education to the centre of contemporary politics the Government has revealed a grasp of both its structural and its ideological significance. In structural terms we can see increasing differentiation within the education system. In ideological terms there are two main features. First, there is 'the ideology of the structure' – that is, the ideology of individualism and competition;[66] and secondly, there is the ideological aspect of the educational process itself, including both the curriculum and hidden curriculum of schooling. Along with the media, education is a key route to the thoughts and values of people within nations.

It is lessons such as these which must now be acted upon by those who share alternative visions of society and of the purpose of education systems to those views which are currently dominant and are reflected in the Education Reform Act 1988. In the way that the demands for state schooling and for comprehensive non-selective secondary education were developed in and by the labour movement, so it is now again essential for educationists to work with and through groups and organizations which represent those whose aspirations and interests are under attack in the current upheavals. Out of such discussions both a broad framework and a detailed plan must emerge which will reflect the very real social and technological changes which have taken place during the second half of this century and express a re-affirmed commitment to the struggle for social justice in and through education.

NOTES AND REFERENCES

1 An account of 'The Great Debate' is provided by G. Whitty, *Sociology and School Knowledge* (1985) ch. 5. Examples of the 'Black Papers' include C. B. Cox and A. E. Dyson (eds.), *Fight for Education* (1969), *The Crisis in Education* (1969), *Goodbye Mr Short* (1970), and C. B. Cox and R. Boyson (eds.), *Black Paper 1977* (1977). Contributors to the Black Papers included Kingsley Amis, Angus Maude, Cyril Burt, Max Beloff, and Caroline Cox. For a detailed study of the development of education policy after 1944, in the context of the crisis of social democracy, see Centre for Contemporary Cultural Studies, *Unpopular Education* (1981).

2 The inquiry was led by Robin Auld QC. See R. Auld, *William Tyndale Junior and Infants Schools Public Inquiry: A Report to the Inner London Education Authority* (1976). An assessment of the effect of this affair is offered in R. Dale, 'Control, Accountability and William Tyndale' in *Politics, Patriarchy and Practice*, eds. R. Dale et al. (1981) 305.

3 The debate over 'standards' has been inconclusive, with as many reports leading to the view that they are rising as falling.

4 Department of Education and Science, *Education in Schools. A Consultative Document* (1977; Cmnd. 6869).

5 W. S. Fowler (ed.), *Towards the National Curriculum* (1988).

6 R. Dale, 'Thatcherism and Education' in *Contemporary Education Policy*, eds. J. Ahier and M. Flude (1983).

7 A. D. Edwards et al., 'The State and the Independent Sector' in *Social Crisis and Educational Research*, eds. L. Barton and S. Walker (1984).

8 Quoted in J. Fitz et al., 'Beneficiaries, Benefits and Costs: An Investigation of the Assisted Places Scheme' (1986) 1 *Research Papers in Education* 169. See also A. D. Edwards et al., *The State and Private Education: An Evaluation of the Assisted Places Scheme* (1989).

9 E. G. West, 'Education Vouchers: Evolution or Revolution?' (1982) 3 *J. of Economic Affairs* 14.

10 T. Albert, 'The Cheapest Way to Help the Brightest and the Best' *The Guardian*, 23 November 1982.

11 R. Johnson, 'British Education and Monetarism' in *Education under Monetarism*, ed. World University Service (1983). The Manpower Services Commission later became the Training Commission, but as this paper went to press the Government announced its abolition, after a major disagreement with the Trades Union Congress, thus removing from the area of education and training one of the last vestiges of corporatist policy.

12 R. Pring, 'Privatization in Education' (1987) 2 *J. of Education Policy* 289.

13 M. Inman, 'Creeping Privatization?' *Schoolmaster and Career Teacher*, Winter 1986, 5.

14 G. Whitty et al., 'Private Education in England and Wales' in *Private Schools in Ten Countries*, ed. G. Walford (1989).

15 P. Newsam, interview in 'Starting Out', London Weekend Television, 11 September 1981.

16 G. Whitty et al., 'Assisting Whom? Benefits and Costs of the Assisted Places Scheme' in *Education Policies: Controversies and Critiques*, eds. A. Hargreaves and D. Reynolds (1988).

17 R. Hammond, 'Centres of Excellence', *The Times Educational Supplement*, 13 March 1987.

18 For more details of these policies, see the contribution by the Bristol Polytechnic Education Study Group to *The Day of the Gerbil*, eds. D. Coulby and L. Bash (1989).

19 'Mrs Thatcher enthuses over opting-out proposals' *The Times Educational Supplement*, 18 September 1987.

20   J. Campbell et al., 'Multiplying the Divisions? Intimations of Educational Policy Post-1987' (1987) 2 *J. Education Policy* 369; P. Cordingley and P. Wilby, *Opting Out of Mr Baker's Proposals* (1987).

21   J. Demaine, 'Teachers' Work, Curriculum and the New Right' (1988) 9 *Brit. J. Sociology of Education* 247.

22   This concern was given added weight by the occurrence of what had become known as 'The Dewsbury Affair'. At the beginning of the school year in 1987 national media attention was focused on twenty-five children in Dewsbury whose parents refused to enrol them at the school to which they had been allocated by Kirklees education authority. At this school, Headfield, eighty-five per cent of the pupils were of Asian origin. Overthorpe, the school to which the parents wanted their children to go, was predominantly white. There was much debate about the parents' motivation and in particular whether their actions were racist. However, in making their case, the parents themselves frequently invoked 'parental choice', the right of parents to choose their children's school, which had been such a central part of the Government's rhetoric about improving education. In July 1988, when the case had reached the High Court, the parents were offered and accepted the places they wanted for their children, with Kirklees explaining that they would have lost the case on a technicality and so chose to settle out of court. (See 'Parents win the school of their choice' *The Times Educational Supplement*, 15 July 1988.) On the House of Lords debate, see 'Peers back open policy on enrolment' *The Times Educational Supplement*, 13 May 1988.

23   Fitz et al., op. cit., n. 8.

24   D. Argyropulo, 'Inner city quality' *The Times Educational Supplement*, 1 August 1986.

25   When not dissimilar changes were introduced in the National Health Service they were accompanied by a restructuring of management which introduced personnel trained in accountancy and financial management at a senior level in hospitals and health authorities. No such innovations are being proposed with respect to schools, whether local education authority or grant maintained, although presumably the grant maintained schools will have the power to buy in such expertise.

26   'CTC sponsors to ask for no strike agreement' *The Times Educational Supplement*, 24 June 1988.

27   Department of Education and Science, *Qualified Teacher Status – Consultation Document* (1988).

28   'Bits of paper' *The Times Educational Supplement*, 13 November 1987.

29   Sir Keith Joseph established the Council for the Accreditation of Teacher Education in 1984. See G. Whitty et al., 'Ideology and Control in Teacher Education' in *Critical Studies in Teacher Education*, ed. T. Popkewitz (1987).

30   R. Levitas (ed.), *The Ideology of the New Right* (1986).

31   T. Gurr and D. King, *The State and the City* (1987).

32   'Mr Dunn's version of morality and the curriculum' *Education*, 8 July 1988.

33   G. Seidel, 'Culture, Nation and "Race" ' in *The Ideology of the New Right*, op. cit., n. 30; P. Gordon and F. Klug, *New Right, New Racism* (1986).

34   B. Coard, *How the West Indian Child is Made Educationally Sub-Normal in the British School System* (1971); B. Bryan et al., *The Heart of the Race* (1985) ch. 2.

35   M. Stone, *The Education of the Black Child in Britain* (1981); C. Mullard, *Anti-racist Education: The Three O's* (1984).

36   S. Pearce, *Education and the Multi-racial Society* (1985); F. Palmer (ed.), *Anti-racism, an Assault on Education and Value* (1986); A. Flew, *Power to the Parents* (1987); R. Lewis, *Anti-racism: A Mania Exposed* (1988). Ray Honeyford was the headteacher of Drummond School, Bradford, who contributed articles to the *Times Educational Supplement* and the *Salisbury Review* attacking multicultural education policies. Jonathan Savery taught at the Multicultural Education Centre in Bristol, where there were demands for his dismissal following the publication of an article entitled 'Anti-racism as Witchcraft' in the *Salisbury Review*. Similarly, there were calls for the dismissal of Maureen McGoldrick, head of an infants' school in Brent, after allegations that she had made a racist remark in a phone call to an education officer. Brent, as an authority, came in for much criticism in the popular press

after announcing its intention to appoint 180 teachers with responsibility for developing racial equality in schools. The Dewsbury affair has been described above, n. 22.

37 M. Francis, 'Issues in the Fight against the Education Bill' (1988) 29 *Race and Class* 103; P. Gordon, 'The New Right, Race, and Education – Or How the Black Papers became a White Paper' (1988) 29 *Race and Class* 95; 'Gerbil Issue' (1988) 6 *Multicultural Teaching*.

38 Committee of Inquiry into the Education of Children from Ethnic Minority Groups, *Education For All* (1985; Cmnd. 9453).

39 Jenny Williams has suggested that debate about 'race' and education has to some extent superseded earlier discourse around class inequalities. However, it has become clear that this 'racialization' of education discourse has had far-reaching implications and effects. (See J. Williams, 'Education and Race: The Racialization of Class Inequalities' (1986) 7 *Brit. J. Sociology of Education* 135.)

40 'Raison claims syllabus will bear global perspective' *Education*, 8 July 1988.

41 'Fighting the siege mentality' (1983) 21 *Teaching London Kids* 3.

42 The Hillgate Group, *The Reform of British Education* (1987).

43 S. Sexton, 'No nationalized curriculum' *The Times*, 9 May 1988.

44 Compare Department of Education and Science, *The National Curriculum 5-16 – A Consultation Document* (1987) with Her Majesty's Inspectorate of Schools, *The Curriculum from 5 to 16, Curriculum Matters 2* (1985). The latter talks of 'areas of experiences' and 'elements of learning' rather than the 'subjects' of the former.

45 R. Aldrich, 'The National Curriculum: An Historical Perspective' in *The National Curriculum*, eds. D. Lawton and C. Chitty (1988) 21.

46 Some indication of this tension is revealed in the pronouncements of retired members of Her Majesty's Inspectorate of Schools. See the interview of former Senior Chief Inspector, Sheila Browne, in *The Guardian*, 19 April 1988 and the letter from former Inspector, H. G. Williams, in *The Guardian*, 26 April 1988.

47 Most notably see J. Haviland (ed.), *Take Care, Mr Baker* (1988). See also B. Simon, *Bending the Rules* (1988), and R. Aitken and H. Ree (eds.), *Dear Mr Baker . . . !* (1988).

48 'Reform: marks out of a hundred' *Times Educational Supplement*, 11 December 1987; 'A decisive No to opting out' *The Guardian*, 9 February 1988.

49 A good example is 'State Schools – What the Parents Think' (1987) 131 *Reader's Digest* 35.

50 Goldsmiths' College Media Research Group, 'Loony Lies', BBC2, March 1988.

51 'Christian base to RE would breed intolerance, say heads' *Times Educational Supplement*, 8 July 1988.

52 'Round Brian quiz' *The Guardian*, 19 July 1988. Leading educationists Peter Mortimore and Christopher Ball have both apparently been barred from membership of the National Curriculum Council by the Prime Minister ('Fit Person' and 'Gift rapped' *Times Educational Supplement*, 1 July 1988).

53 Individual profiles on influential right-wing educationists are provided by Peter Wilby and Simon Midgley in 'As the new right wields its power' *The Independent*, 23 July 1987. A directory of some of the notable groups is appended to Gordon and Klug, op. cit., n. 33. The Hillgate Group, which has come into prominence more recently, includes among its leading members Baroness Cox, Jessica Douglas-Home, John Marks, Lawrence Norcross, and Roger Scruton. The influence of different pressures within the Conservative Party are discussed in Dale, op. cit., n. 6.

54 S. Hall, 'No light at the end of the tunnel' *Marxism Today*, December 1986.

55 For an example of the former see E. Laclau, 'Class war and after' *Marxism Today* April 1987. For an example of the latter see H. Wainwright, *Labour: A Tale of Two Parties* (1987).

56 A clear statement along these lines is provided in E. Wood, *The Retreat from Class* (1986).

57 B. Jessop et al., 'Popular Capitalism, Flexible Accumulation, and Left Strategy' (1987) 165 *New Left Rev.* 104.

58 G. Whitty, 'Curriculum Research and Curricular Politics' (1987) 8 *Brit J. Sociology of Education* 109; R. Hatcher, 'From Analysis to Action – Waiting for the Left Sociologists of Education' in *Socialist Teacher*, November 1987.

59 'Broad alliances' have been advocated by Brian Simon and the journal of which he is co-editor, *Forum*, as well as by the teacher unions.

60 Labour Party, *Parents in Partnership* (1988); D.Fatchett, *Education in a Multicultural Society* (1988).

61 'Labour to set up think tank' *Times Educational Supplement*, 24 June 1988.

62 The first of these is Cordingley and Wilby, op. cit., n. 20.

63 'Think tank launched by left' *The Independent*, 27 July 1988.

64 Socialist Teachers' Alliance, 'Draft of an Education Charter for Schools' (1988) 40 *Socialist Teacher* 11.

65 These financial controls were of two kinds: first, the direct restriction on local education authority budgets, secondly (and more recently) increasing central intervention in determining the ways in which money can be spent.

66 T. Wragg, *Education in the Market Place* (1988).

Housing Tales of Law and Space

ANN STEWART* AND ROGER BURRIDGE*

THE STORIES SO FAR

Once upon a time not so long ago an analysis of law and housing would have been accomplished in a fairly slim volume concentrating upon contractual responsibilities of tenure and their historical development, including perhaps a chapter on council houses and the responsibilities of local government. To a large extent 'housing law' was the child of committed practitioners, concentrating their efforts upon the development of legal services for the poorly housed and the assembly of legal rules that were pertinent to such actions.[1]

In recent years housing has emerged as a subject of increasing interest to administrative lawyers. Urban sociology has provided insights into the role of the state in housing provision and the role of the courts in adjudicating the challenge by bearers of private law rights against the interests of collectively consumed services.[2] At the same time the tensions between central and local government and efforts to restructure the Welfare State have been the subject of analysis by administrative lawyers.[3]

Much of this work relies heavily upon a historical analysis of law, and whilst all change inevitably involves a temporal element,[4] an understanding of the possible significance of space is often missing. History explains what the law has become but it does not elucidate where it is.

It might appear trite that this paper calls for an analysis of both phenomena. The legal interventions of Thatcherism demand a historical analysis and assume a spatial one – the law of England and Wales . . . or does it include Northern Ireland or even Scotland? The jurisdictional quibble (if quibble it is) will not be pursued here; it is merely an emphasis of the assumptions that we make about the space of law. Clearly any thorough analysis of the significance of space should synthesize historical development and this paper makes a somewhat crude division. It first sets out to explain the temporal development of the housing legislation of the present Conservative Government and places Thatcher's reforms against the background of previous administrations. In

*The School of Law, University of Warwick, Coventry, West Midlands CV4 7AL, England.

The authors are grateful to Ken Foster and Sammy Adelman for comments made upon earlier drafts of this paper.

this respect recent housing law is presented as part of a continuum, albeit at a radical change of pace, of previous attempts to resolve the tensions of an industrial economy in crisis.

The review of the recent history of housing provides the basis for a consideration of the spatial implications of the legislation. The 'housing law' is that of England and Wales since laws are invariably reducible to jurisdictional boundaries of geographical nation states. Elsewhere it might be asked whether the Thatcher Government reforms can additionally be explained by reference to the position (temporarily *and* spatially) of England and Wales in the global market of monopoly capital.

The significance of space for law upon which we concentrate is the tendency towards the uneven geographical implementation of law. Whilst a historical perspective explains the restructuring of the Welfare State and the debilitation of local government influence, the implementation of the legislation has a precise and discrete geography. The emergence of 'social markets' not only polarizes individuals by income, it also ascribes them to particular localities. The issue of space extends beyond the resource implications implicit in an implementation-centred approach, however, and in the closing section of the article the notion that the substance of law – that is, the interpretation of laws by administrative agencies – itself has a spatial dimension which is explored.

THE COUNCIL HOUSE TALE

The discussion that follows addresses in more detail the pedigree of Thatcherism, with particular reference to the provision of state housing. We would argue, along with others, that state housing has represented historically a significant material gain for certain sections of the working class by reducing the cost of shelter without a commensurate reduction in wage levels.[5] This is not to deny that state housing has also served its purpose of providing a decently housed, relatively healthy, and appropriately located workforce and, as such, is consistent with the efficient accumulation of industrial capital. The attempts by the Thatcher Government to transform the state sector have been directed primarily at dismantling the existing process of collective consumption and democratic intervention. Provision via the state in its present form may be unacceptable ideologically, but state support provided in a non-collectivist, market-based system which destroys the remaining vestiges of material gain is not. We are seeing a transformation through the introduction of 'social markets' rather than a wholesale dismantling of the state sector. This is made easier because council housing is vulnerable at its supposed strongest point: the collectivist elements of public housing have never had a secure foundation because of the limited and ambiguous nature of the state's intervention.

The core collectivist elements of council housing have involved historic cost accounting rather than a current market value basis. Past investment in the stock is held at its fixed historic cost. As a landlord the local authority spreads

66

the rents it charges over the whole of its stock and does not fix them in direct relation to the actual costs of particular dwellings. The loan which is needed to finance building also is not directly related to a specific scheme. A local authority maintains a consolidated loans fund which borrows from external sources. Spending departments borrow from it. The rate of interest charged against a scheme is not the rate on new advances in the year when the finance for the project was raised but the 'pool rate' – the rate of interest on all outstanding debt, which has been lower.[6] In addition central government has provided a general subsidy to the local authority to offset the overall cost of housing.

The boundaries of state intervention have expanded – in some localities and at different historical periods. Dwellings are costly to produce. Servicing the capital debt is the primary financial objective, unlike education or social services, where revenue matters are highly significant. Local authorities have relied very heavily on the private building sector to provide their stock. In some areas they have built up substantial direct labour organizations – directly employed building workforces which have reduced their reliance on the market. Whereas direct labour organizations have monopolized the repair and maintenance work, their contribution to 'new build' programmes has been limited.[7] State housing has always been subject to the vagaries of the construction market with its fluctuating costs and poor record of quality.

Land has never been nationalized. The level of state intervention has varied. Development gain has been regulated but essentially land has remained in the market. State housing has also been vulnerable to the market fluctuations in interest rates despite the buffers provided by collectivism. Rent policy has only redistributed within the existing sector. Rate fund contributions to the revenue account, which spreads the financial burden over the total local population, have been discretionary, thereby permitting substantial differences in material conditions for tenants.

The boundaries between the market and the public core have moved. The high points would be 1923 and 1924 and between 1946 and 1951 when the market was tightly controlled. In the crisis years of the 1970s the level of subsidy needed to sustain the particular boundary was seen in political terms as too high. Nonetheless, the collectivist core remained; tenants individually did not pay the price of the fluctuations in the market, tenants collectively did to some extent.

Over the last nine years the Government has been attempting to transform the Welfare State. There is considerable debate over whether or not these moves represent a complete break with the post-war consensus. The introduction of a 'social market' philosophy into welfare provision – the key elements of which are a choice of service provider exercised by the individual as parent, tenant, or elderly person, and using either income or a state subsidy or both to pay for the service – does change the game. The quality of provision is dictated by the individual's ability to pay. Under a social market regime the collectivist mediation is lost.

Part of the Government's strategy is to use the possibility of an alternative form of provision as a threat to the public service to transform itself, and to facilitate this approach by adopting financial regimes such as 'internal markets' which mirror the market. The introduction of a social market philosophy is made easier in the housing field because it has a longer history than in other Welfare State services. On the demand side housing associations, ready-made alternative landlords, have been supported by the state for two decades. On the supply side individual means-tested subsidies have been available since the 1930s although they only became mandatory through the Finance Act 1972.

It would, however, be inaccurate to suggest that the Government has had a coherent strategy over the last nine years. Policy has developed in an *ad hoc* manner. Central government has learned lessons from the experience of the 1970s, has experimented and learnt again during the 1980s. A great deal has depended on the state of the financial market and the building societies' role within it. The mechanisms required for a social market are not yet all in place although the Housing Act 1988 represents a major step forward. The recently published consultation paper entitled *The New Financial Regime for Local Authority Housing in England and Wales* represents the next step.[8] Further legislative moves will probably be required to 'redefine' homelessness. The present subsidy system which provides mortgage tax relief and Housing Benefit will need to be transformed into an individual housing allowance – a housing token. It is also not at all clear that the strategy will succeed in its own terms. It depends heavily on the state of the financial sector, the ability to manipulate housing associations, and the strength of opposition from interested groups.

Two phases of the development of Conservative housing policy are discernible, the first of which covers 1979-1986.

1. *Conservative Government Housing Policy 1979–86*

The boundaries between the core and the market were quickly moved in relation to intervention in the land market. In 1980 the new Government quickly disposed of the Community Land Act 1975.[9] Five years later development and land tax were abolished.[10] The pressure on local planning authorities to release land for private development has increased. They are expected to engage in close consultation with builders and developers and to ensure that there is sufficient land allocated to meet the needs of the housebuilders for the following five years:

> Essentially the government's objective has been to establish a market-led planning system with the role of local authorities as that of aiding private developers and facilitating private development.[11]

The building industry did not fare as well in the earlier part of this period. This was due entirely to the major economic recession and in particular the very dramatic drop in public expenditure. The Department of the Environment's review of direct labour organizations was transformed into Part III of the Local Government Planning and Land Act 1980. Under these provisions authorities are required to keep accounts on a commercial – that is, trading – basis. In addition, the Secretary of State for the Environment has powers to ensure that direct labour organizations make a profit on capital employed (presently five per cent). Direct labour organizations are obliged to compete directly with private contractors: they can only undertake work (above a specified value) after tendering against at least three outside contractors. The Secretary of State for the Environment is also empowered to ask for a special report on the operation of the direct labour organization and consequently may direct that it cease trading altogether or in specific areas of work. These measures formed the prototype for the enforced tendering for six additional services contained in the Local Government Act 1988.

Housing suffers the most in any attempt to control public expenditure generated by local authorities because it constitutes by far the largest spending block. The Local Government Planning and Land Act 1980 empowered the Secretary of State for the Environment to impose a capital expenditure ceiling on each local authority. Local authorities still put in an annual bid to central government for a housing allocation to allow them to borrow money through the Housing Investment Programme. They are now able to supplement their Housing Investment Programme allocation with capital receipts from sales. The proportion of receipts which can be used in any one year is prescribed by the Secretary of State for the Environment. The overall effect of these direct controls has been to halve expenditure between 1979-80 and 1986-7. Allocations through the Housing Investment Programme (which in effect sanctions borrowing) are one-fifth of the 1979 level. Receipts – that is, capital assets – now finance seventy per cent of total expenditure. The overall effect is to maintain an allocation system which is based on general principles of needs assessment, while providing windfall profits to specific localities. The London Borough of Tower Hamlets has virtually no capital receipts, whereas Bromley has unspent millions of pounds sterling.

The response of the local authorities, particularly the Labour-controlled councils, was to point to the need to invest in the decaying physical fabric. They produced through the Association of Metropolitan Authorities a series of reports highlighting the defects in different types of public housing stock. Individual local authorities produced equally compelling statistics. The Department of the Environment responded with its stock condition survey in 1985. The results showed the need for £19 billion investment in the public sector. Expenditure was needed in every category of stock from the early 1920s houses to the 1960s tower blocks. The Government's response was to suggest a change in ownership and increased use of private capital.

The Government had learnt from the débâcle of the Clay Cross affair in the 1970s that a direct attack on rent levels could lead to direct opposition. The Housing Act 1980 introduced a new subsidy system for housing based on the same deficit financing principle without intervention on individual rents. It is, however, essentially the same system as that proposed by the previous Labour administration. In effect it has abolished any general subsidy for council housing. Rents now must cover the outgoings on the housing revenue account unless the local authority makes a contribution from the rates. This has become more difficult as a result of the central government intervention on rates culminating in the rate-capping of some authorities. The cost to authorities of subsidizing rent in lost grant is often enormous. The power to do so is about to be lost.

Rents rose very substantially in this period and continue to do so. Councillors have been obliged to make these decisions and have found it hard politically to place the blame on central government. The rent of the majority of council tenants is now subsidized individually through Housing Benefit. The separate systems for rebating the rent of public and private tenants were amalgamated in 1982 and the responsibility for administering the system was transferred to the local authorities. One element in harmonizing public and private sector rents was thereby achieved. The rent levels matter less to those in receipt of full Housing Benefit. While easing the political pain of rent rises this change in subsidy system has further undermined the collectivist nature of council housing.

Rent levels are most significant to those not in receipt of Housing Benefit. The flagship of the Housing Act 1980 was the right to buy. This measure enabled council tenants who saw the advantages of owner-occupation to achieve that goal at a very substantial discount. It was a vote winner and it has proved very popular with the skilled working-class tenants who might in different circumstances or location have been owner-occupiers from the outset. Larger discounts were made available in 1984 and 1986.[12] The Housing Act 1980 set up a system which minimized the chances of local authority opposition and gave the Secretary of State for the Environment very wide powers in default.[13] Some local authorities made half-hearted attempts at administrative resistance but they were put under heavy pressure by the Department of the Environment which monitored the system with unaccustomed zeal.

In comparison, the other new rights in the Housing Act 1980 pale into insignificance. In essence the Government adopted a watered-down version of the Housing Bill prepared by the Labour Government in 1979. The security of tenure provisions remained, the collective consultation mechanisms were reduced to a bare minimum.[14]

Against the background of this scorched earth policy some local authorities tried to take the initiative by improving services in an attempt to maintain their credibility as managers of a public service. This often involved management reorganization to localize the point of delivery of the service. Sometimes it involved tenant participation in management. Councils attempted this at a time when there was a growing attack on their ability to manage. In 1985 the Centre for Policy Studies published a pamphlet entitled *Trust the Tenant*. Its author argued that if property were transferred out of public ownership, it could then be used as a mortgageable asset. Tenants could form co-operatives, take over their own management, and raise money. They would be both better managers and financiers. In 1985 the Audit Commission published its report, entitled *Managing the Crisis in Council Housing*. The report made it abundantly clear that many local authorities were poor quality managers and could be far better if they adopted some market management techniques.

Central government missed no opportunity to chastise for high levels of arrears or overspending or, indeed, underspending – but the attack was of a general nature. Central government essentially did not know a great deal about the way local authorities managed their stock. Local councils traditionally have exercised wide discretion in management, unfettered by outside interference from courts or central government. The Department of the Environment set up the Priority Estates Project in 1984 to provide assistance to local authorities in managing their troublesome estates. Consultants were allocated to willing local authorities who were thereby given access to a small additional capital allocation. These projects experimented with tenant management, financial decentralization, and new repair systems. The project was renamed Estate Action in 1986 and schemes were required to consider private sector involvement, usually through the transfer of existing stock. It was a fluid period in which the role of the private sector was explored, particularly the part which housing associations could play. The Housing and Planning Act 1986 provided the legal powers to enable those schemes which involved privatization to go ahead. Voluntary sales of blocks could go ahead with the consent of the Secretary of State for the Environment.

In the face of financial controls local authorities had tried again to circumvent the legislation by a wide range of devices. They often found that they could obtain access to private sector capital for housing schemes if they surrendered ownership to housing associations and merely retained allocation rights over dwellings. Building societies were looked on as the main potential financiers. Their powers were extended by the Building Societies Act 1986 to allow them to become involved in direct funding of housing schemes. They had already played a major role in funding the sales of council houses. They were now heavily encouraged by central government to become involved with housing to rent and with the upturn in the economy they had more than adequate funds to do so.

By the end of 1986 the local authorities had been severely weakened. They were now often seen as providing an inefficient and unpopular service. Tenants had been encouraged to consider alternative management with the clear advantage that, unlike their present landlord, the new management would have access to funds. The general subsidy had all but disappeared and so had over one million of the most financially able tenants. The authorities had not been able to take the initiative. The attempts at managerial change had been directed by central government towards tenurial change.

2. Conservative Government Housing Policy From 1986 Onwards

Central government confidence in its ability to intervene increased after 1986. This strength is reflected in the White Paper on housing which preceded the Housing Act 1988. The Act is a major initiative. It takes forward a number of the earlier experiments. Public sector tenants will be able to choose to transfer to a new landlord. Housing associations are to provide the alternative. The Housing Corporation has been given the task of persuading the housing associations to take over the public stock. First, however, they themselves are required to be more market-based. Ironically, until now their financial position has been envied by local authorities. They have received around eighty-five per cent of their capital costs in the form of a government-funded Housing Association Grant. This level is being reduced and will be topped up by private finance which the Housing Corporation will organize on their behalf. The level of grant they receive in future will be reduced in general to between thirty and sixty per cent. The task of fixing this is again given to the Housing Corporation. All rent restriction has been abolished for new private and housing association tenancies to facilitate their new role. The assured tenancy which first appeared in the Housing Act 1980 has been adapted to enable landlords to regularly renegotiate market rents. Few believe that the deregulation of the private rented sector will bring about much of an expansion. Clearly there is a role for what is now being called the 'mobility' sector to house affluent mobile people, particularly in London and the south-east of England. Nonetheless, housing association rents had to be deregulated in order to attract private financiers.

The Housing Act 1988 also established housing action trusts which will operate in the same manner as urban development corporations. They will be managed by a board appointed by the Secretary of State for the Environment. The stock will be transferred from local councils to housing action trusts after a vote by tenants. Over a period of three to five years the stock will be improved and sold off to housing associations, private landlords, or to the sitting tenants.

The Housing Act 1988 seeks to provide housing choice for tenants in a market context. Clearly housing associations are a compromise. They are a ready-made alternative with a reasonable record of providing housing. They are not democratically managed and have no collectivist element. Nonetheless, they are non-profit-making and state supported. The Housing Corporation is a quango and is far more tied to the centre than local authorities which as yet have a separate source of income.

Local authorities are set to lose another of the elements which separated them out from other landlords. In the Local Government and Housing Bill 1989 the Government proposed to 'ring fence' housing revenue accounts: local authorities will be unable to subsidize rents through the rates. The housing revenue account will then be an asset-based account, ready to be stripped by any likely contender. Nevertheless, it is highly unlikely that a power will be given to use this account as security for private investment. But, if it were, historic cost accounting will also be lost.

The aim is to introduce 'social markets' into the housing sector. Not all the mechanisms are yet in place. If this legislation is successful there will possibly be a choice of landlords in the market. Nonetheless, the tenant in receipt of state benefits has little incentive to seek the most 'efficient' landlord in market terms. The subsidy is generally paid irrespective of the rent level (although there are powers presently to restrict payments to fair rent level; the Housing Act 1988 does give a new role to the rent officer to oversee benefit levels when they are provided on the new market rents.) The tenant, however, gains nothing in choosing a cheaper landlord. Tenants are likely to choose the landlord whom they judge will provide the best service, the most important aspect of which will be repairs. The Housing Benefit system will need to be transformed into a housing allowance payable to the tenant before the social market is fully established. There is already considerable debate over the concept of a universal housing allowance payable to all irrespective of tenure which would replace mortgage tax relief and Housing Benefit.

3. *The Legal Framework*

The 1960s and 1970s saw considerable intervention by governments in the owner-occupied market but little direct intervention in the public housing sector other than in the ill-fated Housing Finance Act 1972.[15] There has, however, been an unprecedented level of direct interference with the financial aspects of local authority housing provision in the period of the Thatcher Government. Ministers have been provided with extensive discretionary powers to oversee all areas of local authority activity. 'Quasi-legislation' such as financial accounting procedures generated by the Audit Commission and bodies such as the Chartered Institute of Public Finance Accountants take on an added significance. A sense of a wider financial accountability dictates many policy decisions. The rolling back of the state has involved a considerable amount of state intervention.

The local authorities are told that their function is to become one of strategic overseer and regulator but if the present strategy is successful much of this regulation will pass to other statutory bodies, to housing action trusts and to the Housing Corporation. The latter will oversee the transfer of stock from the public sector to housing associations or private landlords. Its consent will be needed in both cases. Environmental health responsibilities will remain with the local council at least until such time as it is privatized. The Housing Corporation has recently issued its draft tenants' guarantee, a guidance to be issued under the Housing Act 1988.

The Housing Corporation states that the aim of the guidance is to define clearly standards and expectations for registered housing associations. In deciding whether there has been mismanagement in a housing association the Housing Corporation will be obliged by the legislation to take into account a housing association's record of compliance with the guidance.

4. *Opposition?*

There has been little evidence yet of opposition specifically directed at housing policies. During the 1970s there was some attempt to analyse the housing question in terms of production as well as consumption, and some discussion of the problems of production took place in mainstream politics: the Community Land Act 1975 tackled weakly the land question and the excesses of the secondary banking sector were curbed. In the 1980s opposition has come from some large urban Labour-controlled local authorities[16] and from the relatively unorganized tenants' movements.[17] The Centre for Local Economic Strategies has organized research over the last three years as well as run a campaign under the rubric of 'homes and jobs'.[18] Their aim has been to promote the idea of economic activity to meet socially-defined need to make the link between satisfying housing need and creating and improving the quality of jobs. Nevertheless, these represent the exceptions to the 'social market' rule. The parliamentary opposition argues within the same consumption-led paradigm. As a result the debate tends to focus on the relative importance of the local authorities or other bodies to regulate the market and the powers which the local authorities would need to operate a market-led service.

The most coherent responses to the present round of legislative proposals have been set within the same social market context. A paper by the chairman of the Association of Metropolitan Authorities' housing committee has argued for a tenure-led strategy in which local authorities as landlords would be able to compete on equal terms in the market with the other landlords. The Association of Direct Labour Organizations has argued for a similar position. Each involves an extension of local authority powers to operate more widely in the market. The public sector tenants' movement has been jolted into action. It is, however, dominated by people who have experienced private landlordism at first hand; there is a conspicuous lack of involvement of younger tenants. Local councillors also tend to fall within the younger age range and are the first generation in power not to have had direct experience of the private market.

The lack of coherent opposition is despite the obvious problems in the housing market. Owner-occupied housing costs are the highest for over twenty years and much attention is paid to the 'pricing out' of workers in London and the south-east of England. There is once again a 'land question' in the south-east of England and the Home Counties. Planning and controlling land release is very much on the agenda. Estate agents are extremely unpopular and are being threatened with state regulation. The building industry is severely over-heating, thereby contributing to the national balance of payments crisis through its massive import of materials and to inflation through the bidding up of wage levels.

At a different level there has been considerable evidence of popular resistance to urban conditions in specific localities – in Brixton, Handsworth, Toxteth, and Broadwater Farm. These protests have shown that tenure has less significance in itself than location. At its crudest, Handsworth is predominantly owner-occupied, Broadwater Farm is a council estate. The condition of the houses, however, reflects the marginalized population housed within the location.

Our account of the Thatcher years suggests that it is too early to write of them as the end of the series on the Welfare State. If there has been a transformation in the process of accumulation of capital that has altered the form of the modern state, then the short sight of history is too blurred to focus upon housing as a commodity form that substantiates such theories.

We suggested earlier that the emergence of a housing policy from the Thatcher Government was hesitant and opportunist. It was inspired more by an adherence to time-honoured Conservative tenets of a property-owning democracy. The picture of that policy as two parts ideology, one part economic expediency, now emerges more clearly. In 1974 when Thatcher was spokesperson on the environment she promised a mortgage interest rate of 9.5 per cent, the abolition of rates, and enforced council house sales.[19] The 1979 Conservative Party manifesto on housing was little more than an articulation of these slogans, appearing in the section 'Helping the Family'. The right to buy council houses was applauded in the Queen's Speech as providing 'the prospect of handing something on' to children and grandchildren. Only later does the slogan materialize into part of a policy of debilitating local government and reducing public expenditure. The right to buy, staunchly upheld by the courts,[20] became a symbol of anti-municipalism. The state rolled out to flatten local democratic dissent, principally by maintaining a stranglehold on local government finance.[21] The tactic suited many of the other objectives in hand: it was an attack on the form of collective consumption that council housing constitutes; it disintegrates the unitary interests of council tenants and dissipates their organizational potential over one landlord; it transfers public subsidy from the democratic control of local councils to the boardroom policies of building societies and banks; it can be sold as the exemplar of individual choice; and it can be justified as a pillar of the monetarist demand for reduced public expenditure. The latter claim emerged as the rallying cry for a more general attack on local democracy.

Owner-occupation through council house sales as presently financed offers great financial advantages to many. As has recently become clear, however, it has also produced windfall income for central government. In its original conception, with large discounts to tenants (amounting to some £5.6 billion by 1986),[22] the sale of council houses was not directed towards the proceeds of privatization, and was prompted by political party prejudice rather than cost accounting. The implications of such a policy were not lost on the Treasury and the proceeds of council houses sales accounted for over half the total privatization proceeds between 1980 and 1986. Forrest and Murie conclude that 'the general tone and shape of the policy has been increasingly dictated by economic rather than housing policy considerations'. The dramatic rise in house prices has given further credibility to Conservative housing policy, as receipts from sales and re-evaluation of the remaining housing stock has enabled the Department of the Environment to pay off prematurely some of its housing debt and increase subsidy for both the Housing Corporation and hard-pressed local authorities.[23]

Underlying this temporary injection of funds is a long-term policy of reduction of subsidy in the production of houses. Secretary of State Nicholas Ridley's announcement of increased cash for renovation was accompanied by the Treasury announcement that support for housebuilding in 1990-1 will be cut by more than £300 million.

The prognosis for the poorly housed, the housed poor, and the houseless is that their condition can be expected to deteriorate. The Government's remedy of pressurized purchase is apparently running out of buyers. Forrest and Murie[24] have mapped out the pattern of sales. The better houses in the better areas become privatized. Thus, typically mixed-tenure estates are created in the suburbs whilst a common feature of inner city areas is the ghettoization of a marginalized underclass, at present living predominantly in council housing. As the polarized city emerges, however, they are at pains to point out that tenure structure is not necessarily crucial to this process.[25] For them the 'important element in the polarized city is the increasing spatial concentration of different groups irrespective of tenure'.[26] We would agree. The Thatcher Government's objective is to destroy whatever material gain council housing provided for certain sections of the working class coupled with its collectivist elements. State support for housing will continue but it will probably be provided through the developing social market which subsidizes the poor who are increasingly distinguished by space rather than tenure. The implications of law and policy for the spatial organization of social relations is the subject to which we now wish to turn.

SPACES OF LAW

Thus far we have suggested that the Thatcher Government's housing policy emerges from a convenient congruence of economic policy objectives and a determination to prevent local democratic processes from interfering in the business of national reconstruction. The tension between central and local relations is essentially a manifestation of the spatial distribution of power, and the struggle of central government to overcome the uneven social, political, and economic circumstances within the country. The texts of recent housing legislation allows for an interpretation that law has a role in 'the uneven process of development that derives from the particular characteristics of capitalism'.[27] Duncan and Goodwin in their analysis of local-central state relations as a product of underlying social causes draw upon recent work by Smith[28] and Harvey[29].

These writers, drawing upon earlier theories of the development of capitalism,[30] maintain that uneven development is not merely a product of pre-existing and natural variation. As Duncan and Goodwin explain:

> Uneven development is not, therefore, simply that types and quantities of socio-economic activities vary from place to place so that there will be an imbalance between them. Rather, uneven development in space and time refers to the uneven process of development that

derives from the particular characters of capitalism. Indeed, uneven development in space and time is central to the processes of capitalist production and social reproduction. Development in one place and time is causally linked to underdevelopment elsewhere, development in one area of life is causally linked with underdevelopment in another, and the conditions that both create lead to further uneven development.[31]

The process is of capital forever seeking out new territories to maximize the exploitation of surplus value. As it does so, it creates infrastructures – roads, railways, factories, houses – in its efforts to increase productivity, before the search moves on for cheaper areas. The process is as evident in the empty cotton mills of north-east England and the busy machinists of the Far East as it is in the still lathes of Birmingham and the humming computers of the M4 corridor.

The shifts are not inexorable, however, and people intervene to protect their community of jobs and homes and strive to maintain a geographical stability. State intervention moulds markets, systematizes welfare, and subsidizes housing in an effort to establish what Harvey calls a 'spatial fix'.[32] Theories of uneven development to date have tended to deal with law, if at all, as only a peripheral consideration. Nevertheless, the spatial fix, be it European Community, nation state, or local council, is a compound of both social and physical structures for which law provides a key binding agent.

The recent interest amongst sociologists in the significance of space, in contrast to time, has not yet permeated into analyses of law. This is perhaps surprising since the concept of the state 'remains the fundamental concept through which territoriality is expressed'[33] and laws are always defined by reference to their territorial jurisdiction. The thesis that we wish to pursue is that the uneven pattern of nation state laws is replicated to some extent at a sub-national level, giving rise at times to 'local law'. Space does not allow for a thorough rehearsal of such a thesis, nor have we developed one, but an analysis of legal intervention in housing policy under the Thatcher Government can be used to sketch in broad outline such a phenomenon. We illustrate it by reference to three key areas in housing: council house sales, housing conditions, and homelessness.

As we have attempted to show above, however, the form of state intervention in housing in England and Wales requires an understanding of the peculiar needs of capital in those two countries in a period of economic restructuring. We might go further and compare it with the legal intervention in Scotland – broadly similar, but does constitutional history provide the total explanation, and why are there similarities or differences in the legislation? – or undertake a comparative analysis of housing law in Scandinavia, the United States of America, or Zimbabwe. It may be that such studies would reveal not only the significance of temporal development but also of the influence upon law and policy of the space that each state occupies in the international division of labour. Thus, the study of housing in Colombia and Mexico by Jaramillo and Schteingart[34] suggests that state intervention is required in those countries in a period of urbanization and industrialization reminiscent of some of the issues (control of interests of landed capital), although they emphasize the difference in form that such intervention takes between the two countries. Analyses such as these indicate that models built upon post-industrialized nations are selective and that, in the Jaramillo and Schteingart study in particular, the relationship between housing production and state intervention is explicable not only by reference to the history of industrialization in those localities, but should also acknowledge the significance of the location of the sites of expropriation in a global economy.

A comparison of the differing expressions of law amongst nation states is only referred to here as a very obvious illustration of the spatial distribution of laws.

The concept of local law is not new. During the development of industrial capital and the emergence of urban Britain, the uneven spatial enforcement of laws via the techniques of private Acts of Parliament or by-laws was common. The development of railways is one example and the Public Health Acts owe their existence to by-law protection in the Metropolis and other cities such as Liverpool. The adoption of model by-laws gradually emerged into nationwide enforcement. Indeed, the concept of the universality of laws (within a nation state boundary, of course) would seem to be an emphasis that occurred particularly with the emergence of the idea of the rule of law. It has generally been accepted amongst all but the most naive of the judiciary that the model of national norms is tempered by an uneven distribution of the resources of enforcement. These would include both the divergent provision of agencies for enforcement and also the unequal distribution of legal advice. The idea of local law with which we are concerned goes beyond unmet legal needs and underfunded environmental health departments. It extends to the suggestion that during periods of crisis law is instrumental in the uneven and unequal distribution of national resources, and that while the normative form of many laws pretends towards national equality, the individual rights that are the vehicle for recent housing policy effectively convey spatially-defined uneven benefits.

The example of council house sales has already been raised. Forrest and Murie conclude that 'the right to buy has proved to be merely one episode [sic] in a procession of legislative and policy measures designed to affect increased central control over local authorities'. Their analysis shows that the erosion of local authority discretion in the provision of housing has heightened the geographical divisions in council house ownership between north and south, inner city and suburb, tower block and terrace. Their clear but complex charts of council house sales follow the uneven contours: 'The decaying council estates in the inner city and urban periphery are high rise monuments to that uneven development.'[35] The mechanism is the nationally available norm of the 'right to buy', but its selective localized consumption creates a pattern of disadvantage.

The uneven implementation of the legislation which regulates housing conditions results in a similar differential distribution across England and Wales, although in this instance it emerges through local interpretations of law. The yardstick of housing renewal and subsidy is the standard of unfitness, presently described in section 604 of the Housing Act 1985. Conceived as a norm to justify the clearance of unhealthy and dangerous houses, it has been transformed in recent years into a norm for evaluating whether or not buildings should qualify for grant. In this respect, the standard is usually implemented by local government environmental health officers. Many of these officers acknowledge local variation in their interpretation of the standard, varied largely according to the requirements of local housing stock and patterns of tenure.[36] In spite of a legal duty to inspect their areas, lack of resources reduces their role to one of reaction, and this in turn adds further impetus to the definition of a local standard, honed by the demand for their services and the amount of grant subsidy allocated by central government. The remedy for unfitness is related to the cost of repair as a proportion of the market value of the house. Recent variations in the increases in house prices have exaggerated the possibility of local differentiation in the interpretation of unfitness to the extent that a house which is unfit in Maidenhead might not be unfit in Maesteg.[37]

In this example, it is likely that there has always been scope for 'local' unfitness standards, although the disparities have become more apparent as housing subsidy is reduced and house prices fluctuate. The significance of the example is that housing subsidy must be apportioned according to legitimated criteria if it is to avoid the taint of a national norm evenly and equally implemented. The practice, however, reveals uneven application. Arguably, at certain times, nationally adjusted implementation would result in all housing subsidy for substandard housing being applied to a few areas, with large parts of the south-east of England receiving little if any support.

The contrast between national and local interpretation in this instance is starkly illustrated because the unfitness standard has a complementary role as the barometer of national housing progress in the National House Condition Surveys which are periodically conducted. A tension accordingly arises between the central government requirement of evaluating national housing stock and controlling public expenditure and local demands for combating housing disrepair, particularly when this is perceived as a service of local government.

Proposals to 'simplify' the unfitness standard[38] will render it less susceptible to local interpretation. The standard of 'fitness for human habitation' contained in the Local Government and Housing Bill 1989 is more objective in that an overall assessment is no longer required. To be 'unfit', a house must fail on at least one criterion. Coupled with the recommended shift to means testing, the role of local government in the regulation of housing conditions will be transformed into that of an agency for evaluating the financial eligibility of applicants against a redefined and narrower standard of unfitness (or tolerability).

The final example of local law is the operation of the Housing (Homeless Persons) Act 1977. Like the unfitness standard, the technique adopted is that of broad statutory duty, with detailed implementation relegated to a code of guidance (interpretation of unfitness is elucidated by a ministerial circular).

Although heavily litigated in its early years, the courts have recently declined intervention in all but the most unreasonable interpretations of the duty. The resultant broad discretion enjoyed by local authorities has led to wide disparity in local interpretation.

The leaked report by the Centre for Urban and Regional Studies[39] suggests that the influences upon interpretation are not unlike those affecting the implementation of unfitness procedures. A crucial factor is the lack of local authority accommodation, tempered by the political complexion of authorities, itself a reflection of the socio-economic structure of localities.

This broad and hesitant exploration of the spaces that define housing law could be dismissed as no more than an acknowledgement that policy administration is tempered to meet local needs. The significance of the theory of uneven development, however, is its insistence that unevenness is not a pre-existing and natural condition, but a product of capital expansion. The implications for more generalized theories of legal intervention rest upon whether the phenomenon of local law is more predominant in times of economic crisis and restructuring. If law has a role in establishing the spatial fixes that people create to stave off the instabilities of the rampaging shifts of capital, it would be expected to retreat at times when those spatial fixes were being dismantled. This might explain the early intervention of the state via by-laws in the creation of safer and more sanitary cities in the nineteenth century, broadening into the fullness of the post-war Welfare State. It might equally explain the response of the present Government to the crisis of the 1970s. Similar mechanisms to the private Acts of Parliament and by-laws of the nineteenth century emerge in reverse today as whole regions are legally singled out for economic treatment (enterprise zones, urban development corporations, and so on). There has, however, been no wholesale retreat into deregulation of the housing market, but rather, as Duncan and Goodwin argue, a rolling back of the local state and a retreat into the central government shell. Thus there has been a shift from regulation by local government, epitomized by the sanitary inspector, to exercise of discretionary power and service provision. State subsidy of housing action trusts is a reaffirmation of the need for state intervention and welfarism as a crucial concomitant to the strong state represented by the modern police. It is illustrated in the efforts by the Department of the Environment to establish a housing action trust at Broadwater Farm.[40]

State provision of housing services for sections of society can be expected to continue, particularly in localities of underprivilege. This may take the form of council housing for the elderly and unemployed or it may be in the form of subsidy via the non-elected Housing Corporation. Whatever the form, the solution will require a degree of local control, management, and legitimacy. This will be achieved by devolving responsibility for the allocation of state resources (subsidy) to non-elected representatives, drawing heavily upon the business community.

The cohesive framework of national norms and display of universal individual rights are crucial to the process. The unevenness of wealth distribution must be seen to be within the law and the concepts of fair distribution with which the rule of law is imbued. The process is inherently unstable, however, and the tenant from the desperate Wood End estates of north Coventry or wherever is bound to suspect that the law is different down the road, or in the next town, or down south. . . .

NOTES AND REFERENCES

1 For an early exception see I. Jennings, 'Courts and Administrative Law – The Experience of English Housing Legislation' (1936) 49 *Harvard Law Rev.* 426.
2 P. McAuslan, 'Administrative Law, Collective Consumption, and Judicial Policy' (1983) 46 *Modern Law Rev.* 1.
3 M. Loughlin, 'Recent Developments in Central-Local Government Fiscal Relations' (1982) 9 *J. of Law and Society* 253.
4 For a discussion on 'the significance of space' see J. Urry, 'Social Relations, Space, and Time' in *Social Relations and Spatial Structures*, eds. Gregory and J. Urry p. 20.
5 Various contributions to *Political Economy and the Housing Question* (1986).
6 See S. Merrett, *State Housing in Britain* (1979).
7 A large urban direct labour organization might have undertaken at its peak sixty to seventy per cent of the new construction work.
8 This proposes to 'ring fence' housing revenue accounts to prevent rate subsidies. The proposal is now included in the Local Government and Housing Bill 1989 Part VI.
9 Local Government Planning and Land Act 1980 s.101 (except in Wales).
10 Finance Act 1985 s.93.
11 M. Loughlin, *Local Government in the Modern State* (1986) 141.
12 Housing and Building Control Act 1984; Housing and Planning Act 1986.
13 Their efficacy was clearly demonstrated in *Norwich City Council* v. *Secretary of State for the Environment* [1982] 1 All E.R. 737.
14 Tenants have a right to be consulted over matters of housing management. This does not include rent fixing, and the landlord decides generally on what constitutes a matter of housing management (Housing Act 1985 s.105).
15 McAuslan, op. cit., n. 2, p. 5.
16 One clear example of an alternative view was Liverpool City Council between 1984 and 1987. It decided to build its way out of a housing and employment problem by concentrating its capital allocations on an extensive 'new build' programme for publicly-owned houses to rent. It met with very substantial criticism. This was partly due to Liverpool's overall stance on the rate-capping issue and the nature of its political leadership. It could, however, be argued that it was also due to the dominance of consumptionist politics which now means that there is an unease with mass anything and is translated into criticisms of design, participation, and choice.
17 CASE UK (the Campaign Against the Sale of Council Estates) is the most notable national movement. The success of the tenants of Hulme in Manchester in resisting the imposition of a proposed housing action trust is another example.
18 The centre is located in Manchester and is funded by a number of local authorities to provide research and information on economic and social issues which are of relevance to local authorities. It publishes a bulletin entitled *Local Work*. Sheffield City Council has commissioned its own substantial research report which looks at all the elements involved in the provision and maintenance of decent quality homes. See A. Stewart, *Planning Homes and Jobs: The Sheffield Report* (1988).
19 Quoted in R. Forrest and A. Murie, *Selling the Welfare State: The Privatization of Public Housing* (1988) 31.
20 McAuslan, op. cit., n. 2.

21 Reported in Forrest and Murie, op. cit., n. 19, p. 9.
22 Reported in Forrest and Murie, op. cit., n. 19, p. 9.
23 Statement of Nicholas Ridley MP, 'Council home sales boost cash for renovation' *The Daily Telegraph*, 2 November 1988.
24 Forrest and Murie, op. cit., n. 19.
25 id., p. 195.
26 id., p. 168.
27 S. Duncan and M. Goodwin, *The Local State and Uneven Development Policy* (1988) 62.
28 N. Smith, *Uneven Development* (1984).
29 D. Harvey, 'The Geopolitics of Capitalism' in *Social Relations and Spatial Structures*, op. cit., n. 4.
30 Smith, op. cit., n. 28, p. *x*ff.
31 Duncan and Goodwin, op. cit., n. 27, p. 62.
32 Gregory and Urry, op. cit., n. 4, p. 153.
33 Harvey, op. cit., n. 29, p. 143.
34 S. Jaramillo and M. Schteingart in *Capital and Labour in the Urbanized World*, ed. J. Walton (1985).
35 Forrest and Murie, op. cit., n. 19, p. 80.
36 R. Burridge, 'The Discrete Setting of Housing Standards' (unpublished paper delivered at W. G. Hart Workshop, Institute of Advanced Legal Studies, June 1987).
37 D. Ormandy and R. Burridge, *Environmental Health Standards in Housing* (1988).
38 Department of Environment, *Home Improvement Policy: The Government's Proposals* (1987).
39 'Homeless rise blamed on housing shortage' *The Guardian*, 31 October 1988.
40 ' "Opt-out" plan for riot estate' *The Observer*, 3 July 1988.

'It All Really Starts in the Family. . . .': Community Care in the 1980s

JANE LEWIS*

Community care has been something of a 'motherhood' issue in the thinking of both left and right. But during the 1950s and 1960s when writers such as Peter Townsend were making moving and well-founded pleas for the de-institutionalization of elderly and mentally ill people, Richard Titmuss sounded what is a by now well-known note of caution:

> What some hope will one day exist is suddenly thought by many to exist already. All kinds of wild and unlovely weeds are changed, by statutory magic and comforting appellation, into the most attractive flowers that bloom not just in the Spring, but all the year round. . . . And what of the everlasting cottage-garden trailer, 'community care'? Does it not conjure up a sense of warmth and human kindness, essentially personal and comforting, as loving as the wild flowers so enchantingly described by Lawrence in *Lady Chatterly's Lover*?[1]

As Titmuss recognized, community care carries an appeal based on a mixture of nostalgia and the promise of loving kindness, but, as he warned, good community care does not come cheaply. Yet a recent document published by the Government on the subject has at the centre of its arguments in favour of community care a calculation that the care of a frail elderly person costs the state £135 per week in a domiciliary setting and £295 per week in a National Health Service geriatric ward.[2]

Support for community care as a cheaper option has gathered force during the 1980s for two reasons. The first reason is the publicity accorded the demographics which show that between 1971 and 1981 alone the number of people aged over seventy-five years – the age group commonly agreed to be in need of most care – increased by twenty per cent, and by the year 2001 the numbers of people aged over seventy-five years are projected to rise by thirty per cent and of those over eighty-five years to almost double.[3] Secondly, it may be argued that the promotion of community care is integral to what Malcolm Wicks has described as the Thatcher Government's attachment to 'an inter-connected trinity of family, private market, and voluntary sector'.[4] For while the concept of community care is, as I shall argue in the first part of this paper, nothing if not confused – involving as it does contributions from local authorities, the National Health Service, the private sector, the voluntary

Department of Social Administration, London School of Economics, Houghton Street, London WC2A 2AE, England.

83

sector, neighbours, friends, and kin – the most important boundary in provision is between the formal and the informal sectors. The main reason why community care is cheaper is because so much of the work is done by informal carers – principally by kin, but also by friends, neighbours, and volunteers. Furthermore, it has been one of the major contributions of feminist social policy analysis to point out that in practice community care means family care, and family care means care by women.[5]

Within the formal sector, a further crucial distinction is rapidly increasing in importance: that between the public and private financing and provision of care. Notwithstanding the rosy picture that has been painted of community care, more and more of those who can afford it have been entering private residential homes. Indeed, the increase in the number of private old people's homes represented one of the most significant amounts of privatization within the Welfare State during the first two terms of the Thatcher Government. Not surprisingly, there are seven times as many private nursing home beds in the south of England as in the north.[6] However, paradoxically, an element of public finance which is now in the form of Income Support has also provided an impetus to the expansion of private residential care. In 1986 the Audit Commission drew attention to the fact that those in receipt of Supplementary Benefit may choose to live in a residential home and have all or part of their expenses paid by the Department of Health and Social Security, thus 'saving' local authorities the cost of providing care in a local authority home.[7] The Audit Commission viewed this as an anomaly working against the community care initiative, and Department of Social Security practice in this area is currently confused.[8] The recent Griffiths Report, entitled *Community Care: An Agenda for Action*, favoured providing public finance only after means testing and assessment of the individual's need for care by social services departments.[9] Were this practice to become more closely controlled, and were we also to see an extension of domiciliary services provided by the market begin to parallel the boom in private residential care, then provision of community care would soon follow a two-tier model and become stratified by ability to pay. Thus, while many on the political left would continue to support the principle of community care as an essentially humane policy, it must be recognized that as presently constituted its main prop – unpaid family care by women – together with the developing trend towards more mixed and socially stratified provision, accord well with the aims and objectives of the Thatcher Government.

THE MEANING OF COMMUNITY CARE

The focus on the importance of community care is itself relatively new. In the work on the needs of elderly people sponsored by the Nuffield Foundation immediately after the Second World War, more attention was paid to institutional provision than anything else.[10] This was despite the recognition that between ninety-five and ninety-eight per cent (estimates varied) of elderly people lived independently, but was in keeping with the authors' pre-occupation with elderly people as an unproductive and dependent group. Similarly the National Assistance Act 1948 had much more to say about residential care than it did about community services. As Means and Smith have remarked, the late 1940s were distinguished by a singular lack of imagination about forms of care other than residential types.[11] This attitude changed during the 1950s and there developed substantial agreement that old people should remain in their homes as long as possible, with Townsend arguing on grounds of the increased happiness of those elderly people enabled to remain at home.[12]

But as Ungerson has recently noted, 'the issue of what, in reality, constituted "community care", and even what might constitute it if ever there were adequate co-ordination between the two bureaucracies of health and welfare' has been neglected.[13] In part this may be attributed to the fact that the idea of community care was born of a reaction against institutional care. It was supposed to provide the love and warmth that empirical investigation showed institutional care to lack, but as Bulmer has shown, the 'common sense' assumptions it was based on were often fallacious.[14] Most often, advocates of community care have referred implicitly to a series of networks – formal and informal – whose efforts require co-ordination. The Barclay Report on social work, for example, identified community in this way, and argued that social services should work in close co-operation with informal networks.[15] This expression of the idea of a 'partnership' between the formal and informal, or, in other variants on the theme, 'interweaving' care, have become increasingly frequent. In his keynote speech to the Directors of Social Services at Buxton in September 1984 the Secretary of State for Social Services, Norman Fowler MP, signalled a change in responsibilities of social services departments broadly in tune with this thinking – the aim would be to switch their emphasis from providing services to the task of co-ordinating social care, whether issuing from private, voluntary, informal, or formal sectors.[16] This did not materialize, in part perhaps because it was far from clear as to what exactly was meant by it: whether the emphasis was to be placed on linking the formal and informal sectors, or on increasing the contributions of sectors other than the public – that is, the informal and private. Certainly, in practice it has proved very difficult to construct meaningful links between the formal and informal sectors. Not only is the formal sector subject to considerable conflicts between the interests of the local authorities and the National Health Service, as well as between public and private provision, but the Government's policy has also tended to view informal and publicly provided formal care systems as alternatives, implying that the former should in large part replace the latter.

Formal provision of community care has been condemned by the Audit Commission as inadequate and incoherent.[17] In the first place, there has been little agreement between providers as to what constitutes community care. To the National Health Service, local authority nursing homes are a part of community care, but to local authorities residential homes lie 'outside' the 'community'. Indeed, this sort of confusion has been part of the internal experience of the National Health Service as well. When the Government first began to talk seriously about community care in the context of the mentally ill, it used the term to refer to services located in the community rather than in institutions.[18] But the mid-1970s saw an attempt to extend the concept of 'community' to include the hospital. Indeed, the reorganization of the National Health Service was intended to promote the integration and rationalization of services inside and outside the hospital,[19] the motive being twofold: to improve the co-ordination and quality of care, and to shift resources from the expensive acute hospital sectors to the community in the hope of holding down spiralling hospital costs. But as the 1986 Audit Commission report reveals, such a shift in resources never took place and community care policy has been one of muddling through. Similarly, within the local authority sector between 1974 and 1981, the share of personal social services expenditure devoted to community care as opposed to day care or residential care declined slightly, whereas expenditure on the other two categories increased. Furthermore, when hospital costs continued their inexorable rise, integration of services as a strategy for cost control was abandoned and by the late 1970s and early 1980s governments sought to limit costs in all areas of service delivery. It follows that greater emphasis was put on the need to encourage informal care.

The Audit Commission stressed both that provision of community care is uneven between different authorities and that provision has not kept up with the rundown of long-stay institutions. The commission pointed out that funds for bridging the transitional phase – that is, for building up community care at the same time as residential care is run down – have been limited. And, of course, present systems for distributing rate support grant act as a deterrent to the expansion of community-based services in many local authorities. The Audit Commission summarized the situation neatly: 'Local authorities are in the position of having to invest – often attracting Ministerial criticism for increasing staffing levels in the process – in order to enable the NHS to save money.'[20] The commission recommended, first, that local authorities take primary responsibility for mentally and physically handicapped people, with resources for these groups being transferred from the National Health Service; secondly, that a joint board under a single manager be established to oversee provision for elderly people in a particular area with funds provided by both the National Health Service and local authorities; and thirdly, that the National Health Service take primary responsibility for mentally ill people. Such an arrangement would significantly increase the responsibility of local authorities, and prove impossible to fulfil in the absence of a commitment to increase central government grant. The position is also complicated by the now complete lack of coterminosity between local authority and National Health Service administrative boundaries, a state of affairs not unrelated to central government's determination to reduce the power of local government.

The Griffiths Report also favours increasing the responsibility of local authorities for community care and recommends provision of a 'specific grant' from central government of forty to fifty per cent of the costs of an approved programme of community care. It is also possible to sense in this report a certain wistfulness for coterminous local authority and National Health Service boundaries. The Griffiths Report openly declared its intention of sidestepping the issue of relationships and responsibilities at the local level between particular authorities, focusing instead primarily on central/local government relations. Immediate reaction to the report expressed the belief that it would not find favour with government ministers because of the role it proposed to give the local authorities. However, the report can be read as advocating considerably greater central control. While Griffiths is anxious to avoid central government 'prescription', it is nevertheless central government that will provide the 'framework' within which local authorities operate. It appears that this framework consists of, first, the setting of overall aims of community care programmes, and secondly, the allocation of block grant subject to central government approval of local authority programmes. Local accountability thus becomes in effect accountability to a proposed Minister of Community Care. It is by no means clear that this degree of central control will be sufficient to ensure the implementation of the recommendations of the Griffiths Report. But the document represents an interesting example of the way in which the Thatcher Government's restructuring of social policy has repeatedly endeavoured – in the Griffiths Report on the National Health Service implemented in 1984 and arguably in the General Education Reform Bill 1987 – both to pass responsibility for provision to the local level and to tighten central control, while publicly emphasizing only the first of these.

The Griffiths Report did not deal with the level of funding, and the report provides no guidance as to how the size of community care budgets of local authorities is to be determined. But given, first, that the demographic picture means that the demand for care will inevitably grow, and secondly, that Griffiths contemplates a level of specific grant under fifty per cent in order to indicate that 'the primary responsibility for community care should lie with local government',[21] the prospects for local government look gloomy, especially with the advent of the poll tax. With this, any increase in expenditure to improve services for those in need will require a disproportionate increase in the tax levied on those same people. The logic must be as Walker has argued: that public provision of community care will become residual.[22] Indeed, the picture emerges in the Griffiths Report of the social service departments giving shape to Norman Fowler's 1984 vision – coordinating care provided by informal carers, the voluntary sector, the private sector, and, as a final resort, the public sector. Private provision of domiciliary services, as opposed to residential care, has not yet reached significant proportions. If significant inducement is given to their growth in the future, then serious issues regarding the present inadequacy of regulation (given only passing mention in the Griffiths Report) as well as equity will arise.

The prospect of greater privatization in the provision of formal services should be seen as the latest addition to a long-standing commitment on the part of the Thatcher Government to reduce the part played by the public sector. The central pillar of policy on community care has been, and must remain, the idea that the informal sector must bear the major part of the burden of community care. A consultative document published in 1978, entitled *A Happier Old Age*, stressed the importance of family links in old age, while continuing to emphasize the importance of a 'joint approach' to care on the part of formal and informal agencies, recognizing that there might be limits to the community's capacity to care.[23] The 1978 Wolfenden Committee Report on the future of voluntary organizations provided firm support for informal and voluntary care: 'We place a high value on this system of care, both because of its intrinsic value and because its replacement by a more institutional form of caring would be intolerably costly.'[24] The 1981 White Paper, entitled *Growing Older*, reflected the Thatcher Government's increasing concern to limit the obligations of the state:

> Whatever level of public expenditure proves practicable, and however it is distributed, the primary sources of support and care for elderly people are informal and voluntary. These spring from the personal ties of kinship, friendship, and neighbourhood. They are irreplaceable. It is the role of public authorities to sustain and, where necessary, develop – but never to displace – such support and care. Care in the community must increasingly mean care by the community.[25]

The document argued that families were best placed to understand and meet the wide variety of personal needs of the elderly person and admitted that this 'may often involve considerable personal sacrifice', particularly where the 'family is one person, often a single woman caring for an elderly relative'. Unlike the literature of the 1950s and 1960s, the burden falling on women was acknowledged, but women were also being effectively told that they had no alternative but to shoulder it.

As Walker has suggested, current government strategy rests in large part on the idea that there are untapped sources of informal care which can be called into play to attend to the needs (great and small) of an increasing population of old and very old people.[26] But the demographics of the female caring population, explained by Moroney as early as 1976, as well as the already powerful injunction to care experienced by women, makes this a dubious proposition.[27] More volunteer help might be forthcoming,[28] but after a certain point, when personal care tasks require increasing skill and strength, the part played by voluntary helpers of all kinds becomes secondary and their role tends to be circumscribed. Indeed, the kind of help that can be expected from neighbours and friends is severely limited by convention and by the taboos surrounding intimate personal care tasks. Friendships are more likely to provide emotional support than practical help, but friendships are increasingly difficult to maintain as the caring task becomes more demanding for the primary carer. As Allan has noted, because friendship is usually based on sociability and enjoyment, it does not automatically translate into help with personal care tasks.[29] Neighbours are more likely to give practical help, but are rarely asked to help with personal tending. If they are asked to help regularly, for example by sitting with an elderly person, some reciprocity is usually felt to be required. Most commonly, as Willmott has noted, neighbours will perform some form of surveillance – for example, while a carer is out at work.[30]

The burden of caring for someone at home rests firmly on the person identified as the carer. Qureshi and Walker's research has revealed the existence of a perceived hierarchy of preferred carers with the daughter the firm first choice in the absence of a spouse.[31] Once the carer has been identified, the part played by other family members is often extremely limited; brothers may be expected to provide some financial assistance where possible and sisters to give some help with respite care, but for the most part the carer finds herself on her own. Indeed, the research of Evandrou et al. has shown that daughter carers received by far the lowest level of publicly provided formal services, such as home helps and meals on wheels.[32] Thus, care by the community translates most often into care by a single carer, usually female, and informal care is more likely to be an alternative to formal care than just one of many interlinked forms of community provision.

GENDER AND COMMUNITY CARE[33]

Cutting across the many issues posed by community care must be the fact that it is deeply gendered. At the most fundamental level, it is a matter of women caring for women, and Walker has remarked on 'the close coincidence of status and interest between elderly dependants and the women they depend on'.[34] That is, carers share a dependent status as a result of their restricted access to the labour market. In both the formal and the informal sectors the people doing the work of caring will usually be female and in both sectors their work is undervalued. In the much publicized Kent experimental scheme to give locally based social workers control of a budget to buy goods and services to meet the needs of clients, one of the most controversial elements was the pocket-money wages paid to the (female) helpers.[35] Nor is there any evidence of a greater commitment to state financial support for carers. While Mrs Jackie Drake won her case for the invalid care allowance to be paid to married as well as unmarried women carers before the European Court in the summer of 1986, had the Social Security Act 1986 been in force her claim for the allowance would have disqualified her mother (for whom she was caring) from receiving the higher premium payable under the Income Support scheme. Indeed, as Land has commented, the lack of provision for carers must be seen in the context of tax and social security systems that provide incentives for particular kinds of support in the family.[36] Finally, in regard to the informal sector alone, the sorts of networks among neighbours, friends, and kin that policy makers often assume to exist and seek to mobilize are in fact women's networks.[37]

Women's work, particularly as unpaid carers in the home, is the bedrock of government policy on community care. As the 1981 White Paper entitled *Growing Older* made clear, it is assumed that women will care for physically and mentally impaired family members. This begs the question of preferences that carers and persons cared for may have. There is little evidence as to those of the latter, but the investigation by West et al. of the care preferences of a random sample in three Scottish areas revealed only a limited preference for informal care without the involvement of paid helpers, indicating a high degree of awareness and anxiety about the burden that is likely to fall on an informal carer.[38] An extremely important aspect of the Griffiths Report is its failure to provide any mechanism through which the client's preferences may be heard. The emphasis is on the construction by local authorities of packages of care (from whatever source) suitable for the individual after due assessment. There is no provision for the person needing care to appeal the assessment, yet part of the rhetoric of Thatcherite policy has been 'consumer sovereignty'. In this the Griffiths Report reflects the inevitable tension between a commitment to enhancing consumer choice and an attempt to meet need by rationally determined criteria.[39] It may be noted that the recent Wagner Report on residential care has shown itself to be rather more conscious of the important issue of client preference.[40] In regard to carers themselves, the crucial question becomes whether the decision to care represents a genuine choice.

In the immediate post-war decades, the assumption that female family members would provide the support needed by the elderly was explicit and unquestioned. Means and Smith cite examples of geriatricians and politicians in the 1950s who expressed the belief that it was part of women's normal role and duty to care for the elderly.[41] Similarly, in acclaiming the family bonds revealed by his study of family in London's East End, Townsend concluded that people with families, especially daughters, made few claims on the state and that it would therefore be counterproductive 'if the state, through housing and other policies, separated individuals from their kin and thus made more professional services necessary'.[42] No consideration was given to the burden falling on women carers. Indeed, as in other areas of government policy such as income maintenance, governments tended to fear that any additional help provided by the state would sap the family's incentive to provide. One reason for the slowness in developing the home help and meals on wheels services lies in the belief that these were areas of support properly confined to the family. Townsend's work on the (atypical) family structures of Bethnal Green stressed the power and authority wielded by women in the private sphere of the family and the extent to which this was derived from their caring role. However, recent feminist analysis of the position of women carers has suggested that 'compulsory altruism' is a more accurate description of their situation.[43] In other words, women care because of their socialization as women and for want of acceptable alternatives. This interpretation raises the further issue as to whether community care can ever be non-sexist.

In fact women's feelings about caring are often profoundly ambivalent, reflecting their desire to care and bitterness at the material and emotional costs that they bear in order to do so. Both patterns of socialization and structural constraints have resulted in women internalizing the injunction to care. Graham has pointed out the extent to which the caring role provides women with part of their feminine identity; it is more than another species of work.[44] Gilligan has argued that the feminine personality comes to define itself in relation to and in connection with others more than does the masculine personality, which is defined primarily through separation.[45] In this construction, concern for others rather than self – an ethic of care – becomes central to understanding femininity. Such a concern for others is not necessarily some kind of happy altruism. As Gilligan points out, women may also judge themselves by their capacity to care. Thus, failure to do so, for whatever reason, commonly induces guilt. In addition, from a materialist perspective, women have a much more limited range of opportunities open to them than do men. Both Gilligan and Graham are suggesting that the injunction to care is seated deeply in the female personality as well as being elicited by a close relationship, usually with kin. We can thus begin to understand why the injunction to care is so powerful and why the approach taken by those who treat the work of caring as simply non-market work that women voluntarily choose for its intrinsic satisfaction is inadequate. Women's willingness to care is considerably more complex than a decision to opt for a labour of love rather than money. It may be as Elshtain suggests that women consciously decide that the private world of home and family has greater integrity and has more to offer than any other.[46] This view depicts women's willingness to care positively, seeing it as part of an intrinsically female culture and value system that is sometimes represented as being of a higher moral order than that of the public sphere of men.

Recent British feminist literature on caring prefers to draw the conclusion that the caring ethic should become the property of men as well as women.[47] For not all women experience the injunction to care positively. Many experience conflicting demands on their capacity to care – from husbands and children as well as elderly or otherwise dependent kin – or tensions between the demands of others and emergent desires for self fulfilment. Perceived failure to juggle these demands successfully and thus to fulfil the injunction to care may result in guilt and unhappiness. It is well known that carers are especially prone to use the word 'guilt' to describe their feelings. Indeed, Ungerson and Land and Rose have suggested that it is very hard to know where the love ends and the guilt, or compulsory altruism, begins.[48] In other words, there will in all probability be 'costs' to caring, and the extent of these are not easily susceptible to the kind of measures favoured by economists. Certainly it is possible to estimate the amount of income foregone by women who give up work to care, as Nissel and Bonnerjea have effectively shown.[49] They estimated that the carers in their sample forfeited an average of some £4,000 a year in income (1980 rates) by staying at home to care. Carers may feel very bitter about such material losses. They may also nevertheless feel glad that they cared. The strain on their material resources, their own health, and the possible tensions between the work of caring and other aspects of their lives has to be balanced against the powerful injunction to care and the guilt if it is ignored.

Carers hold feelings of affection and obligation in a delicate balance. Indeed, affection shades imperceptibly into duty when a phrase like 'Well, it's

91

your mother' is used to explain the decision to care. Ties of obligation between family members are commonly based on delicate notions of reciprocity. Historians have pointed out that these do not necessarily operate on the basis of current exchange, but rather between generations, and may vary between social classes and ethnic groups. The process of re-negotiating a relationship between family members when an elderly person becomes increasingly frail is fraught with difficulty, especially if the quality of the relationship has been historically poor. As Finch has stressed, 'the delicate balance between dependency and independence for which people apparently aim in their family relationship' has been ignored by government policies that seek to make families take more responsibility for their members.[50] Even in cases where the carer is unequivocally committed to caring, it is rare that she will either wish or be able to care without help from the formal sector. Studies suggest that a majority of women carers want to care but do not want to see themselves as the alternative to publicly provided services. They want both support from paid helpers in the form of domiciliary and institutional care – from home helps, district nurses, institutions providing respite care and day care – and in many cases the security of knowing that when the burden grows too great and they can no longer cope that there is good quality hospital care available.

Most studies of informal care have been of the snapshot variety, but such evidence as there is reveals that the burden of caring may be lengthy and impose considerable constraints on the carer's extra-caring life, both in terms of her own career possibilities and in terms of the environment she might wish to provide for other family members; caring for an elderly dependent person and caring for children, in particular, are not always compatible tasks. My own recent biographically-based study of forty-one carers found that the period of full care, defined as that period during which the person cared for required such personal tending as to make it impossible for the carer to leave her for more than an hour or two other than with a substitute carer, varied from six weeks to twenty-two years, with a period of between two and five years being most common.[51] However, full-time caring was usually preceded by periods of semi-care, during which carers felt they should not leave a dependant for extended periods of time, and by part-time care, during which they managed to balance personal tending with paid work. These periods of caring may be lengthy and have obvious implications for the spontaneity of family life for parents and children and for the carer's job performance, mobility, and promotion chances. Furthermore, a recent study of 657 elderly people and their carers showed that sixty per cent of the main helpers experienced some effect on their own health.[52] The effects on other family members, particularly children, who may witness a painful deterioration – whether physical or mental or both – in a beloved grandparent has received scant attention.

One measure of the burden borne by informal carers is the fact that in many caring situations where either the person cared for qualifies for the attendance allowance or the carer qualifies for the invalid care allowance, the person cared for would be considered too disabled to be cared for adequately in a residential home.[53] The needs of carers for ready support from the formal sector are therefore great and vary both over the course of the individual caring cycle and between carers. However, there is little evidence that in practice caring has been effectively shared, despite the interest expressed by ministers in the Department of Health and Social Security in broadening the responsibilities of social services departments such that they promote the interweaving of care. The experience from the carers' perspective is more likely to be one of isolation, lack of information, and, all too often, of inappropriate help when assistance is offered. For example, while it is true, as Levin et al. suggest, that carers require more help in respect to bathing the elderly and infirm, if the carer feels that the bathing attendant violates her elderly relative's sense of due proprieties, the help will be rejected.[54] Some carers want financial help rather than services, others want more domiciliary services, others more respite care in order to enable them to maintain an extra-caring identity. Above all, carers with carefully planned caring routines need help they can rely on. If the timing of transportation to a day care centre is erratic, then carers often end up shouldering the responsibility themselves. The problems of seeking institutional care for a dependant when the carer can no longer cope (something that carers find very hard to admit), and of coming to terms with the aftermath of a period of intensive personal tending are also extremely difficult. As the report of the Audit Commission noted, paid helpers are often inadequately trained to work in the often contested territory of domiciliary care.[55] The Griffiths Report noted the importance of the staffing issue, but downplayed the degree of training that might be required. The report suggested that elderly people's need for help in dressing and with shopping and cleaning could be met by essentially unskilled labour 'particularly school leavers, YTS etc.',[56] thus displaying remarkable insensitivity to the difficulties helpers encounter when working with the elderly and infirm. It must be acknowledged that, in the past, formal publicly provided support was often inappropriately delivered, but Griffiths provides little ground for optimism about the future.

Informal care for the elderly is often lauded because it is flexible. By this is usually meant that it is more responsive to the needs of the dependant. This may be true, but the caring routines that must be established by an informal carer are often remarkably inflexible. Different carers need different kinds and combinations of help; some want institutionally provided respite care every few weeks or every few months, while some want domiciliary care overnight or for a couple of hours each day. And as Levin et al. have demonstrated, meeting these needs is crucial to preventing carer stress and breakdown.[57] Fear has often been expressed that state support for informal carers will result in formalizing the informal. This is only likely to be the case if by their inflexibility statutory services dragoon carers into frameworks not of their own choosing, but it must be recognized that effective support of each and every carer requires careful assessment and must necessarily be a highly individualized and costly business.

If caring is to represent a genuine choice for women rather than a species of social engineering, then those who want to care must be better supported. Brody's research based on longitudinal data gathered in the United States of America indicates that most young women both desire to care for their parents when they become elderly and expect to have equal opportunities with men in the public world of work.[58] However, the trend towards diminishing public provision will involve women who decide to care in ever-increasing sacrifice of their own aspirations. For women who neither wish nor feel able to care, and for carers who feel they can no longer cope with their caring responsibilities there must be an institutional alternative. Booth's view that there is no institutional model without harmful effects is not only profoundly gloomy,[59] but runs counter to the way in which many of those who can afford it have been opting for the kind of institutional care available in the private sector. Choosing to care involves there being a choice not to care, and that in turn cannot be a genuine choice unless institutional care is high quality. At present, the Government seems determined to increase the scope for market provision without an equal determination to regulate private providers. The scenario for the future is therefore bleak, for if local authority provision of community care is to become residual, with the family and market the two major providers, then women's 'choice' to care is, for the vast majority of working- and middle-class women, going to disappear. Furthermore, the burdens on carers must surely increase.

NOTES AND REFERENCES

1 R. Titmuss, 'Community Care: Fact or Fiction?' in *Commitment to Welfare*, ed. R. Titmuss (1968) p. 104.
2 Audit Commission, *Making a Reality of Community Care* (1986).
3 J. Ermisch, *The Political Economy of Demographic Change* (1983); M. Wicks and M. Henwood, *The Forgotten Army: Family Care and Elderly People* (1984).
4 M. Wicks, 'Enter Right: The Family Patrol Group' *New Society*, 24 February 1985.
5 J. Finch and D. Groves (eds.), *A Labour of Love* (1983).
6 A. Walker, 'Tendering Care' *New Society*, 22 January 1988.
7 Audit Commission, op. cit., n. 2.
8 'DHSS U-Turn on Community Care' *New Society*, 26 February 1988.
9 Department of Health and Social Security, *Community Care: An Agenda For Action* (1988; chairman R. Griffiths).
10 B. S. Rowntree, *Old People* (1947); J. H. Sheldon, *The Social Medicine of Old Age. Report of an Inquiry in Wolverhampton* (1948).
11 R. Means and R. Smith, *The Development of Welfare Services for Elderly People* (1985).
12 P. Townsend, *The Family Life of Old People* (1957).
13 C. Ungerson, 'Gender Divisions and Community Care – A British Perspective' (1985; paper given at an ESRC-sponsored conference at the University of Kent at Canterbury).
14 M. Bulmer, *The Social Basis of Community Care* (1987).
15 P. Barclay, *Social Workers: Their Roles and Tasks* (1982; Report of Working Party of the National Institute for Social Work).
16 M. Bulmer, 'Can Caring Come Together?' *New Society*, 4 July 1986.
17 Audit Commission, op. cit., n. 2.
18 S. Ayer and A. Alaszewski, *Community Care and the Mentally Handicapped* (1984).

94

19 J. Lewis, *What Price Community Medicine?* (1986).
20 Audit Commission, op. cit., n. 2, para. 57.
21 Griffiths Report, op. cit., n. 9, para 6.23.
22 Walker, op. cit., n. 6.
23 Department of Health and Social Security and Welsh Office, *A Happier Old Age* (1978).
24 Baron John Wolfenden, *The Future of Voluntary Organisations. Report of the Wolfenden Committee* (1978).
25 Department of Health and Social Security, Secretaries of State for Scotland, Northern Ireland, and Wales, *Growing Older* (1981; Cmnd. 8173).
26 A. Walker, 'Community Care: Fact and Fiction' in *The Debate About Community. Papers from a Seminar on Community in Social Policy*, eds. A. Walker, P. Ekblom, and N. Deakin (1986).
27 R. M. Moroney, *The Family and the State: Considerations for Social Policy* (1976).
28 H. Qureshi, D. Challis, and B. Davies, 'Motivations and Rewards of Helpers in the Kent Community Care Scheme' in *Volunteers: Patterns, Meanings, and Motives*, ed. B. Hatch (1983).
29 G. Allan, 'Friendship and Care for Elderly People' (1986) 6 *Ageing and Society* 1.
30 P. Willmott, *Social Networks. Informal Care and Public Policy* (1986).
31 H. Qureshi and A. Walker, *The Caring Relationship* (1988).
32 M. Evandrou, S. Arber, A. Dale, and N. Gilbert, 'Who Cares for the Elderly?: Family Care Provision and Receipt of Statutory Services' (paper presented at the Annual Conference of the British Society of Gerontology, September 1985, at Keele University, published in part in *Dependency and Interdependency in Old Age: Theoretical Perspectives and Policy Alternatives*, eds. C. Phillipson, M. Bernard, and P. Strang (1986).
33 This section draws on material that is developed further in J. Lewis and B. Meredith, *Daughters Who Care* (1988).
34 A. Walker, 'Care for Elderly People: A Conflict Between Women and the State' in *A Labour of Love*, op. cit., n. 5, p. 111.
35 For a description of the scheme see D. Challis and B. Davies, *Case Management in Community Care* (1986).
36 H. Land, 'Social Security and Community Care: Creating "Perverse Incentives" ' in *Social Security and Community Care*, eds. S. Baldwin, G. Parker, and R. Walker (1988).
37 J. Finch, 'Comunity Care: Developing Non-Sexist Alternatives' (1984) 9 *Critical Social Policy* 6.
38 P. West, R. Illsey, and H. Kelman, 'Public Preferences for the Care of Dependency Groups' (1984) 18 *Social Science and Medicine* 287.
39 J. Twigg, 'Social Security, Community Care, and the Griffiths Report: Reflections on a Debate' in *Social Security and Community Care*, op. cit., n. 36.
40 Department of Health and Social Security, *Residential Care: A Positive Choice. Report of the Independent Review of Residential Care* (1988; chairman G. Wagner).
41 Means and Smith, op. cit., n. 11.
42 Townsend, op. cit., n. 12.
43 H. Land and H. Rose, 'Compulsory Altruism for Some or an Altruistic Society for All?' in *In Defence of Welfare*, eds. P. Bean, J. Ferris, and D. Whynes (1985).
44 H. Graham, 'Caring: A Labour of Love' in *A Labour of Love*, op. cit., n. 5.
45 C. Gilligan, *In a Different Voice. Psychological Theory and Women's Development* (1982).
46 J. B. Elshtain, *Public Man and Private Woman* (1981).
47 For example, see Finch and Groves, op. cit., n. 5.
48 Ungerson, op. cit., n. 13; and Land and Rose, op. cit., n. 43.
49 M. Nissel and L. Bonnerjea, *Family Care of the Handicapped Elderly: Who Pays?* (1982; Policy Studies Institute Report No. 602).
50 J. Finch, 'Social Policy, Social Engineering and the Family in the 1990s' in *The Goals of Social Policy*, eds. M. Bulmer, J. Lewis, and D. Piachaud (1989).
51 Lewis and Meredith, op. cit., n. 33.
52 D. A. Jones, C. R. Victor, and N. J. Vetter, 'Carers of the Elderly in the Community' (1983) 33 *J. of the Royal College of General Practitioners* 707.

53 Audit Commission, op. cit., n. 2.
54 E. Levin, I. Sinclair, and P. Gorbach, *Supporters of Confused Elderly Persons at Home* (1983).
55 Audit Commission, op. cit., n. 2.
56 Griffiths Report, op. cit., n. 9, para. ix.35.
57 Levin et al., op. cit., n. 54.
58 E. Brody, P. T. Johnsen, M. Fulcomer, and A. M. Lang, 'Women's Changing Roles and Help to Elderly Parents: Attitudes of Three Generations of Women' (1983) 38 *J. of Gerontology* 597.
59 T. Booth, *Home Truths. Old Peoples' Homes and the Outcome of Care* (1985).

'A Better Partnership between State and Individual Provision': Social Security into the 1990s

PETE ALCOCK*

THE POST-WAR LEGACY

Social security, the provision through the state of some form of monetary support for sections of the population, has been the central feature of welfare provision within Britain since the early developments of a capitalist wage economy. From Speenhamland to the workhouse or from insurance to Income Support, therefore, both the amount of state support to be provided, and the forms under which provision is made, have been the focus of debates and struggles about the proper role of the state in providing for its citizens.

There are those who have argued that poverty and social security are indeed inevitable (and irremoveable) aspects of any wage economy.[1] However, both the forms and the amount of state provision for income support have in practice varied considerably throughout the development of the British state. Rights to benefit guaranteed by the state, irrespective of proof of desert, have generally been argued to be examples of high points of state commitment, and minimal discretionary provision to be examples of limited state involvement in cash welfare. Not surprisingly, provision of state-guaranteed rights through insurance, based on the recommendations of the Beveridge Report, were therefore a major part of the so-called post-war welfare settlement.[2]

Much has been written about the principles of state support contained in the Beveridge Report,[3] and much has been made of the failure of post-war social security policy to adhere to those principles over the ensuing forty years.[4] Certainly by the late 1970s they had not served to stem the contradictions or the criticisms of state social security policy. And despite the ideals of comprehensive insurance provision the social security provision of the 1970s was largely based on a means-tested support, which continued to be both divisive and stigmatizing.

Insurance provision had also, of course, always been based upon state support for working-class male breadwinners unable to earn wages on the labour market.[5] Benefits were therefore based not only on need, but also on proof of availability for work; and benefit levels, especially for the long-term

*Department of Applied Social Studies, Sheffield City Polytechnic, 36 Collegiate Crescent, Sheffield, South Yorkshire S10 2BP, England.

unemployed, were relatively low in order to maintain the incentive to undertake low-wage employment where this was available. This reinforced the underlying role of state welfare in supporting labour discipline. But it also compounded the unequal treatment under the state welfare system of women and Britain's black population, who, as a result of their exclusion from employment and insurance, have had to rely more heavily on means-tested support.

The overlap of the wide range of insurance-based and means-tested benefits for different groups of claimants inevitably led to extreme complexity within the benefit system and to much confusion about potential entitlement amongst those who were forced to rely on it. Confusion alone was bad enough, but worse – it meant that many people failed to realize the need to claim at all; this resulted in large numbers of claimants not receiving all the support to which they may have been entitled. The Government's own estimates of this problem of low 'take-up' put the levels of payment at between fifty and seventy-five per cent of those entitled for some means-tested benefits. Low levels of take-up were also a product, however, of the depressing and even hostile environment of state benefit dependency in the late 1970s, fuelled by media hysteria that extensive and complex state support was a soft touch for forgers and scroungers.[6]

These complex and contradictory developments of post-war social security provision had by the late 1970s, therefore, produced a state scheme that was riddled with problems and inconsistencies. And by the time the Thatcher Government first came to power in 1979 it inherited a system which could command no support from either the claimants who depended on it, the administrators who tried to operate it, or the tax-payers outside it who had been encouraged to believe that they were being asked to meet an open-ended bill. Furthermore, by this time social security had escalated to become by far the largest single item of state public expenditure. For a government openly committed to monetarist targets and reductions in public spending, the challenge of social security reform was therefore an obvious one, and one which was quickly undertaken.

CUTS OR RESTRUCTURING

In 1980 the new Conservative Government introduced two pieces of social security legislation which attempted to rationalize and reduce the complex provision of the 1970s. Rationalization came in the form of the regularization of the previously largely discretionary Supplementary Benefits scheme, although this did also result in some reductions in entitlement.[7] Reduction came with the severing of the link between pensions and earnings (in future they would only rise in line with price inflation), and later in the direct cuts to the major National Insurance benefits, notably by the phased withdrawal of the Earnings-Related Supplement to short-term benefits. These were the first cuts to major benefits for fifty years, and yet – perhaps, a testimony to the declining importance of insurance-based benefits – they did not attract much opposition even in Parliament, where only a handful of Labour MPs attended the final reading of the Social Security Bill.

However, the cuts in benefit could not stem the increasingly rapidly rising costs of the social security budget, resulting primarily from the growing numbers of unemployed claimants produced by economic policies. Indeed, in the light of the massive increase in benefit dependency in the early years of the 1980s the changes to benefit entitlement introduced could be, and were, characterized as penny-pinching trifles.[8] And that they confirmed the central role of means-testing within state welfare provision was really only a continuation of a trend which was already well established within the post-war benefits system.

In 1982, however, these benefit cuts were accompanied by some structural changes in the form and administration of social security provision. Means-tested support for housing costs in the form of rent and rates rebates was unified and rationalized under the auspices of local authority administration of local benefits. The change proved disastrous for claimants as local authorities struggled under the weight of their new income maintenance responsibilities; but it provided the appearance, at least, of a reduction in control by the central state.[9] National Insurance provision for short-term absence from work due to sickness was also removed from state control and replaced by Statutory Sick Pay, to be provided by employers. Initially this was limited to sick pay for six weeks (although this covered the majority of such absences), but it was later extended to twenty-six weeks.

Certainly these early reforms did not meet the demands of some of the more far-sighted proponents of New Right welfare policy, who were supposedly informing the Thatcherite strategies for reform. As early as 1971 Rhodes Boyson MP, a minister during the early period of the Thatcher Government, had written of the need to reduce all state dependency to a minimal means-tested role in order to foster individual self-help.[10] And by the early 1980s Charles Murray, the New Right guru of the United States of America, was advising senior government policy-makers on the need for the state to foster free enterprise directly through the provision of minimal public support.[11] Ideas such as these were also discussed in the seminars of the Centre for Policy Studies, founded in the 1970s by another government minister, Sir Keith Joseph MP, to provide a forum for the development of New Right policy initiatives in welfare.

Some of the clearest prescriptions for social security reform from the New Right, however, came from the work of the Adam Smith Institute, which was established in 1979. It undertook a major review of state welfare policy, called the Omega Project, and produced both analysis of the supposed short-comings of post-war social security policy and proposals for its radical reform.[12] The Omega Project pointed to the confused goals and inefficient complexity of the social security scheme, and to their deleterious effects on private provision and work incentives. They focused in particular on state pensions provision, criticising both its moral intentions and its funding framework. Their recommendations were for the abolition of all existing major benefit provision, including the State Earnings-Related Pensions Scheme (SERPS) which they described as a 'costly mistake'.[13] In place of these benefits they recommended that state provision should be limited to a basic minimum means-tested benefit. For those of employment age this would be linked directly to the taxation system, and would be set against earnings to provide an (albeit limited) incentive to engage in waged employment. For those over pension age, this minimum state support would be the subject of compulsory contributions for those who could pay (the state would provide for those who could not); but those who wished to provide personal pensions for themselves over and above the state minimum level could, if they wished to, contract out of the scheme.

Interestingly the radical proposals of the Adam Smith Institute for social security reform compared in breadth with other radical reforms being suggested at the same time both by the politicial centre[14] and the radical left[15] – all of whom were agreed that the existing complex and contradictory system could only be improved by the introduction of major change. And, although the institute's proposals were much more radical and far-reaching than the changes brought about by the benefit cuts and restructuring undertaken during the first term of the Thatcher Government, their themes of minimal state welfare, support for low-wage employment, and the encouragement of individual and work-based protection – in short, the encouragement of private provision for income support – were beginning increasingly to dominate discussion of benefit policy within government circles.

Of course, encouragement of private welfare provision within state social security was hardly an innovatory development in the 1980s. Beveridge himself had always been committed to the desirability of permitting and encouraging private arrangements for income maintenance to supplement state provision through the National Insurance scheme; and the growth in work-related private superannuation schemes for additional pensions for those in secure employment had begun in earnest in the late 1950s and was already big business before 1979. Furthermore, as Papadakis and Taylor-Gooby have pointed out, privatization measures which merely transfer the administration of income support from the public to the private sector, as in the case of sick pay, do not guarantee any reduction in state expenditure (because of the subsidies still maintained) or state control (because of the legal regulation still required).[16]

However, the economics and legalities of the private provision of welfare are only parts of a political and ideological strategy to redefine the expectations and responsibilities of collective state support. And, after the successful re-election of the Thatcher administration in 1983, it was becoming clear that such political and ideological restructuring was to become the major feature of the strategy for social security reform.

Commitment to a more fundamental restructuring of social security provision was first signalled by the establishment in 1984 by Norman Fowler MP, then Secretary of State for Social Services, of a series of four public reviews of benefit provision. The reviews covered pensions, Housing Benefit, Supplementary Benefit, and benefits for children and young persons. They were, according to Norman Fowler MP, to be 'the most substantial examination of the social security system since the Beveridge report forty years ago', although their government-dominated membership and their apparently limited remits suggested the expected scope of their examination had already to some extent been predetermined.[17]

Suspicions of the limited remit of the reviews appeared to be confirmed in June 1985, when the review reports (with one exception) appeared, with Cabinet endorsement, as a Green Paper outlining proposed social security reforms.[18] The Green Paper set out proposals for 'a new and better structure for our social security system' and concluded that there was 'widespread dissatisfaction' with the present system.[19] In his statement introducing the proposals to the House of Commons on 3 June, the Secretary of State for Social Services said that his programme of reform would 'establish a better partnership between state and individual provision'.

Although no direct examination of the National Insurance scheme had been included in the review process, the proposed reforms recommended further significant reductions in the scope of insurance-based benefit provision. These included the extension of sick pay to twenty-six weeks, the replacement of Maternity Benefit with statutory maternity pay, the replacement of Widows' Benefit with lump sum payment, and (as suggested by the Adam Smith Institute) the abolition of SERPS and its replacement with private personal pensions. Most of the major recommendations for benefit reform, however, came in proposals to rationalize and to simplify income-related – that is, means-tested – benefit provision. These included the replacement of Supplementary Benefit with a new benefit called Income Support, and the aligning of entitlement to this benefit to means-tested support for low-wage families (through the new Family Credit) and for rent and rates (through Housing Benefit). Reform of income-related benefits was claimed to be a necessary response to the complexity and confusion which surrounded existing provision, and a desirable means of targeting limited responses onto those groups most in need of state support.

Much of the proposed simplification of means-tested benefits was to be achieved, however, by the abolition of entitlement to extra needs-related payments for special needs, and their replacement with blanket premiums for certain groups of claimants such as families, pensioners, and those with disabilities. As critics pointed out, it was more than likely that without significantly increased benefit levels (which were not promised) such simplification and targeting would lead to much hardship for large numbers of existing claimants.[20] Others argued that the central role for means-tested benefits which this implied would only compound existing problems of divisions and stigmatization within the benefits system, and further entrench its support for low wages through the operation of the poverty trap.[21]

The Government's own belief in the ability of the reformed social security scheme to meet the needs of all claimants itself seemed to be belied by the proposal to introduce, alongside entitlement to weekly benefit, the possibility of the payment of grants or loans to claimants from a cash-limited and discretionary Social Fund. This feature of the proposed reforms attracted perhaps the most widespread disapprobation, including criticism from the Government's own Social Security Advisory Committee. It seemed to presage a step backwards towards judgemental decisions by state officials about entitlement to state benefit, based upon nineteenth-century notions of the 'deserving' and the 'undeserving poor'. As Stewart and Stewart pointed out, it also threatened to cross the boundaries between social security and social services.[22]

Although the reforms proposed in the Green Paper were nowhere near as radical as those suggested by the Adam Smith Institute, they did embody a significant shift towards minimal state welfare and the direct encouragement of individual protection through employment and the private market. However, even these more limited plans did not attract the support of all the potentially powerful patrons of private welfare. Both the Confederation of British Industry and the National Association of Pension Funds opposed the abolition of SERPS. Not all employers had welcomed the transfer of responsibility for sick pay to the workplace, and neither they nor the pension funds were keen to take on the potential pension needs of those who did not already benefit from employment-based superannuation provision. For insecure, temporary, and part-time employees the state pension scheme provided a cost-effective back stop to private occupational schemes, and the removal of this cushion to the private market was more than some of its most influential supporters were prepared to risk.

In spite of its early resolve, therefore, the Government decided to bow to these more pragmatic assessments of the viability of private welfare; and in the White Paper which followed in December 1985 and outlined the changes that were planned following the consultative process, the proposal to abolish SERPS was replaced by a commitment to reduce future payments under it, and to provide additional incentives for individual private pension pro-vision.[23] Reduction in the scope of coverage had been suggested by the Adam Smith Institute as a temporary, but less desirable, alternative to the abolition of SERPS.[24]

The reversal of the decision to abolish SERPS may also have been a response to the widespread opposition from the Labour Party and poverty lobby to the suggestion of reneging on a cross-party commitment to the state scheme, which had only been introduced a few years earlier in 1978 and was not planned to achieve full operation until after 1998. However, this was not conceded in the White Paper, and does not appear to concur with the Government's dismissal of such opposition to the other changes proposed in

102

the Green Paper, all of which were included intact in the Social Security Bill which followed the White Paper and was introduced into Parliament in 1986.

The Social Security Bill was one of the major legislative measures of the latter part of the Thatcher Government's second term. And, although one or two minor amendments to it were introduced in the House of Lords and conceded in the House of Commons, it had received the Royal Assent by July 1986, just over two years after the review process had begun, and took its place on the statute book as the most fundamental reform of social security policy since the 1940s.

However, with a couple of minor exceptions, the reformed social security scheme did not come into force immediately in 1986. Implementation of the sick pay and maternity pay provisions was delayed until April 1987; and implementation of the major reforms to income-related benefits and to pensions was put back until April 1988. The ostensible aim of this delay was to give benefit administrators time to prepare for what would be almost wholesale changes in law and practice – the hurried introduction of reforms in 1980 for Supplementary Benefit and 1983 for Housing Benefit had created widespread chaos and confusion amongst claimants and officers alike. However, it also gave the planned reforms a more important political profile, for in June 1987 the Prime Minister called a General Election.

The existence in legislative form of the Government's plans for social security reform, which had been widely condemned by the opposition parties when first introduced, provided a platform for these measures of privatization and minimal state welfare to become a major issue in the 1987 General Election campaign. Curiously, however, this was not to be: the Government made little of their plans to reform benefits; and the opposition parties, with little to propose in alternative to those plans other than tinkering with the now discredited post-war scheme, were unwilling or unable to raise the low profile of welfare politics.

Whether more fundamental alternative plans for reform could have deflected support for the Government's plans is now, however, only a hypothetical question. For in June 1987 the Thatcher Government was triumphantly returned to power for its third term. In his preface to the 1985 White Paper on reform, Secretary of State Norman Fowler MP had claimed confidently that support for the need for reform had been won: 'The debate is not whether social security should be reformed but how it should be reformed.'[25] With their return to power in 1987 the Government could convincingly claim that they had demonstrated support for the direction and detail of reform too.

CONTINUOUS REVIEW

The Social Security Act 1986 is an example from the Thatcher Government's second term of the kinds of fundamental restructuring of welfare provision which are going to be experienced in a number of other areas of social provision during a more radical and more confident third term of office, as the other contributions to this special issue of the *Journal of Law and Society* make clear. By the time the reforms were finally introduced in April 1988 the true extent of the reductions in benefit for some claimants were only just beginning to register with opposition MPs and some Government back-benchers. Debate in Parliament highlighted some of the most extreme cases, and back-bench anger at these examples eventually extracted a minimal concession over transitional protection for some pensioner claimants and the level of the upper capital limit for loss of entitlement to Housing Benefit. However, need for and direction of fundamental reform was unchallenged and seemingly unchallengeable.

Even before the Social Security Act 1986 had been implemented, however, the new Secretary of State for Social Services, John Moore MP, had made it clear that the process of reform was by no means over. In his first major speech on 26 September 1987, he referred to the need to keep social policies under permanent review and stressed that the Government's commitment was to ensure a march of the Welfare State 'away from dependence towards independence', encouraging people to 'use their talents to take care of themselves and their families'. This rhetoric is much closer to the views of Rhodes Boyson MP and Murray than the earlier limited reforms of benefit entitlement, and appears to be based upon a definite ideological and political commitment to undermine the 'benefit dependency culture'.

Although it appeared to attract much support in the research carried out as part of the reviews of social security policy in 1984-5,[26] universal benefits such as Child Benefit do not fit readily with a minimalist role for state welfare. Support for Child Benefit in the renewed assault on benefit dependency was always likely to be lukewarm at best. In autumn 1987 it was announced that Child Benefit was not to be up-rated in 1988 in line with inflation, presaging perhaps further reductions in the future to reduce its monetary and therefore its political value, as had happened previously with funeral and maternity grants. And in a speech to the Institute of Directors in June 1988 the Secretary of State for Social Services reiterated the need to target state support on the weak and vulnerable and said that 'hard questions' still remained to be answered.

Further gradual reduction also appears to be the policy with what is now left of National Insurance benefits. A new Social Security Bill was introduced in 1987 to tighten up on the contribution conditions for entitlement to short-term National Insurance benefits. And regulations were brought in to extend the period of disqualification from Unemployment Benefit to twenty-six weeks for those deemed to be voluntarily unemployed.

What the policy developments of the Thatcher Government's third term have already made increasingly clearer, however, is the direct relationship between economic and social policy planning of income maintenance provision. There have, of course, always been contradictions between the economic and social policy objectives of post-war social security measures; but these contradictions are now under concerted attack.

The attack has most recently been predominantly orchestrated by the Department of Employment – under the control of ex-Social Services Secretary Norman Fowler MP – in the Employment Act 1988 and the accompanying White Paper entitled *Training for Employment*.[27] The aim of the measures contained in these documents is to replace the plethora of training and job creation schemes for long-term unemployed claimants with a unified training programme, administered by a revamped Training Commission, replacing the old Manpower Services Commission. The new training programmes – 600,000 a year – will be a mixture of employment experience and work-related training, carried out as far as possible in employer-based placements, tailored to the needs of the individuals concerned. Rather than receiving wages, however, those on training placements will continue to be paid their means-tested benefit entitlement plus a supplement of between £10 and £12 per week depending on their circumstances, from which up to £5 of work expenses may be deducted.

This new 'benefits-plus' basis of remuneration for job training is intended to make such placements more attractive to claimants with large families, whose means-tested benefit entitlement might otherwise put them above the rather meagre wages paid under previous job creation schemes. However, it is a clear example of benefit policies serving the economic needs of a wage labour market. Norman Fowler MP made it clear in the debates on the Employment Bill that the Government now felt that there were plenty of job opportunities there for those willing and able to take them, and that claimant advisors interviewing long-term unemployed claimants would now be able to point out the potential entitlement of wage support benefits such as Family Credit in helping unemployed people decide how best to respond to the opportunities for independence.

The Employment Act 1988 contains a measure permitting the Secretary of State for Employment to designate the new training placement as approved training under the Social Security Act 1975. In these circumstances refusal of a training place would constitute voluntary unemployment under the terms of the Act, and would render the claimant liable to a twenty-six week disqualification from benefit. When pressed in the House of Commons about the Government's intentions to make the benefits-plus training programme compulsory in such a manner, the Secretary of State for Employment would only state that the Government had no intention to designate the scheme under the Social Security Act 1975 at the present time.

Such compulsory work for benefit does exist in the 'workfare' schemes in the United States of America, and Norman Fowler MP is known to have studied the operation of these schemes. His assurances about the present time may, therefore, be no more than that. In any event, the work of Restart counsellors and claimant advisors may operate as a powerful indirect pressure on claimants to undertake placements offered by the Training Commission. Furthermore, the precedent of youth training provision offers an ominous prospect here. Youth Training Scheme places were initially undertaken voluntarily under the guidance of careers advisors; but in the Social Security

Bill 1987 entitlement to Income Support for young people aged sixteen to eighteen years was removed in order to ensure that, if not in employment or full-time education, they were required to undertake a placement on the Youth Training Scheme. This was justified by the Government as tackling the culture of benefit dependency at its roots. It is no change in principle to tackle it further up the tree, too, if other measures are not entirely successful.

FREEDOM OF CHOICE AND A PRIVATE MARKET IN WELFARE

What the developments in social security policy and employment policy during the first year of the Thatcher Government's third term make abundantly clear is that Thatcherite strategies involve the joint planning of social and economic policy measures to meet economic, political, and ideological aims which are fundamentally at odds with pre-existing forms and practices of state welfare. With the benefit of hindsight, it is now also clear that such strategies underlay the earlier, more limited reforms of the Thatcher Government's previous terms of office, and were a central focus of the much-vaunted review of social security provision in 1984-5. Now they are merely to be carried forward more vigorously with a direct assault on the benefit dependency culture.

Of course, to what extent these aims have thus far been achieved is a debatable point – the call of John Moore MP for a continuous review of social policy suggests that the process of reform may be an enduring one, and there is no guarantee that the future holds only the prospect of further success. Furthermore, whether they have fundamentally altered the economics of state support for income maintenance is also open to question – certainly they have not reduced the proportion of public expenditure required for social security benefits. Indeed, in 1988-9 public expenditure on social security is planned to rise in real terms by £430 million to a total of £48 billion – its highest level in both relative and absolute terms.

However, there can be little doubt that these developments do constitute a fundamental challenge to the previously predominant political and ideological assumption that the aims of social policy were to be determined by independent social investigation and that measures would then be gradually adapted in order better to meet these aims – if and when economic circumstances allowed. Founded, it is argued, on the belief in a post-war political consensus over the central role of state welfare, this assumption has appeared to justify an incremental or progressive model of change and development in welfare policy within agreed guidelines. The Thatcherite attack on welfare provision is, at heart, an attack on such a model of change.

This model had been identified by the Prime Minister herself as a form of 'creeping socialism'. And the political and ideological objectives of Thatcherite welfare reform are directed at reversing these collectivist incursions into the market economy as much as they are aimed at the narrower objectives of balancing or reducing budgets for state expenditure. In this sense the continuous review process can better be seen as a form of decremental reform of state welfare, or, conversely, as an incremental return to freedom of choice and a private market in welfare provision. The measure of the importance of change, and of its success, therefore, is not primarily that of the speed with which there can be a rolling back of state involvement in welfare provision, but is rather that of the direction in which the provision of state support can be guided and the political and ideological expectations to which that gives rise.

Thus, in spite of initial expectations to the contrary, it is the legal changes to the form of welfare provision – and not the economic pressures on expenditure and consequent benefit cuts – which are at the centre of the Thatcherite strategy on welfare, and which therefore provide the key to any alternative strategy.

There has never been any expectation, then, within government circles, that there could be any complete withdrawal of the state and the law from the provision and regulation of income support. Even the Adam Smith Institute's proposals for radical reform included a basic minimum payment for all from the state. However, there has been a clear attempt to reduce the role of state benefit to such a minimalist provision. There have been cuts and restrictions in entitlement to universal and contributory benefits, and a concentration on means-tested measures which provide a simple and basic income for those who cannot provide for themselves. The rationalization of income-related benefits in the Social Security Act 1986 was a major endorsement of such a goal, and this has involved a significant shift in the role of the law, from seeking to define rights to a range of needs-related support payments to ensuring that only basic categories of need are identified.

For those who can be expected to provide for themselves, both positive and negative incentives have been provided through the development of new legal measures to regulate and encourage private welfare. In the area of pensions the new measures have taken the form of permissive regulations for private individual pension plans as well as financial and legal incentives to pursue them. In the case of temporary absence from paid employment the new measures have taken the form of statutory requirements on employers to make provision for income maintenance, with financial incentives to meet these requirements via reduced National Insurance contributions. In circumstances of able-bodied unemployment the new measures have taken the form of harsh disqualifications for voluntary unemployment, increased investigation and 'assistance' by officers of the Department of Social Security, and the proposed offer of job training for all claimants unemployed for six months or more. For young unemployed people such offers of job training are to be made compulsory; and this remains a legal possibility for unemployed adults too.

Many of these measures involve continued state expenditure, through subsidization, and continued or extended state regulation. However, they shift the focus of state concern with welfare from the direct provision of public support for all contingencies to the provision of a legal framework to encourage, or coerce, individuals to choose private support or protection through employment or the marketplace. That not all will be equally able or willing to exercise such a choice is deemed to be either a misfortune for the individual concerned or a symptom of the individual's irresponsibility; and for these 'deserving' or 'undeserving poor' who remain outside the private market in welfare, minimal state provision will be preserved.

This return to a nineteenth-century philosophy of minimal state welfare for the relief of proven individual poverty is most starkly revealed in the operation of the new Social Fund for the poor.[28] The fund is in part an admission of the inadequacy of the minimal levels of the basic Income Support benefits to meet all the needs of all claimants forced to rely on it. It will provide discretionary grants (for needs related to community care) and loans (to be repaid via deductions from future benefit) to meet urgent and priority needs for expensive items which claimants cannot themselves afford to buy. However, the total number of payments made from the fund will be subject to monthly cash limits allocated to each local office of the Department of Social Security, and within these offices priorities will have to be judged against demand by social fund officers, based on information provided by claimants, social workers, or others. There can consequently be no appeal against refusal to make a payment, though claimants will be able to ask for a review of their request.

Discretion, subject to cash limits, is a fundamental departure from the legal rights to payments for expensive items contained in the Supplementary Benefits scheme. Again, it will involve a shift in the role of the law – in this case from a role of defining needs and rights to one of providing a framework for the exercise of individual discretion. In this new context state support will operate much more along the lines of a form of public philanthropy; and, as Stewart and Stewart have argued, this is likely to include more and more social work involvement in judging the priority needs of claimants.[29] In 1988 a report on community care by Sir Roy Griffiths suggested that in the future responsibility for administering discretionary grants for community care needs might be better transferred to local social service departments. Although this has, not surprisingly, met with mixed reactions in social work quarters, it would be a logical step in the transfer of expectations from state-administered legal rights to social work assistance for the 'deserving poor'.

That a move towards public philanthropy may also foster expectations of private philanthropic endeavour to supplement minimal state support is also an important feature of the gradual redrawing of the boundaries of collective state provision. The Prime Minister herself has extolled the virtues of private charity, freely given, over enforced state redistribution of resources. The limited amounts of benefit under Income Support and the cash restrictions on the Social Fund are likely to increase the pressure on claimants to seek such private charity to meet even fairly basic needs; and early evidence suggests that many organized charities are experiencing such increased pressure on their resources in the late 1980s. Certainly the desirability of private charitable efforts to supplement minimal state provision seems to be a recognized feature of future plans for state support – following the introduction of the Social

Security Act 1986 copies of the *Charities Digest* were sent to all local offices of the Department of Health and Social Security.

Obviously, the new private market in welfare is likely to have significantly different implications for different groups of claimants and potential claimants within Britain. Divisions of gender and race are likely to be particularly acutely accentuated here.

Given their weaker position in the labour market, their greater responsibility for child and adult care, and their generally greater longevity, women are much more likely to be amongst those unable to benefit fully from the labour market and private welfare, and therefore forced to rely on minimal state provision. This process of the feminization of poverty is not a new one;[30] but the new policies for welfare are likely to result in future in a much greater concentration of women within those marginal groups outside the growing private provision of welfare.

Similar further marginalization is also likely to be in store for a large part of Britain's black population. As Gordon and Newnham have demonstrated, black people have already experienced greater suspicion and harassment in the receipt of state benefits, in particular because of suspicions about their immigration status (passport checks) or their right to state benefit (recourse to public funds).[31] These pressures will be heightened as a result of further restrictions on relatives' right to claim public support after joining their families in Britain, contained in 1988 changes to immigration law, and as a result of changed practices within the Department of Social Security over passport checking procedures. Black people also experience lower wages and higher unemployment than their white compatriots, and, as with women, this is likely to result in greater exclusion from the private market in welfare and greater reliance upon minimal state support.

THERE IS AN ALTERNATIVE

Although it is not within the scope of this special issue of the *Journal of Law and Society* to discuss future strategies for welfare or alternatives to the Thatcherite path, there are some clear lessons for any alternative policies for welfare reform in Britain, which flow directly from an appreciation and analysis of 'Thatcher's Law'.

As was argued in the first section, by the time the Thatcher Government first came to power in 1979, the post-war social security scheme in Britain was already defensible in name only. And, indeed, for Norman Fowler MP to claim in the 1985 White Paper on social security reform that the argument over the need for reform had by then been won was no earth-shattering revelation. In spite of this, however, most of the opposition to the Government's policies for welfare reform, most notably within Parliament itself, has concentrated upon castigating these as cuts in or departures from previous benefit provision.

If these were intended as a defence of existing post-war benefits against further cuts they have, perhaps predictably, been largely unsuccessful – such is the lot of opposition. If they are intended as the basis for a future return to prior provisions, however, they are much more worrying. The increasing breadth of Thatcherite reform will make retracing the steps of legal change more and more difficult in practice; but, more importantly, it will make this appear more and more irrelevant in principle.

No realistic future alternative strategy for social security reform could include as the central feature of its plans for legislative change the reintroduction of the Supplementary Benefits system. The Thatcherite strategy to change the agenda of state provision has already achieved the relegation of previous policies for collective support. The intention was to prevent the possibility of going back; and by the 1990s this will undoubtedly have been achieved. Any alternatives to Thatcherism can only therefore look to the future.

By the 1990s freedom of choice and a private market in welfare will be established within provision for income support, and state benefits will be reduced to a minimal philanthropic role. Against such a background the notion of rights to state welfare for all will have to be fought for and won all over again. This does not mean a return to mid-twentieth-century debates about insurance through the state and the prevention of poverty through employment-based contingency planning, however. These limited (white, male) perceptions of collective social security are no longer a legacy, and no longer a viable way forward. It will be a new and different perception of rights, responsibilities, and social justice which provides the effective challenge to individual choice on the private market in the future – if, that is, there is to be any challenge to it at all.

NOTES AND REFERENCES

1   T. Novak, *Poverty and the State: An Historical Sociology* (1988) ch. 1.
2   *Report on Social Insurance and Allied Services* (1942; Cmd. 6404; chairman Sir William Beveridge).
3   See, for instance, P. Alcock, *Poverty and State Support* (1987) ch. 4; A. Deacon and J. Bradshaw, *Reserved for the Poor: The Means-Test in British Social Policy* (1983) ch. 2; T. Cutler et al., *Keynes, Beveridge and Beyond* (1986).
4   See, for instance, S. MacGregor, *The Politics of Poverty* (1981) ch. 2; A. Dilnot et al., *The Reform of Social Security* (1984) ch. 1.
5   See K. Mann, 'The Making of a Claiming Class: The Neglect of Agency in Analysis of the Welfare State' (1986) 15 *Critical Social Policy* 62.
6   See P. Golding and S. Middleton, *Images of Welfare: Press and Public Attitudes to Welfare* (1982).
7   See J. Allbeson and R. Smith, *We Don't Give Clothing Grants Anymore: The 1980 Supplementary Benefits Scheme* (1984).
8   Dependency upon Supplementary Benefit more or less doubled between 1980 and 1985 from four to eight million claimants.
9   Rent and rate rebates are not classed as public expenditure.
10 R. Boyson, *Down With the Poor* (1971).
11 C. Murray, *Losing Ground* (1984).
12 Adam Smith Institute, *Omega Project: Social Security Policy* (1984).

13 id., p. 35.

14 See Dilnot et al., op. cit., n. 4.

15 B. Jordan, 'The Social Wage: A Right for All' *New Society*, 26 April 1984.

16 E. Papadakis and P. Taylor-Gooby, *The Private Provision of Public Welfare: State, Market, and Community* (1987) 33ff.

17 See P. Alcock, 'The Fowler Reviews: Social Policy on the Political Agenda' (1985) 14 *Critical Social Policy* 93.

18 Department of Health and Social Security, *Reform of Social Security* (1985; Cmnd. 9517, 9518, 9519).

19 Cmnd. 9517, op. cit., n. 18, Preface.

20 See R. Berthoud, *The Examination of Social Security* (1985); Child Poverty Action Group, *Burying Beveridge: A Detailed Response to the Green Paper – Reform of Social Security* (1985).

21 Alcock, op. cit., n. 17.

22 G. Stewart and J. Stewart, *Boundary Changes: Social Work and Social Security* (1986).

23 Department of Health and Social Security, *Reform of Social Security: Programme for Action* (1985; Cmnd. 9691).

24 Adam Smith Institute, op. cit., n. 12, p. 34.

25 Department of Health and Social Security, op. cit., n. 23, Preface.

26 Department of Health and Social Security, op. cit., n. 18, vol. 3, p. 76.

27 Department of Employment, *Training for Employment* (1988; Cm. 316).

28 See H. Bolderson, 'The Right to Appeal and the Social Fund' (1988) 15 *J. Law and Society* 279.

29 Stewart and Stewart, op. cit., n. 22.

30 See C. Glendinning and J. Millar, *Women and Poverty in Britain* (1987).

31 P. Gordon and A. Newnham, *Passport to Benefits: Racism in Social Security* (1985).

'Consensual Authoritarianism' and Criminal Justice in Thatcher's Britain

ALAN NORRIE* AND SAMMY ADELMAN*

INTRODUCTION

The impact of Thatcherism on the criminal justice system may be understood in terms of two apparent paradoxes. The first is that of continuity and change, so that while there have been significant developments in the direction of authoritarian forms of rule under Thatcherism these developments cannot be viewed in isolation from previous periods of British history. Thus, while Thatcherism is authoritarian, it is inaccurate to identify authoritarianism with Thatcherism as a wholly new departure.

The second apparent paradox is that of consensus and conflict. We argue that a central feature of Thatcherism is its ability to draw upon and renovate consensus through conflict. Taking as our particular focus the development of popular perceptions of and relations with the police from the mid-nineteenth century, we argue that a consistent feature of class relations in Britain has been that the criminalization process has operated with the consent of significant sections of the working class as well as the middle class. We then argue that while Thatcherism involves more authoritarian modes of criminalization, it has been able to draw upon a relative consensus across class lines in order to successfully operate a more conflictual criminal justice system.

This essay contributes to a debate about the specific nature of authoritarianism under the Thatcher Government which owes most to the work of Hall and his use of the term 'authoritarian populism'. We discuss this concept in the fourth section of this paper. More recently, Scraton has edited a series of essays entitled *Law, Order and the Authoritarian State* which draws upon Hall's perspective and seeks to apply it through very thorough empirical analyses of different aspects of the criminal justice system. We have drawn on the essays in this book as a resource for writing this paper, but we feel that it lacks a coherent theoretical framework partly because it follows Hall's analysis. Our argument is that the utility of the term 'authoritarian populism' is limited by its derivation from a mode of analysis that unduly privileges ideological and political factors in opposition to the structural and economic conditions within which ideologies and politics operate.

*School of Law, University of Warwick, Coventry, West Midlands CV4 7AL, England.

We therefore use the term 'consensual authoritarianism' provisionally to denote the need to look at the historical material basis of a relative consensus incorporating important sections of the working class and the need to comprehend the contradictory fusion of authoritarianism and consent so characteristic of the Thatcherite project. In making this argument it is important to realize that we are drawing a distinction between those periods of consent (or, indeed, conflict) which manifest themselves in particular historical conjunctures, and a more fundamental and structural level of consent within British society which has existed for over a hundred years and which has its roots in the division of interests within the working class between, very broadly, its better and worse-off sections. While recognizing the need for historical specification of the meaning of the term in different periods, this division within the working class can be designated as one between a labour aristocracy and other, poorer, less privileged sections of the class.[1] Our argument will be that it is this structural division within the working class, allowing for a consensual alliance across the classes and aligning the better-off workers' interests with those of capital, which forms the historical basis for particular historical periods of consent and, to the extent that it is able, defines the limits of conflict within British society. This alliance on the part of the workers assumes different forms in different historical periods, ranging from resistance within limits to overt collaboration. When we talk of issues such as 'policing with consent' or the fashioning of consensus under Thatcherism, we are thinking of a historically identifiable conjuncture of consent which is based upon (and drawn from) a fundamental division within the working class and the historical cross-class consensus to which it has given rise.

CONTINUITY AND CHANGE

The immediate impression one has of the criminal justice system after nearly ten years of Thatcherism is that which Hall identified as a drift into an authoritarian law and order society.[2] This drift – or perhaps development, for there is nothing to suggest that many of the changes have not been deliberate – towards more authoritarian methods of criminalization has occurred throughout the system, taking in the police, the courts, the prisons, and subsidiary parts of the system such as the various branches of the social services through the use of the concept of 'community policing' or 'multi-agency policing'.[3]

While space precludes a detailed catalogue of all these developments, certain key developments may be briefly mentioned.[4] First, in relation to the police, there has been a move towards a more centralized and militarized form of policing in which technologies and organization have been developed, having as their primary aim the containment and suppression of public disorder. Policing for public order, as one police chief has quite candidly admitted,[5] has become the first priority, with the prevention and detection of individual crimes a secondary and subsidiary motivation.[6] As a result of this

113

declared change in police activity, we have also witnessed the more overt politicization of the police as they have become publicly identified with the successive policies of the Thatcher Government, particularly with regard to notions of what is normal, acceptable, rightful conduct and what is abnormal and alien – descriptions which are constructed in terms of class, race, and respectability, an area of ideological conflict in which the impact of Thatcherism has been particularly significant.[7]

Elsewhere within the system, important developments have occurred concerning the processing of defendants brought before the courts as well as the character of the prison system. We have witnessed a tendency for courts at all levels to be seen more clearly as arms of government rather than in their primary ideological role as independent forums for the just resolution of cases. Magistrates' courts, for example, have used their power to grant bail conditions as an auxiliary form of social control in connection with the miners' strike and the peace convoys in the West Country, and have, on various occasions, effectively connived at 'preventive detention' by the police of such groups through their unquestioning acceptance of police remand recommendations.[8] In the higher courts the decisions to prosecute Sarah Tisdall and Clive Ponting,[9] and the willingness of the courts to accept the Government's arguments concerning 'national security' in the Spycatcher case[10] are manifestations not only of the 'identification' of important elements of the judiciary with the policies and ideologies of Thatcherism, but are also the most overt signs of the drift towards authoritarianism in the protection of state secrets, and towards censorship and creeping erosion of civil liberties in this area.[11] The dubious circumstances surrounding trials arising out of the Broadwater Farm riot in 1985;[12] the decision based on grounds of 'national security' not to prosecute police officers in Northern Ireland 'shoot to kill' cases – despite the recognition that there was a case to answer, together with the suppression of Stalker's inquiry;[13] and the recent rejection by the Court of Appeal of the appeal of the 'Birmingham Six',[14] have all raised questions about the administration of justice in Britain in the 1980s. So, too, have the acquittal of police officers on charges arising from the death of John Shorthouse and the serious injuries to Steven Waldorf and Cherry Groce.[15] The period since 1979 has also been noticeable for persistent attacks on the tradition of trial by jury, ranging from the removal of peremptory challenges to more recent indications of a desire to further restrict the choice of a trial by jury for those charged in magistrates' courts.[16]

As regards the prisons, the rise in the prison population (itself arguably an indirect outcome of Conservative social and economic policies);[17] the Government's prison building programme; the changes in the parole rules for violent offenders and drug traffickers serving over five years as well as for certain categories of those serving life for murder; the failure to provide decent regimes within the prisons; the increased emphasis on security within the system;[18] and the heightened repression of increasing protest against prison regimes[19] have all augmented the authoritarian character of the system.

It must also be noted that accompanying these events, trends, and developments there have been substantial changes in the legal frameworks within which the criminalization process occurs. The passing of the Police and Criminal Evidence Act 1984 and the Public Order Act 1986 have both increased the discretion available to police officers in the conduct of their activities in relation to individuals and social groups. The former in particular has extended police powers of detention, stop and search, search of premises, and the creation of roadblocks according to very loosely defined criteria.[20] Justified as involving a balance between police powers and individual rights, this legislation was seen to fail in regard to the latter at its first serious test.[21] As for the Public Order Act 1986, this gives unprecedented powers to the police to ban and impose conditions on marches and to restrict demonstrations and pickets.[22] In addition, under the 'new, improved' Prevention of Terrorism (Temporary Provisions) Act 1984 the original legislation is extended to include within its potential ambit the members and supporters of any organization in the world which uses 'violence for political ends'; in addition, the legislation is made semi-permanent. This means that as well as the political control exercised over Irish politics in Britain,[23] any liberation movement in the world conducting armed struggle, together with its supporters, is potentially affected. Lastly, on the heels of all these other developments, we have the recent announcement that a cornerstone of the trial process, the 300-year-old right to silence, has been abolished in Northern Ireland and will soon be ended in England and Wales.[24]

There is, then, a substantial empirical basis for the claim that the British State has developed an authoritarian mode in the 1980s – that is, a relatively naked emphasis within the criminal justice system upon criminalization and the suppression of resistance, and a relative de-emphasizing of the formal norms and values of individual justice. However, it is important not to oversimplify this development for two reasons. First, it must be noted that while the 1980s mark important changes, there are also substantial continuities between this and previous periods, both recent and not so recent. Thus, we should note that many of the developments of the 1980s are extensions of what had occurred in the 1970s. When Hall wrote about the drift into a law and order society, he was referring as much to the historical period that had immediately passed as to the period that was to come,[25] and the outlines of what Ackroyd and her collaborators called the 'strong state' in Britain were already quite visible in the mid-1970s.[26] Similarly, Poulantzas, in an influential work, identified the phenomenon of 'authoritarian statism', in which the balance between coercion and consent was shifted towards the authoritarian side of the spectrum in this period.[27]

Looking back to the period of the 1970s in Britain, it is possible to view many of the present developments as building upon what happened then, in a different socio-political context. As regards the police, for example, the system of national organization which was so important during the miners' strike was set up in the earlier period in large measure as a response to the successes of the National Union of Mineworkers in the 1974 strike,[28] and the creation of a quasi-military 'third force' of riot-trained police again emanates from the 1970s.[29] Similarly, allegations of police racism, which have been a major cause of riotous resistance to the police throughout the 1980s (and particularly in 1980, 1981, and 1985) were common currency in the 1970s and earlier.[30]

As regards the courts, the consistent and structured injustice confronting working-class people in magistrates' courts was a persistent theme of the 1970s.[31] The recent appeal of the Birmingham Six, together with the cases of the Maguires and the Guildford Four in turn remind us that all of these people were convicted in the earlier period.[32] As far as prisons are concerned, the resistance to jail conditions and maltreatment in the 1980s are no more than the latest chapter in a story that includes, for example, Hull in 1976.[33] It was also in the 1970s that the militarization of prison control began with the institution of Minimum Use of Force Tactical Intervention (MUFTI) squads.[34]

More could be said, but the point has been made: while there are significant differences and changes in the criminalization process in the 1980s, there are also continuities and similarities between the 1980s and developments in the different political conditions of the earlier period. We stress this point because it is important to show that an easy identification of the empirical developments within the criminalization process in the 1980s and the Thatcherite project is not possible. From this it follows that it is not only necessary to be careful in characterizing policies as peculiarly Thatcherite, but it is also important to situate changes that have occurred in the 1980s within a broader historical perspective. Finally, if the reader still requires some persuasion as to the need to confront the continuity between past and present, we cite one historical description of an anti-police riot and its aftermath:

> That evening the Riot Act was read several times and the police and specials paraded the town dispersing enclaves of citizens. Between 10 and 11 p.m. a large crowd rallied at a newly erected church east of Colne, armed themselves with long spear-like iron palisades left over from the construction of the church railings, and entered Colne from Keighley Road. The battle was joined. . . . In the struggle, Joseph Halstead, a special constable and local mill owner, was struck in the head with an iron palisade and killed. Yet again, the police were swept from Colne. . . . The chief defendant in the murder of Halstead was a twenty year old weaver, Richard Boothman. Boothman was tried at the assizes and sentenced to death in March 1841. His sentence was later commuted to transportation. . . . Boothman maintained to the end that he did not murder Halstead. He claimed he had never been a part of the crowd that night, had been arrested after just returning from a neighbouring local feast and that he had been a victim of a case of mistaken identity.[35]

If the events of Broadwater Farm in September 1985 and the subsequent police siege of the estate – involving hundreds of arrests, the disregarding of legal procedures, and the trial and conviction of defendants on the flimsiest of grounds[36] – have a quintessentially '80s' feel about them and therefore symbolize more broadly the nature of the criminalization process under Thatcherism, we should invest Storch's description of events almost 150 years ago with some significance, for it turns the question around: from asking what is distinctive about the 1980s, we should perhaps ask, why does it appear distinctive; for, as we can see, a historical perspective makes easy characterization impossible.[37]

Our second concern with the 'authoritarianism thesis' focuses on the extent to which the development of the 'strong state' has been accompanied not by conflict but by consensus in British society. The 'strong state' involves, by definition, a repressive strategy; it is at the heart of a social order which has become more coercive and conflictual. That this is so is clear to see, whether in the form of anti-police resistance in inner cities, in mining communities, or in republican areas of Northern Ireland. At the same time, however, the development of the 'strong state' has taken place with the acquiescence, at least, and often the substantial support of significant sections of the British population. Police attempts, for example, to establish community partnerships through such initiatives as neighbourhood watch schemes have not, it appears, been wholly unsuccessful, at the very least in their ability to generate the support necessary to the very acts of establishing the schemes.[38] Nor have oppressive police tactics such as those used in the miners' strike or in the quelling of inner city disturbances been met with wholesale condemnation. On the contrary, important sections of the working class in addition to the middle class have been drawn into supporting police actions. Politically, this is most clearly evidenced by the programmes of the Labour Party, whose pro-police pronouncements on law and order issues in particular are designed to win the middle ground of middle-class *and* affluent working-class support.[39] In part, what we have seen in the 1980s has been a successful 'divide and rule' strategy in which divisions between black and white, north and south, rich and poor, employed and unemployed have been exacerbated and manipulated to generate *consent behind the state* amongst certain relatively privileged sections of the middle and working classes for control through conflict *against* other less privileged sections of the working class (the unemployed, blacks and Asians, and workers in struggle) as well as *déclassé* groups such as travellers, students, and peace protesters.

The 'authoritarian state' thesis with which we started thus requires modification in two extremely important ways if we are to understand the criminalization process under the Thatcher Government. On the one hand, it is not nearly so distinctive as the impact of immediate events upon the senses suggests. If Thatcherism entails authoritarianism, so too did 1970s Labourism and the very creation of the bourgeois state. So a simple identification between Thatcherism and authoritarianism will not do. On the other hand, if authoritarianism is to be identified as an important feature of Thatcherism, it is authoritarianism *against* some *with* the consent of others. This 'consensual authoritarianism' clearly requires further consideration.

In the next two sections we will argue that the key to understanding these two problems is to be found within the historical development of British class relations and in the context of imperialism. It is only in this broader context that we can appreciate the specificity of Thatcherite criminal justice.

If we are to situate the present period historically, we must be able to get a 'fix' on the developments that have occurred in criminal justice in previous decades, and, more importantly, the social, political, and economic developments that underpin them. Clearly, in the space of a short article we cannot write a complete history of the criminal justice system of this kind. We want instead to focus on one particular institution, the police, and the historical development in the class basis of modern British society which underlies it. In the process we will clear up some confusion in recent writing about the immediate post-war period.

There is an academic consensus that underlies conservative, liberal, and Left Realist accounts of the historical development of policing in the post-war period. It essentially takes the form of a claim, suitably qualified, that in the immediate post-war period there was a substantial measure of consensus in British society about policing, so that the period can accordingly be seen as a benchmark against which contemporary developments in the direction of conflict can be measured.[40] This view of a 'golden age' of policing has recently been attacked on an empirical basis by Gilroy and Sim,[41] who show that the period in question was, like most of the history of British policing, characterized by conflict.

While there is much substance in this criticism, we feel that it misses two important points – one implicitly, the other explicitly. First, it is the case that the history of policing in Britain reveals not only consistent conflict, but also, after the initial period of imposition, consistent *consensus* among significant sections of the working class, and that *both* conflict and consensus relate to historical developments within the British working class. Secondly, it is the case that while the 'golden age' theorists perhaps overstate their claim, there was a real sense in which the immediate post-war period was one of relative consensus across the classes. What is really wrong with the liberal and Left Realist 'golden age' claim is not that it identifies consensus but that it dehistoricizes a period of *relative* consensus by abstracting it from the economic, political, and ideological conditions upon which it was based. In doing so, it turns a historical moment into a normative ideal which then becomes the basis for a particular political stance.

The post-war consensus, with which we shall deal below, is an important part of the story of modern policing but it must not be allowed to obscure an earlier and more fundamental consensus at the heart of British social relations which occurred as much as a century earlier. It is well known that around 1850 the fear of the 'dangerous classes' as a turbulent mob incorporating *all* elements of the working class gave way to a differentiated awareness of the sectional nature of working-class criminality. Observers began to be concerned with 'diffuse criminality' rather than the 'dangerous classes' so that 'contemporary writing in mid-century London exhibits a sense of relief and victory over the forces of mass violence'.[42] What lay behind this change?

Foster's seminal account of social relations in the first sixty years of the nineteenth century is occasionally referred to by police historians for his vivid and detailed discussions of struggles over control of the police in Oldham in the 1830s and 1840s.[43] What these historians usually ignore is Foster's analysis of why such struggles – often of a violent and bloody kind – abated from 1850 onwards. Partly it was a matter of simple economic recovery, but more importantly it was the product of emerging economic, social, and political divisions within the working class itself. The class became politically and ideologically split by the development of a layer whose position as taskmasters and pacemakers placed them above and in opposition to the mass of workers. This newly developed layer – a 'labour aristocracy' – surrounded itself with a 'cocoon of formal institutions' emphasizing respectable behavioural norms so as to insulate itself from 'the constant ridicule reserved for bosses' men'.[44] As for the mass of ordinary unprivileged workers, Foster describes their position thus:

> ... the essence of the non-aristocrats' culture was a rejection of everything associated with their work-time taskmasters: discipline, subservience, abstinence. Its most characteristic expression was the public house – where no free born Englishman need call any man his master. And protected by dialect, a defence the labour-aristocrat had to do without, it needed no formal institutions beyond the friendly society to handle the most unavoidable contacts with the authorities.[45]

The contrast between 'labour aristocratic' respectability and the non-aristocratic culture of dialect and the public house perhaps suggests the roots of that well-known policing distinction between 'roughs' and 'respectables'[46] refined though it must have been down the years. The quotation also indicates that when Storch's 'domestic missionaries'[47] set about their crusades against pub culture, it was only *one* section of the working class (albeit the larger one) that they directed their energies against and from whom they received continuing opposition.

Foster's work is important because it underlines the material basis for a phenomenon that is recognized by many writers, but whose significance is rarely grasped.[48] That phenomenon is the continuous division in working-class attitudes to criminality and the police. A *consensual* history of policing can be traced from Weinberger's observation that anti-police violence in the 1870s came from only 'a section of the working class' who were opposed to 'police action in connection with licensing laws and with Poor Law policing',[49] through Bailey's observation that in the 1886-7 Trafalgar Square clashes between the police and the poor, the 'respectable' working class were conspicuous by their absence,[50] to Cohen's discussion of the expansion of notions of respectability and public propriety amongst increasing sections of the working class in the wake of New Unionism and the success of Labour politics.[51] Respectability and respect (albeit grudging) for the police were real phenomena having a real material basis in economic and social developments.

The significance to the twentieth century of this nineteenth-century development becomes apparent when one considers the relationship between 'respectable' trade unionism, 'respectable' Labourism, and respect for the

119

'fine traditions' of British policing. This is not a phenomenon that simply appeared during the 1984-5 miners' strike, it is one firmly grounded in historically developed realities. Thus, Geary identifies the commencement of peaceful policing of trade disputes from 1946 but the peaceful *running* of such disputes by workers to the period prior to the First World War, and he relates this latter development to the influence of trades unions and their relationships with the emerging Labour Party – often in the face of great provocation from police and troops.[52] And Weinberger, in an important recent article, shows that in the inter-war period both employed and unemployed workers' organizations were more prone to attack by the police if they could be branded with an unrespectable non-Labourist label such as 'communist'. She writes that police violence 'seemed to have occurred most readily in areas . . . [*inter alia*] where the local labour movement positively rejected all support for the activities of the organized unemployed' and where 'local strikers or the unemployed were regarded as acting under Communist influence'.[53] Such a prejudice, she notes, was as prevalent in the 'respectable' labour movement as it was among Conservatives. In other words, there existed a *de facto* alliance between the police, the Conservatives, and the 'respectable' labour movement by means of which the National Unemployed Workers Movement and sections of the miners' union were isolated and exposed to attack. Empirical similarities between this period and the 1980s may be noted,[54] but the important point here is the underlying material basis not just of class conflict, but of continuing sectional class division, consensus, and collaboration which can be gleaned from the historical perspective. It is within that context that one can understand both the way in which a period of collaboration across the classes – as in the post-war period – can generate a relative consensus in respect of policing, and begin to see the ways in which particular political, ideological, and economic projects such as those of Thatcherism can take root in a soil already prepared for them. We now turn to consider this latter issue in detail.

THE SPECIFICITY OF THATCHER'S CRIMINAL JUSTICE

We began with two apparent paradoxes between continuity and change, consensus and conflict. We argued that the key to understanding these paradoxes was to be found within the historical development of British class relations. The criminal justice system has always been able to rely on support across the classes, most importantly from sections of the working class who, for real material reasons, see themselves as having a stake in the capitalist system. This is borne out by a historical perspective on the history of policing and is given a clear political expression in the view and stances adopted by the Labour Party when it has been in government and in opposition.[55] We agree with Sim, Scraton, and Gordon when they write against 'the romanticized versions of a united homogeneous working class' of:

> . . . the significance and depth of the political and ideological differences within working-class experiences. The fractures and divisions in neighbourhood and workplaces have as

120

much to do with the ideas and politics of patriotism and race, of masculinity and gender, of jobs and materialism, as they have to do with the objective location of paid work, domestic labour or unemployment within the economy.[56]

Unlike these writers, however, we stress the implications of this view for identifying the securing of consent within the working class for state actions. Thus, we do not agree completely that 'an understanding of the processes of criminalization' involves examining how 'consensus is forced rather than forged'[57] because that is only a partial explanation. The key to understanding our two paradoxes resides in the collaboration between significant sections of the working class and the state both at the level of social relations themselves (in particular, the police/public relationship) and at the level of the state (the political role of the Labour Party in and out of government). Herein lies the source of continuity behind the change, of consensus behind the conflict.

Thus far, however, we have not properly addressed the important question of the specific nature of the influence of Thatcherism on the criminal justice system. In this final section, we seek an answer through our use of the concept of 'consensual authoritarianism', and by discussion of Hall's 'authoritarian populism' and the debate it has engendered.[58] Our point of departure takes the form of agreement with Jessop et al. that Hall's 'authoritarian populism' is essentially 'ideologist' in conception. In responding to this criticism Hall characterized authoritarian populism as 'a movement towards a dominative and "authoritarian" form of democratic class politics – paradoxically, apparently rooted in . . . populist discontents',[59] and he located its importance in 'the one dimension which above all others, has defeated the left, politically, and Marxist analysis theoretically, in every advanced capitalist democracy since the First World War':

> . . . namely, the ways in which popular consent can be so constructed, by an historical bloc seeking hegemony, as to harness to its support some popular discontents, neutralise the opposing forces, disaggregate the opposition and really incorporate *some* strategic elements of popular opinion into its own hegemonic project.[60]

Hall accepts that in taking this stance he 'deliberately and self-consciously *foregrounds* the political-ideological dimension' and he recognizes the limited nature of concepts such as 'hegemony' and 'authoritarian populism'. They do not operate at a level of abstraction sufficient to generalize the entire condition of a particular period. They are 'more specific, time-bound, concrete in their reference' so that authoritarian populism can only be 'a partial explanation of Thatcherism':

> It was an attempt to characterize certain strategic shifts in the political/ideological conjuncture. Essentially, it refers to changes in the 'balance of forces'. It refers directly to the modalities of political and ideological relationships between the ruling blocs, the state and the dominated classes. It attempts to expand on and to begin to periodize the internal composition of hegemonic strategies in the politics of class democracies. . . . *It references, but could neither characterize nor explain, changes in the more structural aspects of capitalist social formations.*[61]

It should be noted that there is a crucial difference between this explanation of authoritarian populism as a *descriptive* concept located purely at the level of the *categorization of ideologies* (and thereby conceding that the term 'authoritarian populism' *is* 'ideologist') and the other statement we quoted above. There authoritarian populism was more than just a categorization of ideology, it was a tool for seeing the way *in which popular consent was constructed historically by means of an ideological project*. Hall's claim, then, concerns the real effects of hegemonic projects on class relations, not simply the description of the 'modalities' or the 'internal composition' of particular ideologies. This is a big difference, which brings us onto the principal complaint of Jessop et al. about authoritarian populism: that in considering why a hegemonic project is successful, it is necessary to consider that project in the context of its reception by particular classes and class sections. 'Popular discontents' and 'popular opinion' are not abstractions, they correspond to the views and sentiments of particular sections of the population:

> In emphasizing the specific discursive strategies involved in Thatcherism, authoritarian populism risks ignoring other elements. In particular, it could neglect the structural underpinnings of Thatcherism in the economic and state systems and its specific economic and political basis of support among both people and power bloc.[62]

In contrast with Hall, it is that material basis for the acceptance of authoritarianism that we attempt to incorporate in our term 'consensual authoritarianism'. We do not deny the importance of the ideological forms that authoritarian populism takes, far from it. We do argue that those forms have to be understood within the wider context. For that reason, we do not deny that authoritarian populism has its uses as an analytical tool. But we do assert that it is of limited use in considering the ways in which Thatcherism has achieved the consensus of comparatively broad sections of the British people around its authoritarianism.

We can pursue this line by following Jessop et al. in their argument. We agree with them that there is nothing new in a British national-popular project as such. The British working class has for a long time, as Engels put it, been prepared to '[discredit] itself terribly' by siding with its ruling class. Jessop et al. point out that the Conservative Party has been able to mobilize both the deferential and the self-seeking working class, and that Thatcherism has been extremely successful in harnessing these elements. The success of the Thatcherite ideological project must be seen in the context of pragmatic and extremely real 'interests in lower direct taxation, council house sales, rising living standards for those still in private sector employment, lower inflation, and so forth'.[63] It is amongst those who snap at the bait of private interest and wealth that we should seek the material basis of the acceptance of 'authoritarian populist' ideologies.

We now come to the issue of authoritarianism itself as the other side of the consensus coin, the constructing of support for Thatcher's economic and political strategies against those sections of society who are losers, not winners. We agree with Jessop et al. that the creation of a 'Two Nations' Toryism has had real effects in terms of dividing the working class so that the support of the well-off can be drawn upon while those who experience unemployment and poverty, who are prepared to fight for their jobs and communities, are suppressed under the ideological banners of authoritarian populism. Thatcherism's economic strategy of dismantling the Welfare State in favour of privatization, popular capitalism, and the enterprise culture deliberately unleashes the effects of economic crisis upon those who were at least better able to survive under the old order. Thatcherism seeks not to integrate the poor and underprivileged but to manage their protest. As the effects of other economic policies have taken hold, controls have increased along with protest. The demand for 'law and order' is not a simple paroxysm of popular discontent opportunistically harnessed by Thatcherism. It is a real class response to the management of social conflicts arising from economic policies which have the support, more or less passive, more or less active, of significant sections of the working class.[64] Thatcherite authoritarianism is a product of Thatcherite 'Two Nations' politics and economics.[65]

We can see this if we compare the history of the present period of Thatcherism with the earlier period from 1945-79. Without wishing to endorse any idea of a 'golden age', we can see now with the benefit of hindsight that the earlier period was one of relative consensus. Politically this was formalized in the post-war settlement which established the Welfare State and was run by both 'One Nation' Toryism and the Labour Party on a relatively stable basis. This political consensus overlaid and drew upon the underlying social consensus we have identified at the heart of modern British class relations, symbolically and accurately referred to at the time as 'Butskellism'. This political consensus sought to unify the nation across class lines by providing the promise at least of a measure of support for those who in one way or another became casualties of the system. It was in this context that the immediate post-war period yielded a relative consensus in relation to criminal justice issues amongst others. While the period has been afforded a moral and political significance it by no means deserves, the image of consensus was not a complete illusion. 'Dixon of Dock Green' may be a fiction in both senses of the word, but it was not without a basis in real social developments.

The story of the breakdown of the political consensus (and also to some extent its relationship to the underlying social consent that we have discussed) has been told at length by Hall with his collaborators in his earlier work.[66] *Policing the Crisis* was written before Hall had moved theoretically into the explanation of 'authoritarian populism'. Perhaps for that reason, *Policing the Crisis* appears to us to be a much more rounded analysis of the location of politics and ideology, of a 'crisis of hegemony' within an overall economic context. The 1970s witnessed the failure of Labour's corporatist solution to economic crisis. Its populist 'law and order' slogans, together with moral panics around issues such as mugging, ideologically signalled that failure and provided important legitimations for the move, begun under Labour, towards authoritarianism.[67]

Like the Conservatives, Labour offered a solution to the economic and political crises of British capitalism. But it offered a solution that in the second half of the 1970s was increasingly discredited in practice. Labour offered corporatist consensus which drifted into authoritarianism at the same time as its support for the Welfare State drifted into public spending cuts, the abandonment of a political commitment to full employment policies, and the prioritizing of the fight against inflation.[68] In other words, Labour gradually moved towards the policies which Thatcherism wholeheartedly adopted. Here lies the specificity of Thatcherism as economics, politics, and ideology. It proposes a radical economic solution designed to dismantle the Welfare State, privatize and restructure the economy. It presents this solution under the ideological labels of 'the individual', 'the family', 'the nation', 'law and order', 'the enemy within', and so on. It uses these labels politically to force through its policies, to divide society into 'us' and 'them', the 'productive' and the 'parasitic',[69] rich and poor, employed and unemployed, black and white, male and female, and it is this political/ideological brew, designed as part of a project to set British capitalism to rights economically that lies behind the authoritarian state. It is the radicalism and ruthlessness of the political, economic, and ideological projects of Thatcherism that accounts for the developments in authoritarianism that we have witnessed in the last ten years. There was authoritarianism before Thatcher so that what we experience is importantly a matter of degree. But the ratchet has been turned more than one notch in the process. That Thatcherism has achieved and continues to achieve this scaling up of the authoritarian nature of the state is in part due to Thatcher's ability ideologically to articulate authoritarian ideas in a popular way, but more importantly is due to the fertile social ground upon which these ideological seeds have been scattered. Behind the authoritarian populist ideologies there lie the real material possibilities for consensual authoritarianism within the British class structure.

NOTES AND REFERENCES

1 See footnotes 48 and 64 below.
2 S. Hall, *Drifting into a Law and Order Society* (1980).
3 P. Gordon, 'Community Policing: Towards the Local Police State' in *Law, Order and the Authoritarian State*, ed. P. Scraton (1987).
4 For fuller discussion, see the various contributions to Scraton, op. cit., n. 3, and P. Hillyard and J. Percy-Smith, *The Coercive State* (1988).
5 Geoffrey Dear, Chief Constable of the West Midlands Police (see Scraton, op. cit., n. 3, p. 49).
6 Compare P. Gilroy and J. Sim, 'Law, Order and the State of the Left' (1985) 25 *Capital and Class* 15; also in Scraton, op. cit., n. 3.
7 We have in mind here explicit economic policies to restructure the economy in relation to the newspaper industry (Eddie Shah and the *Stockport Messenger* dispute of 1983-4, Rupert Murdoch and News International in 1986-7) and the mining industry (the miners' strike in 1984-5) which led to overt stances being taken by the police in favour of minorities, sometimes individuals, wishing to return to work, together with the more general notions of normal and abnormal implicit in the identification of inner city areas as being populated by those who are 'different from the rest of society' (Scraton, op. cit., n. 3, pp. 56 and 100), and the marginalization of travellers (the Peace Convoys in 1985-6), peace and anti-apartheid campaigners, and students who by dress and conduct are cast 'beyond the pale'. Compare P. Scraton, 'Unreasonable Force: Policing, Punishment and Marginalization' in Scraton, op. cit., n. 3; N. Davies, 'Inquest on a Rural Riot' *Observer*, 9 June 1985.
8 Hillyard and Percy-Smith, op. cit., n. 3, pp. 295-9.

9   C. Ponting, *The Right to Know: The Inside Story of the Belgrano Affair* (1985).

10 *Attorney-General* v. *Guardian, Times and Observer* [1987] 1 WLR 1250. It appears from newspaper reports that the recent final decision of the House of Lords to accept the newspapers' case was not founded on the belief that the public interest demands publication so much as on the view that since the information concerned is in the public domain anyway, further barring would be ineffectual. For analysis, see G. Robertson, *Guardian*, 14 October 1988.

11 Recent proposals in June 1988 by the Home Secretary, Douglas Hurd MP, to amend the Official Secrets Act (see *The Times*, 30 June 1988) indicate the extent of authoritarian control desired by the Thatcher Government. This legal onslaught is matched by the continuous attempts to undermine the BBC across a range of issues, including the reporting of the air raid on Libya by the United States of America and the showing of programmes such as 'Real Lives' and 'Secret Society'.

12 Amnesty International, *United Kingdom: Alleged Forced Admission During Incommunicado Detention* (1988).

13 Statement by Sir Patrick Mayhew MP, Solicitor General, *H.C. Debs.*, (25 January 1988) and in *Guardian*, 26 January 1988; J. Stalker, *Stalker* (1987).

14 C. Mullin, *Error of Judgement* (1987); *Guardian*, 29 January 1988; *Observer*, 31 January 1988.

15 On the Waldorf shooting, see M. Benn and K. Worpole, *Death in the City* (1986) 55-61.

16 Criminal Justice Act 1988 s. 118; M. Zander, 'Surprising New Moves to Restrict Trial by Jury' *Guardian*, 5 August 1988; see in general Hillyard and Percy-Smith, op. cit., n. 4, pp. 155-60.

17 S. Box, *Recession, Crime and Punishment* (1987).

18 Hillyard and Percy-Smith, op. cit., n. 4, pp. 299-312; J. Sim, 'Working for the Clampdown' in Scraton, op. cit., n. 3.

19 Sim, op. cit., n. 18. In Scotland, the SAS have been used at Edinburgh and Peterhead prisons, and 'élite' riot squads trained to SAS standards have been established. This has occurred on the basis of a conspiracy theory that 'drugs barons' are seeking to destroy Peterhead prison (see *The Scotsman*, 8-11 August 1988). For a more realistic account, see P. Scraton, J. Sim, and P. Skidmore, 'Through the Barricades: Prisoner Protest and Penal Policy in Scotland' (1988) 15 *J. of Law and Society* 247.

20 Such as 'reasonable suspicion' and 'serious arrestable offence'. For discussion, see H. Bevan and K. Lidstone, *A Guide to the Police and Criminal Evidence Act* (1985); for a useful summary, see Hillyard and Percy-Smith, op. cit., n. 4; see L. Bridges and T. Bunyan, 'Britain's New Urban Policing Strategy – The Police and Criminal Evidence Bill in Context' (1983) 10 *J. of Law and Society* 85 for what proved a good prognosis of the likely effects of the legal categories.

21 See above, n. 12.

22 R. Card, *Public Order: The New Law* (1987) ch. 4. See Hillyard and Percy-Smith, op. cit., n. 4, pp. 259-62 for useful summary.

23 C. Scorer et al., *The New Prevention of Terrorism Act: The Case for Repeal* (1985).

24 *Guardian*, 20-21 October 1988. In one dramatic week the Government removed the right of silence, sacked workers at the Government Communications Headquarters (GCHQ) for belonging to a trade union, and banned television interviews with members of legal political organizations such as Sinn Fein. While this article's focus is upon criminal justice, it would be quite wrong to decontextualize the criminal justice issue from the broader developments implicit in these other moves.

25 Hall, op. cit., n. 2. See also S. Hall et al., *Policing the Crisis* (1978).

26 C. Ackroyd et al., *The Technology of Political Control* (1977).

27 N. Poulantzas, *State, Power and Socialism* (1978). Poulantzas's use of the concept 'authoritarian statism' proved influential for Hall's later work on 'authoritarian populism'. We discuss this in the fourth section below.

28 M. Kettle, 'The National Reporting Centre and the 1984 Miners' Strike' in *Policing the Miners' Strike*, eds. B. Fine and R. Millar (1985).

29 C. Lloyd, 'A National Riot Police: Britain's Third Force?' in Fine and Millar, op. cit., n. 28. As the recent substantial *ex gratia* payment by the Metropolitan Police to the family of Blair

Peach reminds us, nine years after his death at the hands of the police during an anti-fascist demonstration in Southall in 1979 (*Guardian*, 8 July 1988). The police continue to maintain their lack of responsibility despite the payment, and no police officer has ever been charged.

30 D. Humphrey, *Police Power and Black People* (1972); M. Cain, *Society and the Policeman's Role* (1973); Institute of Race Relations, *Police Against Black People* (1978); A. Sivanandan, *A Different Hunger* (1982).

31 P. Carlen, *Magistrates' Justice* (1976); A. Bottoms and J. McLean, *Defendants in the Penal Process* (1976); D. McBarnet, *Conviction: Law, the State and the Construction of Justice* (1981) ch. 7.

32 R. Kee, *Trial and Error: The Maguires, the Guildford Pub Bombings and British Justice* (1986); C. Mullin, op. cit., n. 14. For a good review of these and other works in the area, see J. Sim, (1987) 15 *Int. J. Sociology of Law* 225.

33 M. Fitzgerald, *Prisoners in Revolt* (1977); J. Thomas and M. Pooley, *The Exploding Prison* (1980).

34 Sim, op. cit., n. 18; Hillyard and Percy-Smith, op. cit., n. 4, pp. 306-12. It is worth noting that the single really progressive development in recent decades, the Special Unit at Barlinnie prison, was begun in the early 1970s under the Conservative Government, and then undermined by the ensuing Labour Government (see J. Boyle, *The Pain of Confinement* (1984)).

35 R. Storch, 'The Plague of Blue Locusts' (1975) *Int. J. of Social History* 83.

36 See above n. 12.

37 This discussion does not include one of the most important continuities between past and present, the role of the British state in Northern Ireland. The main plank of the state's criminalization strategy remains the Diplock Courts (established in the mid-1970s) and allegations of a shoot-to-kill policy occurred in the 1970s also: see K. Boyle, T. Hadden, and P. Hillyard, *Ten Years on in Northern Ireland* (1980) 27-9. For the interconnection between colony and mainland, see P. Hillyard, 'The Normalization of Special Powers: From Northern Ireland to Britain' in Scraton, op. cit., n. 3. And for an important historical perspective, see M. Brogden, 'An Act to Colonize the Internal Lands of the Island: Empire and the Origins of the Professional Police' (1987) 15 *Int. J. Sociology of Law* 179.

38 P. Gordon, 'Community Policing: Towards the Local Police State?' in Scraton, op. cit., n. 3.

39 P. Gilroy and J. Sim, op. cit., n. 6.

40 T. Critchley, *A History of Police in England and Wales* (2nd ed. 1978); J. Benyon and C. Bourne, *The Police: Powers, Procedures and Proprieties* (1986) ch. 1; I. Taylor, *Law and Order: Arguments for Socialism* (1981).

41 Scraton, op. cit., n. 3, pp. 74-9.

42 A. Silver, 'The Demand for Order in Civil Society' in *The Police: Six Sociological Essays*, ed. D. Bordua (1968).

43 J. Foster, *Class Struggle and the Industrial Revolution* (1974). For critical comment, see G. Stedman Jones, 'Class Struggle and the Industrial Revolution' (1975) 90 *New Left Rev.* 35.

44 J. Foster, op. cit., n. 43, pp. 237-8.

45 id.

46 M. Cain, op. cit., n. 30. See also D. Garland, *Punishment and Welfare: A History of Penal Strategies* (1985) 37-40.

47 R. Storch, 'The Police as Domestic Missionary' (1976) 9 *J. of Social History* 481. For a thorough analysis of the divisions in the working class emerging around the issues of crime and disrespectability in a Welsh town, see D. Jones, *Crime, Protest, Community and Police in Nineteenth-Century Britain* (1982) ch. 4.

48 The exception being P. Cohen, 'Policing the Working Class City' in B. Fine et al., *Capitalism and the Rule of Law* (1979). For a recent analysis of divisions within the working class which returns to the concept of a labour aristocracy, see M. Spence, 'Imperialism and Decline: Britain in the 1980s' (1985) 25 *Capital and Class* 128. The classical reference is to V. Lenin, *Imperialism: The Highest Stage of Capitalism* (1917) especially the Preface to the French and German editions (1920). In arguing for the significance of this distinction, we are not

claiming that those sections of the class which constitute the labour aristocracy always remain the same – plainly that would be absurd in an economic world that has changed dramatically over time. We assert the continued importance of relatively privileged layers within the working class who more easily identify their interests with capitalism and imperialism than the badly paid, the unemployed, those who constitute a 'reserve army of labour'. Nor do we deny the development of new sections of the workforce in the twentieth century such as the 'new middle class' emerging out of the post-war Welfare State. We see these developments, however, as contributing to the strengthening of the divisions first created in the mid-nineteenth century. Compare E. Hobsbawm, *Labouring Men* (1964) 300-3; R. Gray, *The Labour Aristocracy in Victorian Edinburgh* (1976) ch. 10, and *The Aristocracy of Labour in Nineteenth Century Britain* (1983) ch. 8.

49 It was the poorest sections of the class, in particular the youth and the Irish, who opposed the police. Weinberger notes that police assaults were carried out by all classes of labourers but that the semi-skilled were over-represented. She also notes the divisions between the more and less respectable trades, the latter uniting with casual labour in disrespectability and police opposition: B. Weinberger, 'The Police and the Public in Mid Nineteenth Century Warwickshire' in *Policing and Punishment in Nineteenth Century Britain*, ed. V. Bailey (1981) (quotations from pp. 65 and 67). See also the important essay by J. Davis, 'The London Garotting Panic of 1862: A Moral Panic and the Creation of a Criminal Class in Mid Victorian England' in *Crime and the Law in Western Societies: Historical Essays*, ed. V. Gattrell et al. (1980).

50 'The social distinction which had been forged in the mid-Victorian years between the "dangerous" and the "respectable" classes was not thawed by the economic and social crisis of the 1880s.' (See 'The Metropolitan Police, the Home Office and the Threat of Outcast London' in Bailey, op. cit., n. 49, pp. 94-5.)

51 P. Cohen, op. cit., n. 48.

52 R. Geary, *Policing Industrial Disputes 1893-1985* (1985) chs. 3-5.

53 B. Weinberger, 'Police Perceptions of Labour in the Inter-War Period: The Case of the Unemployed and of Miners on Strike' in *Labour, Law and Crime*, eds. F. Snyder and D. Hay (1986) 174.

54 D. Howell, ' "Where's Ramsay MacKinnock?": Labour Leadership and the Miners' in *Digging Deeper: Issues in the Miners' Strike*, ed. H. Benyon (1985).

55 J. Sim, P. Scraton, and P. Gordon, 'Introduction: Crime, the State and Critical Analysis' in Scraton, op. cit., n. 3, pp. 50-9; Gilroy and Sim, op. cit., n. 6.

56 Sim, Scraton, and Gordon in Scraton, op. cit., n. 3, p. 61.

57 id., p. 63.

58 B. Jessop et al., 'Authoritarian Populism, Two Nations and Thatcherism' (1984) 147 *New Left Rev.* 32; S. Hall, 'Authoritarian Populism: A Reply to Jessop et al.' (1985) 152 *New Left Rev.* 115.

59 Hall, op. cit., n. 58, p. 118.

60 id., pp. 117-18.

61 id., p. 119, emphasis added.

62 Jessop et al., op. cit., n. 58, p. 37.

63 id., p. 42. See also p. 49.

64 We refer here to the view of Jessop et al. that 'Thatcherism involves a passive revolution rather than mass mobilization' (op. cit., n. 58, p. 43), a conception that they contrast with the activism that would be present if the Conservatives had 'organize[d] the working class politically'. This seems to us a rather 'politicist' view of the relationship between politics and society. Thatcherism can rely to an extent on a support that may not be politically organized in its favour but which perceives interest in common with its projects. This may be characterized as 'more or less active or passive' – the terms are not wholly satisfactory. Compare Spence, op. cit., n. 48, for whom a modern labour aristocracy has 'the most immediate material interests in upholding existing industrial priorities, financial priorities, and a continuing commitment to the world imperialist system' (p. 134). The recognition of an identity of economic interests transforms the way in which one understands the character of

political organization and its articulation with social forces.

65 Compare Jessop et al., op. cit., n. 58, p. 52: 'There is an authoritarian element in the Thatcherite programme. But it is much better interpreted in terms of the problems of economic and political *crisis-management*, than in terms of a generalized authoritarian populism.'

66 Hall et al., op. cit., n. 25. Hall summarizes his early position in his reply to Jessop et al., op. cit., n. 58, p. 116.

67 id. Described by Hall as a 'pragmatic and creeping authoritarianism': see Jessop et al., op. cit., n. 58, p. 35.

68 Jessop et al., op. cit., n. 58, p. 40.

69 id., p. 50.

The Privatization of Industry in Historical Perspective

The sale of state-owned industrial assets by the Thatcher Government promises to be the most radical restructuring of British industry at least since 1951. About £13 billion had been raised by the end of 1987 with an average of £5 billion a year until 1990 planned from the future sale of the water and electricity industries. The great public utilities of gas and telecommunications have been returned to the private sector and even industries which have made losses for decades – coal and railways – look as if they may become candidates for privatization.

How fundamental the Thatcher Government's privatization policy is may be appreciated by noting that state ownership of industrial assets has been advancing from mid-Victorian times. It is true that the nationalizations of the 1945-51 Labour Governments marked a quantum jump in the process, but the subsequent Conservative Governments accepted the changes, with the exceptions of road haulage and iron and steel. Having been elected with a doctrine of rolling back the frontiers of the state, the Heath Government of 1970-4 left office with a larger portfolio of state industrial assets than that with which it had begun. In this perspective the Thatcher Government's reversal of the process by privatization appears a thoroughly reformist policy.

The purpose of this essay is to offer an explanation for and an evaluation of the previous trend and for the reversal after 1979. Three broad possibilities offer themselves. First, the long-term tendency was based on errors that were only fully appreciated after 1979; secondly, privatization is a mistaken policy that neglects the lessons of history; and thirdly, the underlying conditions that had warranted state ownership had changed by the beginning of the 1980s and new policies were therefore justified.

In a nutshell, the first option most closely accords with the evidence. The explanation for the long-term trend in the nineteenth century is that there were genuine problems with the performance of certain industries, especially with gas, water, telegraphs, and railways. Competition did not seem to work and, in the absence of controls, private monopoly appeared to provide unsatisfactory levels of service at excessive prices. When controls were imposed, other forms of inefficiency emerged. Municipalization was an effective short-term solution

Department of Economic and Social History, School of Economic and European Studies, University of Hull, Hull, Humberside HU6 7RX, England.

for industries which only required local networks (gas, water). It was no answer for industries which required national networks (telegraphs, railways). In both cases the long-term effects of state ownership before 1914 were probably harmful; the statutory monopolies which local and national governments acquired held back the development of new industries (electricity supply and telephones). Regulation of privately-owned monopoly industry was not obviously more successful. In the four decades before the outbreak of the First World War, the railways maintained an uncoordinated structure – the legacy of competition – without the vitality of the early competitive industry.

Contrary to their general reputation, the years between the world wars were a creative period in innovative and effective industrial organization. The railways were at last restructured before being returned to private ownership after their war service, a national electricity grid was managed by the government-established Central Electricity Board which should be a model for the Thatcherite electricity industry, and the British Broadcasting Corporation (BBC) met with the sort of acclaim that nationalized industries had not received since the adulation of the Post Office in the 1860s. Even the curbs upon bus competition had their positive aspects, as bus users nowadays are coming to appreciate. In general, mounting pressure for state ownership, as a solution to unemployment or to improve the distribution of income, was resisted on efficiency grounds.

The hurried nationalizations of 1945-51 established a framework for the public corporation which proved inadequate. Nationalized industry performance since the early 1950s continued to meet with a great deal of criticism, despite three White Papers.[1] Apart from this general background which predisposed the Conservative Party to reforming the nationalized industries in some way, there are three principal explanations for the turning point in policy. The first explanation is the changed attitude to unemployment; secondly, there is a related commitment to the Public Sector Borrowing Requirement and the contribution to its reduction which assets sales could make; and the third explanation is the probable desire to constrain union power which was at its strongest in the public sector. Additional attractions of the policy were that privatization could be represented as a means of regenerating British industry and creating a more stable share-holding democracy.

The timing of the policy shift can be traced to the coincidence of high unemployment and inflation during the mid 1970s which broke confidence in traditional Keynesian macro-economic solutions. Tighter budgetary controls and monetary targets were, in effect, enforced by the International Monetary Fund in 1976 through the Letter of Intent that the Chancellor of the Exchequer was obliged to write. These controls and targets precluded the generous subsidies which the nationalized industries had come to require. Thatcher then inherited a budgetary discipline which Heath mistakenly thought he could avoid by floating the exchange rate in 1972.

Much more consideration and experience underlies the privatizations that are terminating state enterprises than went into the organization of the nationalized industries of 1945-51. The performance of privatized industry, on a commercial definition, may be expected to improve both for that reason and because the goals of the new enterprises are simpler, being primarily financial. Whether the industries will be able to avoid the problems that originally gave rise to their acquisition by the state depends largely upon the new regulatory institutions and rules established since 1983. These are genuine innovations and generally mark an advance on the achievements of the Victorians or those of the inter-war period. That is why the second option for evaluating nationalization and privatization over the last century and a half may probably be rejected.

Technology has changed, but in some industries the scope for competition has been improved by reductions in minimum efficient size (for example, the impact of microwave transmission in telecommunications); in other industries the minimum efficient size has increased (such as the need for a national gas distribution network). The railways no longer have a monopoly on long-distance land transport but a national grid, which can be an industry entry barrier, has become necessary for electricity. On average, neither the need for supervision of competition nor the scale of the enterprise which would have to be nationalized, if that were judged preferable to regulation, has diminished. The third option mentioned above as a possible explanation for the shifts of industry between the private and the public sector may therefore be eliminated.

VICTORIAN STATE ENTERPRISE AND INDUSTRIAL REGULATION

A simplistic explanation for the trend in state ownership before 1979 would appeal to socialist ideology, in particular to clause 4 (section 4) of the Labour Party's constitution and to the party's electoral strength or weakness. In a historical perspective this response is clearly inadequate since the movement for the state ownership of industry began before the foundation of the Labour Party. More fundamental and longer-term forces than the political colour of particular governments have been at work, both to increase state ownership since mid-Victorian days and to reconfigure political opportunities by the time that Thatcher came to power.

Before the industrial revolution, state ownership of industrial assets was miniscule because industrial assets in total were small. The scale of the production units was also typically small; perhaps the largest were the government dockyards. None the less, the state aimed to exercise a pervasive influence on the economy through the regulation of wages and certain prices such as freight rates.[2] A distinctive device for raising revenue and securing government objectives was the granting of statutory monopolies to private sector enterprises, the best known of which was the East India Company. In practice, communications were so poor and the costs of enforcement so high relative to the available resources that there was considerable flexibility in the regulated economy. New enterprises could be set up away from long-established centres of population where traditional controls were imposed by both governments and unions. That was the pattern of the transformation of industrial activity in the first half of the nineteenth century.

Some state industry continued in an unreformed style. Mid-Victorian management of supplies to the armed forces were a byword for inefficiency. Ten or twelve tons of soldiers' buttons never taken from their wrappers could be disposed of as scrap metal.[3] Having sold Her Majesty's Ship *The Medway* in Burma, the Government then paid the buyer for the spare stores on the vessel a sum double the purchase price of the ship.[4] Other state industry was revolutionized. The Post Office had been operated as a state monopoly with the right to tax postal users for the benefit of state revenue. Rowland Hill's 1840 reform abandoned this principle in favour of the provision of a public service.[5] The success, in terms of volume if not of revenue, of the 1840 price cut ultimately owed a great deal to the private railway service which markedly speeded up deliveries. As far as the public were concerned, though, by the 1860s the Post Office was a successful example of state enterprise which showed the private enterprise telegraph system in a poor light.

From the mid century the number of telegrams sent soared but two decades later it was still dwarfed by the volume of letters. Although prices fell whenever a new firm entered the industry, commercial users continued to make adverse comparisons with certain state-owned continental telegraph administrations, complaining of high tariffs, duplication of offices, and poor service.[6] When industry entry occurred, competition was intense. The incumbent telegraph company persuaded the Admiralty to pull up a rival's cable across the English Channel and itself paid men to dismantle a competitor's land lines.[7] This type of competition was hardly in the public interest.

In the far larger railway industry the optimality of competition between private firms was also questioned. Nobody contested that the companies had rapidly extended the new transport facility across the country. What was debated was whether rates were as low as they could be and whether services between competitors were adequately co-ordinated.[8]

The Railway Act 1844 dealt with these concerns both by introducing a form of service and fare regulation, 'the Parliamentary train', and by a provision under which any new railways built after 1844 could be compulsorily purchased by the state at any time beyond twenty-five years after they had been established. Railways were a form of industry which was so different from anything that had gone before that new measures were needed. Gladstone and the Board of Trade had doubts as to whether 'arms' length' regulation in the Railway Act 1844 would provide a permanent solution, and therefore wished to leave open the option of direct state control through ownership.

Among the defining experiences of the industrial revolution, rapid and intensive urbanization was prominent. Adequate water supplies became essential if the new agglomerations were not to become hotbeds of disease or

132

to be ravaged by fire. When particularly disastrous fires or epidemics did break out, the private water companies were blamed. Only six of the fifty private water companies provided adequate supplies in the 1840s according to the Select Committee on the Health of Towns, a finding which subsequent cholera outbreaks seemed to support.[9] Newcastle's first cholera deaths in the 1853-4 epidemic occurred well ahead of London's. According to the Cholera Commission this was most probably because of malpractice by the local water company. Despite having been set up to provide a source of water independent of the polluted Tyne, the company had supplied contaminated water from the river. Neighbouring Tynemouth, which did not use Tyne water, escaped the epidemic. Twenty years after, Newcastle's high death rate and poor sanitary conditions were still being blamed on the deficiency and poor quality of the company's water.[10]

Everywhere in the country fires were not brought under control quickly because of a lack of water. In the first half of the nineteenth century a two-hour wait for the water to be turned on was not unusual. Under these conditions a fire in a crowded industrial town could be disastrous. 800 homes were destroyed and fifty-three people killed in the Newcastle fire of 1854.[11] In most towns disease and fire risk gave an impetus to municipalization. The Newcastle and Gateshead Water Company was more politically astute than most and, by appointing a number of councillors to the board of directors, managed to hold off state ownership until the present day.

A similar evolution was experienced by the gas industry, although a higher proportion of Victorian gas companies became regulated local monopolies rather than state enterprises. In the early days where competition was strong, as in London, four or five sets of gas mains could pass under one street. Allegedly this replication both encouraged the neglect of apparatus, low gas pressure, and the inaccuracy of meters, and enhanced the risk of escaping gas and the incidence of serious accidents.[12] By the mid century when competition had largely disappeared, general maximum prices and dividend provision for gas companies was introduced by central government legislation. More sophisticated regulation was inaugurated in 1875 with a sliding scale according to which the dividend had to be reduced if prices were raised.[13] This may have reduced the extent of municipalization but it did not prevent the spread of local state ownership.

In gas and water supply, unit costs fell as the scale of operations increased.[14] The distribution networks that gave rise to this characteristic were only local. The organizational choice was therefore between a regulated local private monopoly or a municipally owned enterprise.

In telecommunications and railways, national networks were involved so that organization of necessity was large, and state ownership had to be central government ownership. During the public debate in the later 1860s, linked with the deliberations of the Royal Commission on Railways of 1866, the state declined to assume ownership of the railways under the terms of the Railway Act 1844. That the railway interest was well represented in Parliament was no doubt a contributory factor, but the sheer size of the undertaking made the nationalization of the railways a daunting prospect. Instead, increasingly close regulation of services, tariffs, and working conditions were imposed. This particularly British solution seems to have been responsible for the continuing extremely high capital costs of British railways relative to those of other countries; it failed to rationalize the structure that had emerged under competition, instead freezing an arrangement that a freer market might eventually have reorganized.[15]

By contrast the Victorian state acquired the entire private telecommunications network in 1870 and conferred upon itself a statutory monopoly. This last was necessary because business groups, such as the Edinburgh Chamber of Commerce, wanted and achieved a uniform tariff regardless of the distance or the route along which a message was sent, as the Post Office offered. Since the costs of transmission were not uniform, this pricing policy would, in the absence of statutory entry barriers, have encouraged private enterprise to offer services only on profitable routes. The Post Office service there would have been undercut and the Post Office would have lost the source of the subsidy for the unprofitable routes. A particular attraction of this nationalization was the possibility of using post offices as telegraph stations at no extra cost. Surprisingly, no consideration was given to the Post Office reaching an agreement with private telegraph companies to operate such an arrangement, as the telegraph companies had with the railways. Apparently even the Victorian state took but did not give away.

The experience of the telegraph system after the 1870 transfer to the state was a precursor of the nationalization process after 1945. The service was extended into unprofitable areas, tariffs were reduced in response to political pressure, and wages were rapidly raised. Soon the postal service was subsidizing a greatly expanded telegraph system for no obvious good social reason.[16] When a comparison is made with the alternative organization – the private regulated Victorian monopoly – the superiority of either is debatable. Productivity growth on the regulated railways slowed down both in comparison with the earlier period and with contemporary performance in the United States of America.[17] At the local level, matters seemed more satisfactory. The cost efficiency of private and municipal gas companies was similar.[18] That is to say, companies under different ownership and facing similar economic environments would supply a similar output at a similar cost. The advantage of the municipal enterprise then was that it would be unlikely to exploit customers by raising prices as much as would a profit-oriented private firm.

The Victorians had identified the problem of natural monopoly that their technology had produced and the wider repercussions of inadequate service in industries such as water. They experimented with a number of organizational responses which included local and national state ownership and the regulation of services and prices of privately owned companies. State ownership at the local level seemed satisfactory but subsequent experience, discussed below, showed there were serious adverse long-term consequences. In any case, for services that required a national network municipalization was impossible, while the other possibilities had considerable drawbacks.

THE SECOND INDUSTRIAL REVOLUTION AND THE CENTURY OF TOTAL WAR

Victorian technical progress had augmented the minimum efficient size of the firm and created the problems identified above. The next wave of technology, based on electricity and the internal combustion engine, diminished the problem in some respects and increased it in others. The internal combustion engine ultimately provided the means of eroding the railways' monopoly but electrical developments required a national unitary organization for electricity supply. The new technology also revealed a further difficulty with the Victorian solutions to the natural monopoly problem. Both the British electricity supply and the telephone service ran into barriers created by the first wave of state ownership, statutory monopoly. In both cases the state had acquired monopoly rights over earlier related technologies and was therefore able to constrain the development of the newer services.

Anxious to avoid losing revenue from their gas companies, local authorities limited the expansion of private electricity companies.[19] Conservative and Liberal Governments during the 1880s prescribed that electricity franchises should revert to the local authority after a fixed term. Local authorities which chose to operate their own electricity stations were restricted to supplying their own administrative area. As the technology advanced, these quickly became too small to support generating stations which would supply electricity at the minimum possible cost. Electricity prices were therefore considerably higher than those of Germany and the United States of America, and the use of the related technology consequently spread more slowly.

At national government level similar constraints were placed upon the telephone by virtue of the statutory telegraph monopoly. Telephone companies were first restricted to a radius of five miles so that the telegraph would not lose long-distance traffic. Continual public complaints about the quality and price of the service led the Post Office to relax controls and then to tighten them. Municipal telephony was tried and failed with one notable exception, the Hull network founded in 1904. First the privately owned trunk lines were nationalized in 1895 and then the entire system was acquired in 1912.[20] Telephone usage remained low in relation to the level of economic development. The government department was not a suitable form for an organization that had to undertake large long-term investments.[21] Although an attempt was made to remedy some of the deficiencies after the First World War, the difference was hardly perceptible.

By 1907, substantial portions of gas, water, and electricity were owned by the state, along with most of the telecommunications networks, the postal service, and the naval dockyards; but the proportion of total employment in state industry was still small, at about 7.4 per cent (see Table 1). Adding in the tightly regulated railway sector would roughly double the numbers employed in the state-regulated sector, but the overall size is still not great. More important for understanding the post-1945 acquisitions is the recognition that only the Post Office was a giant corporation in terms of the numbers employed in a single organization. In comparison with the Americans or Germans, throughout the twentieth century the British remained weak in designing large-scale industrial companies, whoever owned them.[22]

TABLE 1. State Employment and Output in the Census of Production Industries 1907

	Employment	Gross Output	Net Output	Percentage of industry net output
Government Shipbuilding (incl. dockyards and lighthouses)	25,580	6.46	2.49	
Royal Ordnance	14,533	3.36	1.45	
Naval Ordnance	1,118	.083	.077	
Miscellaneous (Army Clothing Factory, Army Bakeries, etc)	2,329	.51	.18	
H.M. Telegraph and Telephone	10,171	2.87	n.a.	
H.M. Post	202,193*	18.7 **	n.a.	
H.M. Office of Works	5,668	.63	n.a.	
Local Authority (Building)	185,286	20.02	n.a.	
Gas (local authority)	28,574	10.77	5.73	33
Water (local authority)	17,389	8.46	7.35	81
Electricity (local authority)	14,119	5.73	3.59	64
Trams and Light Railways (local authority)	12,434	1.74	n.a.	57+ (73)
Total	519,394	79.33		
TOTAL NATIONAL	6,984,976	1765	712	
State percentage of the total	7.4	4.5	—	

* 1910 total for post and state telecom minus 1907 state telecom employment. **1910.
+ proportion of gross output, ( )indicates proportion of employment. Values in £ million.
(Source: *Census of Production 1907, 56th Report of the Post Master General 1910*, P.P 1910.45)

Strategic or defence considerations were a new element in state ownership of industry in the twentieth century. Churchill's purchase on behalf of the British Government of British Petroleum shares in 1914 was intended to assure the continuity of oil supplies after the Royal Navy's conversion from coal fuel.[23] Four major air companies were amalgamated under government sponsorship in 1924 into the subsidized Imperial Airways because of the role for air power demonstrated during the First World War.[24] Eleven years later British Airways was formed and also received a subsidy for the same reason. Under the identity of the British Overseas Airways Corporation, the two companies were nationalized in 1939. Largely with government financial support, British Dyestuffs Corporation had been established in 1918 because of the British weakness, revealed by the war, in this technology related to explosives.

136

Direct state control of transport and industrial facilities during the war imposed a new responsibility upon government for post-war restructuring especially in the coal mines and railways. Nationalization was considered and rejected as irrelevant.[25] The railways, reorganized into much larger regional monopoly groups, were returned to the private sector. In 1938, after great industrial conflict, coal royalties were nationalized with a view to facilitating the rationalization of an industry still operated by private enterprise.

In general, the inter-war years were notable for a refusal to accede to pressure for state ownership. The iron and steel industry was granted tariff protection on the condition that it rationalize itself and improve efficiency. The instrument of this reorganization, the Iron and Steel Federation, was founded in 1934.[26] The view that competition was not an unambiguous good similarly did not commit the government to state ownership in road transport but led instead to regulation and entry barriers. Competition between private bus operators often involved racing between bus stops which was unsafe and ultimately inconvenient to users.[27] Entry to this industry and to a lesser extent to freight road haulage was therefore limited in 1930. Three years later the London Passenger Transport Board became the largest public corporate employer.

In newer industries, state corporations – the Central Electricity Board and the British Broadcasting Corporation (BBC) – were rather effective during the inter-war years. Established in 1926 to build and administer the national grid, the Central Electricity Board was intended to rectify the deficiencies of the nineteenth-century industry by co-ordinating and selecting the most efficient generating stations, whether they were private or public. A measure of the board's success was that, whereas outside the national grid suppliers the municipal power stations were less efficient than comparable private stations, those municipal generators chosen to supply the grid were as efficient as private suppliers.[28] The statutory monopoly conferred on the BBC in 1922 was justified by the limited bandwidth available for broadcasting and for cultural and educational reasons.[29] The substantial independence from government of the BBC probably contributed to the greater impact upon society than the output or employment might suggest.

Equally interesting was the institutional response to beam wireless international communications. Wireless competition with the state-owned Pacific Cable ultimately led to a reduction of British government-controlled industrial assets, albeit under pressure from other governments of the British Empire. To pre-empt possible nationalization proposals by an imperial conference in 1928, Marconi and the Eastern Telegraph companies merged their respective competing wireless and cable interests in a company, formed in 1929, which also bought state-owned cables and leased the British Post Office beam stations. In exchange for shares in Cable and Wireless, the British Government transferred the freehold of these stations to the company in 1938.[30]

From 1906 the Labour Party had been presenting nationalization Bills in Parliament and in 1918 adopted the policy of nationalization in clause 4 of the party constitution. Clause 4 seeks an equitable distribution of income through state ownership. During the inter-war years, Labour only formed a majority government in 1929-31, which was not an auspicious time for nationalization, given the economic views of the day. Had electoral fortunes been different, more state ownership might have been expected in these years on income distributional grounds – a new motive in historical terms. Even without a full term of office for a Labour government, by the outbreak of the Second World War state influence over industry had become greater than before the First World War. State ownership of assets had not increased proportionately but, driven by technology and defence, had expanded none the less.

Technological progress made the Second World War far more capital-intensive than the First World War had been. A much greater industrial mobilization was necessary, with more detailed – but not invariably more effective – state control over industry.[31] In comparison with civilian production the problems of the war economy are simple. The state decides what has to be produced in order to win the war and commandeers the required resources. Mistakes can be made but the problem is essentially technological; how best to use the national resources to achieve a single end. Peace-time production lacks this simplicity, for no single body can determine what goods and services people would select, given a free choice and their fixed money incomes. The outputs are potentially much more varied and so are the production processes. Mistakes in resource use by a war economy based on physical planning with inadequate information are unlikely to surface, since they will be judged prejudicial to state security.

The upshot is that the war-time experience of physical planning tended to create an administrative hubris that carried over to the peace time. There was a widespread belief that large units were more efficient than small ones.[32] Because of the monopoly problem, the policy issue was whether the units would be directly controlled through state ownership or whether some form of indirect control through regulation was preferable. A landslide majority for the Labour Party in 1945 provided further ideological support for nationalization, buttressed by the voting power within the Trades Union Congress of the coal, railway, and transport unions.

Little thought had been given to the reorganization of large-scale nationalized industries or to their management. When he assumed ministerial office, Emanuel Shinwell was amazed at the absence of any plan for nationalization which he could follow.[33] Nationalization meant different things to different groups, and the resulting organization reflected this. The absence of discussion about practicalities allowed the consensus to be maintained. Nationalization was seen as a means of financing investment for reconstruction from war damage. It was to be a means of 'co-ordinating' the transport and energy industries, a term which to railway workers meant reducing job losses from road transport competition.

The 'Morrisonian' corporations were statutory monopolies with the Government as their sole shareholder and sole banker.[34] Boards of nationalized industries were responsible to Parliament for the overall financial position and government ministers had powers to control investment and borrowing. Precisely what goals these corporations were supposed to achieve was only partly clarified in the ensuing two decades and, even then, government policy often diverted corporations from these objectives. Nationalized industries were instructed at least to break even 'taking one year with another' and they were to be operated 'in the public interest'.[35]

The upward leap in the size of the state sector as a result of this burst of nationalization may be seen by comparing the 1907 totals in Table 1 with those of Table 2. About two million workers (or more than ten per cent of total employment in 1951) were added to the public sector. The largest of the new units, such as the National Coal Board or the British Transport Commission, employed more than three times as many workers as the Post Office. Dissatisfaction with the Morrisonian framework was expressed in parliamentary debates and in questions in the House of Commons during the 1950s. Economists noted the irrationality of the arrangements for national resource

TABLE 2. The Principal Nationalizations 1940–51

	Vesting date	Approximate figure for total employees 1950
The British Overseas Airways Corporation (BOAC)	1 Apr. 1940	16,000
The British European Airways Corporation (BEAC)	1 Aug. 1946	7,000
The National Coal Board (NCB)	1 Jan. 1947	730,000*
The British Transport Commission	1 Jan. 1948	890,000
The British Electricity Authority (BEA) and Area Electricity Boards	1 Apr. 1948	170,000
The Area Gas Boards and the British Gas Council	1 May 1949	140,000
The Iron and Steel Corporation of Great Britain	15 Feb. 1951	235,000 (Nov. 1951)

* Excluding workers in ancillary activities.

(Source: H.A. Clegg, 'The Nationalized Industries' in *The British Economy 1945–1950*, eds. G.D.N. Worswick and D.H. Adys (1952))

allocation and governments were concerned about the large losses made in the early years by the National Coal Board and the British Transport Commission. Financing new investment in nationalized industries was liable to interfere with the Exchequer's national debt operations. These concerns culminated in the 1961 White Paper which drew up rate of return on net asset objectives for most industries. Borrowing requirements continued to rise; the 1964 Labour Government therefore initiated a series of discussions and studies which generated another White Paper in 1967. The principles of a test discount rate on new investment and marginal cost pricing were introduced. Partly because of the practical difficulties of identifying marginal costs, the pricing policy was generally neglected. In addition, government prices and incomes policies required delays in price increases in 1966-7 and, because of price restraint, many nationalized industries accumulated large deficits from 1970-3.[36]

Policies of rolling back the frontiers of state intervention were at first embraced by the Heath Government of 1970-4. Rhodes Boyson MP, later a junior minister in the Thatcher Government, edited in 1971 a volume devoted to the failure of state industries and the need to return them to a competitive framework.[37] Rising unemployment and bankruptcies quickly diverted the Heath Government's attention from its original policies. Instead, a Keynesian remedy of expansion and a floating exchange rate was tried. Shipbuilding, aerospace, and the motor industry all provided unexpected entrants to the state sector as British manufacturing declined in the 1970s. The trend was accelerated by the next Labour Government which entirely nationalized aerospace, shipbuilding, and iron and steel, and set up the British National Oil Corporation as a means of monitoring and controlling the development of the North Sea oil fields.

Despite this ambitious programme the administrative and organizational principles of nationalized industries remained basically unchanged. The 1976 report of the National Economic Development Office on the nationalized industries contrasted the failings of the United Kingdom's nationalized industry organized on the 'arm's length' philosophy with the relative success of France, the Federal Republic of Germany, and Sweden, where information was exchanged more frequently and at a number of levels.[38] The 1978 White Paper replaced the test discount rate for individual projects with a five per cent rate of return for investment programmes as a whole. Each industry was also required to publish performance indicators such as productivity and unit cost indices. The Labour Government did produce an organizational innovation in the form of the National Enterprise Board which held shares in a considerable number of companies, including International Computers, with a view to compensating for what some saw as the inadequacies of the capital market for risky projects. This approach to industrial policy was quickly discarded in the Thatcher Revolution after 1979.

THE THATCHER REVOLUTION

Privatization of state industries was not mentioned by the Thatcher parliamentary opposition in its first policy statement published in 1976 and entitled *The Right Approach*. The 1979 General Election manifesto emphasized the party's opposition to more nationalization – a traditional Conservative theme – and the intention to return aerospace and shipbuilding to the private sector. This was no more radical than the treatment of the steel and road haulage industries during the 1950s, but the announced willingness to sell shares in the National Freight Corporation might have been taken as a harbinger of more far-reaching policies. The tide had fully turned by 1983. Reform of the nationalized industries was central to economic recovery, according to the manifesto of that year. The Thatcher Government asserted that transferring industries to private ownership enhanced their alertness. More would be transferred, therefore, and they would be exposed to real competition. Only 'substantial parts' of British Steel were to be returned to the private sector. Water and railways were not mentioned at all, while gas (ironically) and electricity were considered candidates for the introduction of competition rather than privatization.[39]

As these policy statements imply, during the Thatcher Government's first term only those relatively small companies were sold which operated in competitive markets. After 1983 new regulatory institutions and rules were established and the really big sell-offs of British Telecom and British Gas took place (see Table 3). That privatization policy was only formed slowly is shown by the two Telecommunications Acts of 1981 and 1984. The first partly liberalized the market, the second privatized and introduced competition in basic telephone service. Only in 1986, with the White Paper on water privatization, were all the Government's objectives for privatization fully stated.[40]

TABLE 3. Major Public Asset Sales 1979–88

Company	Date of Sale	Net Proceeds (£ million)
British Petroleum (BP)	1979, 1983, 1987	290*, 565*, 7,200
British Aerospace	1981, 1985	43, 346
Cable and Wireless	1981, 1983, 1985	182, 263, 600
Britoil	1982, 1985	627, 425
Enterprise Oil	1984	380
Jaguar	1984	297
British Telecom (BT)	1984	3,916
British Gas	1986	2,546
Trustee Savings Bank (TSB)	1986	1,360*
British Airways	1987	900*
British Technology Group /National Enterprise Board (sale of shareholdings)	1984-7	306
British Airports Authority	1987	1,281*
Rolls Royce	1987	1,360*
Rover	1988	− 397***
British Steel	1988	12,000*

* = gross proceeds. TSB and Jaguar proceeds retained by the organization and not the Government.
** = gross proceeds. Bank of England buy back scheme reduced net proceeds.
*** = government aid of £547 million minus £150 million purchase price.
(Sources: C. Veljanovski, *Selling the State* (1987); J. Vickers and G. Yarrow, *Privatization; An Economic Analysis* (1988); *Financial Times*, 26 November 1988; *Independent*, 15 July 1988; H. M. Treasury, *The Government's Expenditure Plans 1988-9 to 1990-1* (1988; Cm. 288) 56.)

From the Government's viewpoint a great attraction of privatization was that it allowed the Public Sector Borrowing Requirement target to be fulfilled without imposing the stringency that would otherwise be required. Price stability was a major goal of the Thatcher Government and the Public Sector Borrowing Requirement was the chief plank in the monetary strategy to achieve this end. Any wavering would have sent the wrong signals to the markets. Yet it soon became clear that the target was inappropriate and excessively deflationary. Selling nationalized industry assets actually has the same monetary consequences as government borrowing by selling bonds. The Public Sector Borrowing Requirement target conflated current account spending with capital.

The monetarist doctrines underlying the target provided the theoretical backing which was at the centre of the policy shift on state ownership. Once it was accepted that there was a natural rate of unemployment which the state could only reduce by improving the working of the market, the Government was able to absolve itself from responsibility for job losses from commercializing state enterprises or from refusing to bail out failing large private sector employers. Of course, the ideological change did not occur in a vacuum. The experience of macroeconomic 'fine-tuning' in the 1950s and 1960s, culminating in the 'stagflation' of the 1970s, provided the background, as Callaghan's conversion from Keynesianism showed.[41] Deteriorating British economic performance prepared the ground for the policy shift on privatization as it did on monetarism.

Dissatisfaction with the great state corporations was an equally significant contributory cause. Increasing financial demands of nationalized industry made privatization look more attractive, first when the International Monetary Fund imposed limits on domestic credit expansion in 1976, and subsequently when similar monetary targets were adopted by the Thatcher Government. Keith Joseph MP, who was particularly close to Mrs Thatcher, was impressed by telecommunications liberalization in the United States of America. He was also anxious to break what he saw as the unions' hold on the national 'jugular vein', the telecommunications network. During the process of trying to reform British telecommunications, the difficulties of finding an institutional arrangement by which the state industry could raise capital without a Treasury guarantee eventually pushed the Government into considering the sale of the entire telecommunications organization. With this enormous flotation successfully completed, there was little reason why other utilities should not go the same way.

Governments are not always able to implement their chosen policies. Their ability to do so often depends upon the support or acquiescence of influential lobbies. So it was with privatization. Top nationalized industry management had privileged access to specialized information essential for successful privatization.[42] Their resistance could at least have proved embarrassing for the Government. So long as the policy did not involve a break-up of the industry (and an appeal could be made to natural monopoly arguments which are borne out by Victorian industrial experience), freedom from changing and arbitrary government restrictions on pricing and investment was a pleasing prospect for top management. Employment legislation, high unemployment, and the perception that times were going to be lean in state industries (reinforced by Monopolies and Mergers Commission investigations from 1980) altered the relative advantage of the private sector. Even so, trade union pressure would have caused a reversal of the policy had Labour been elected in 1987.[43]

Competition was clearly not a major interest of the Government in the massive sale of British Telecom and British Gas. If it had been, the corporations would have been broken up before sale. Public concern about their monopoly power delayed electricity privatization until a proposal to divide the Central Electricity Generating Board had been formulated. Some unease about the lack of competition and the abuse of monopoly power was demonstrated by the creation of industry-specific regulatory bodies, beginning with the Office of Telecommunications (Oftel), but their formal powers have been weak.[44] Even Oftel, which has greater authority than the Office of Gas Supply (Ofgas), has had to rely on publicity, moral suasion, and the personality of the Director General rather than on formal proceedings to ensure fair competition.[45] In part, this limitation was intended to avoid the expensive, legalistic, and cumbrous regulatory system used in the United States of America; this system was being called into question at the same time as the privatization policy was begun. The conservative movement in economics and ideology maintained that competition was a natural state of affairs in the long run, so long as governments did not obstruct it.[46]

Had the Government broken up British Telecom and British Gas, monopoly power and profits could have been reduced but so too would the sales value of the companies. Competition and revenue were at odds. Only profitable enterprises could be sold without government subsidy, yet the state industrial portfolio largely consisted of three types of assets, for each of which profitability raised different problems. The three groups were: (i) natural monopolies which could increase profitability by exploiting consumers; (ii) large companies that had failed the market test yet had strategic or employment value; (iii) organizations whose activities were not all clearly marketable despite being socially valuable.

The earlier Victorian state acquisitions, reversed during the Thatcher Government's second term in 1983-7, fell into the first group. In gas, water, telecommunications, electricity, and railways, unregulated competition between companies was inefficient or had proved unsustainable. Private monopoly was likely to be more interested in profits than in the well-being of the consumer, and therefore some regulation had to be imposed. For smaller units the restrictions were imposed through state ownership. Larger enterprises remained in private hands but subject to controls. These are the industries which will test the effectiveness of the new regulatory institutions. Public complaints about the service provided by the flagship of privatization, British Telecom, at the very least indicate that the regulators will have a demanding job.[47]

In the second category falls British Leyland, now called Rover. Such companies had been turned round under state management, or their profitable components had been hived off and sold separately – as with Jaguar

– or the return to profitability and the associated job losses were left to the new and subsidized owner. British Aerospace was charged £150 million in 1988 for the purchase of Rover, to which was attached £547 million of state aid and the writing off of all but £100 million of the company's debt.[48] Moving Rover out of the public sector has proved expensive, but the Government no doubt believes that it is less costly in the long run than continuing support for the company. Here privatization makes the best of a bad financial job.

In the third group lies the water industry and possibly railways and coal. Ten water authorities in England and Wales will be sold in 1989. Their operations will be supervised by an Office of Water Supply analogous to Oftel and Ofgas. A National Rivers Authority will assume responsibility for flood protection, pollution control, and water resource planning. The costs of inadequate water regulation in 1853-4 show how important the tasks of these bodies will be. No competition is being introduced into the industry but emulation by independent boards may operate in much the same manner.

Railways and coal have been loss-making industries for many years – in part to ensure that the reduction of the labour forces had the least harmful effect upon employees and the regions, in part because of other alleged benefits to the economy which private enterprise would not or could not take into account, and in part because of the strength of the industry unions. Turning these industries into saleable properties requires that these reasons are no longer compelling, because either conditions or values have changed.

Privatization has paid scant regard to the wider social impact of industry, probably because the notion is a Pandora's Box. For many years the configuration of the telecommunications network was influenced by the desire not to allow any individual exchange to be too large in case it was eliminated by enemy action. With privatization this consideration ceases to be relevant to network design. Defence considerations have not generally bulked large, however. More importantly, state industry objectives have included the extension of service to as many customers as possible at the same price regardless of cost (the universal service obligation). Local employment has often been an even tighter short-term constraint upon state industry management, if not an objective.

Arguments can be advanced that private enterprise manages assets more efficiently than the state. If this were so, the market would be willing to pay more for them than they are worth to the state and everybody would gain from privatization. In fact efficiency improvements began under the stimulus of impending privatization and are largely attributable to the clarification and narrowing of enterprise objectives.[49] Experience with the Victorian telegraph industry suggests that the pressures on state enterprise in the long term would make this improved performance hard to sustain. Admittedly, the government department (for telecommunications) and the Morrisonian public corporation were perhaps especially vulnerable to political interference which other forms are possibly not.

What privatization has almost completely ignored is the income distribution motive for state ownership, enshrined in clause 4 of the Labour Party

144

constitution. The Thatcherite view is that what matters is the distribution between the state and private individuals or families, not the distribution between individuals. Neither nationalization nor privatization has made much difference here. Confiscation of privately-owned industrial assets would have produced a more equal interpersonal income distribution, but instead £2.6 billion was paid in compensation during the nationalizations in the period 1945-51. The 'gift' of privatized shares on an equal basis to taxpayers or voters would have created a more egalitarian income distribution as well as giving the population a stake in capitalist enterprise.[50] The need to window-dress the Public Sector Borrowing Requirement restricted the redistribution to special offers for buyers of small numbers of shares. This largesse did extend share ownership – adult shareholders trebled between 1979 and 1987 – but hardly influenced the pattern of wealth and income. In the state industries neither industrial subsidies nor prices failing to reflect costs have proved particularly effective means of influencing income distribution in a desirable direction. The impact of special prices is hard to predict or control; British Telecom's low user rebate, intended to help low income households, conferred the greatest benefit upon second home owners.

The most likely redistribution of income through state industries is in favour of groups with the greatest bargaining power. Customers of state-supported industries find prices below cost agreeable so long as the cost of the subsidy is spread among others as well. Workers and management appreciate higher wages partly financed by general taxation. Clearly the policy chosen depends upon the extent to which the government is representative of interests as a whole and how liable it is to be swayed by pressure groups. In turn, this is likely to depend upon the size of the unit of government. Large governments present more opportunity for the lobbyist than small ones, and representative municipal government is less prone to subsidize local industries than national government.

In comparison with the nationalizations of 1945-51, the big privatizations have been relatively slow and considered. This means that the organizers of successive flotations will be able to benefit from the experience of previous privatizations. The effect can already be seen in the reductions in the speculative gains made from new issues.[51] The potential variety of arrangements will offer yardsticks for individual industries which the pervasive Morrisonian corporate form did not. Even if efficiency does not improve faster than in the best periods of the old regime, reduced government interference with management or with related activities that impinge upon statutory monopolies can be expected to raise the average pace of productivity growth. Then the question remains as to whether the abandonment of the social and employment objectives of the Morrisonian corporations more than offsets such gains. Even if the relevant magnitudes were known, which they are not, valuations placed upon them will differ and render a final judgement controversial.

CONCLUSION

Although technology has greatly changed since mid-Victorian times, the characteristics (principally high fixed costs) that make for difficulties in sustaining competition have become if anything more pervasive in industry. The remarkable policy shift on industrial ownership since 1979 cannot be explained in these terms. The key is rising nationalized industry costs meeting greater financial stringency and ideological change that breaks with the political consensus of the long post-war boom.

The vague directives and constraints to which the post-1945 public corporations were subject inevitably encouraged inefficiency when judged by market criteria. They may well have limited the attainment of any major objectives at all; labour relations were not transformed as the architects of the nationalized industries had hoped. As faith in the ability of governments to influence the level of employment waned in the 'stagflation' of the 1970s so the scope for industrial reform which cost jobs was enhanced. Monetarist policies favoured reducing the Public Sector Borrowing Requirement by selling state assets even though with a more consistent target they would not have done so. Success required more than one period of office, for a Labour Government would have reversed the early moves. The 'Falklands factor', by which Mrs Thatcher swung back into popular favour, proved an essential ingredient for the fulfilment of a long-term privatization programme.

Inspection of the evidence of industrial regulation before 1914 offers an indication of the likely success, in its own terms, of the new regime. On the one hand, there were planning benefits from unitary control in certain industries in which distribution networks were crucial. A private monopolist could not be left in charge of such an industry untrammelled by a concern for consumer well-being. Establishing suitable rules and procedures for enforcement proved difficult and therefore 'internalizing' regulation by bringing the regulators and the regulated into one body – the state industry – was an obvious solution. On the other hand, state industry was not necessarily efficient; there could be upward political pressure on wages and downward pressure on prices at least at the national level, causing deficits or reductions in service. The statutory monopoly that invariably accompanied state ownership tended to retard subsequent technological progress, including the telephone and electricity supply. Private ownership with regulation – the Thatcher Goverment's approach – is therefore preferable on this count, which is of fundamental importance for economic development in the long term. Widespread and persistent complaints about the quality of service provided by privatized firms could ultimately call this conclusion into doubt and begin another cycle of transferring industrial assets between state and private hands.

NOTES AND REFERENCES

1 H.M. Treasury, *Financial and Economic Obligations of the Nationalized Industries* (1961; Cmnd. 1337); *Nationalized Industries: A Review of Economic and Financial Objectives* (1967; Cmnd. 3437); and *The Nationalized Industries* (1978; Cmnd. 7131).

2   D. C. Coleman, *The Economy of England 1450-1750* (1977) ch. 10.

3   W. S. Jevons, 'The Railways and the State' in *Essays and Addresses by Professors and Lecturers of the Owen's College Manchester* (1874) 475-6.

4   id.

5   M. J. Daunton, *Royal Mail: The Post Office Since 1840* (1985); Post Office, *The Post Office: An Historical Summary* (1911).

6   J. L. Kieve, *Electric Telegraph: A Social and Economic History* (1973); J. S. Foreman-Peck, 'Competition, Co-operation, and Nationalization in the Early Telegraph Network' (1989) 31 *Business History* (forthcoming).

7   Post Office, *Prospectus and Directors' Report of the United Kingdom Telegraph Company* (1861; Post Office Archives, Post 81/105); Submarine Telegraph Company, *Report of Committee of Enquiry, February 1861* (1861; Post Office Archives, Post 81/105).

8   J. S. Foreman-Peck, 'Natural Monopoly and Railway Policy in the Nineteenth Century' (1987) 39 *Oxford Economic Papers* 699.

9   British Parliamentary Papers, *Report from the Select Committee on the Health of Towns* (1840).

10 R. W. Rennison, *Water to Tyneside: A History of the Newcastle and Gateshead Water Company* (1978).

11 id.

12 R. Millward, 'The Emergence of Gas and Water Monopolies in Nineteenth Century Britain' in *Salford Discussion Papers in Economics* (1986).

13 Committee on Industry and Trade, *Survey of Industries* (1928) vol. 2, 304-333.

14 M. E. Falkus, 'The Development of Municipal Trading in the Nineteenth Century' (1977) 19 *Business History* 134.

15 Foreman-Peck, op. cit., n. 8.

16 Kieve, op. cit., n. 6.

17 G. R. Hawke, *Railways and Economic Growth in England and Wales 1840-1870* (1970) 302-3; A. Fishlow, 'Productivity and Technological Change in the Railroad Sector 1840-1910' in *Output, Employment, and Productivity in the United States after 1800*, ed. D. S. Brady (1966), *Studies in Income and Wealth*.

18 R. Millward and R. Ward, 'The Costs of Public and Private Gas Enterprises in Late Nineteenth Century Britain' (1987) 39 *Oxford Economic Papers* 719.

19 I. C. R. Byatt, *The British Electrical Industry 1875-1914* (1979) ch. 12; Committee on Industry and Trade, op. cit., n. 13.

20 The legislation covering nationalization was enacted in 1905.

21 J. Foreman-Peck, 'Competition and Performance in the UK Telecommunications Industry' (1985) 9 *Telecommunications Policy* 215; C. R. Perry, 'The British Experience 1876-1912: The Impact of the Telephone During the Years of Delay' in *The Social Impact of the Telephone*, ed. I. de Sola Pool (1977).

22 The British preferred trusts or holding companies to large integrated corporations. See L. Hannah, *The Rise of the Corporate Economy* (2nd ed. 1983).

23 M. Kent, *Oil and Empire: British Policy and Mesopotamian Oil 1900-20* (1976) 38-49.

24 H. J. Dyos and D. H. Aldcroft, *British Transport: An Economic Survey from the Seventeenth Century to the Twentieth* (1969) ch. 13.

25 The majority of the 1919 Sankey Commission on the coal industry recommended nationalization but was ignored by the Government. A select committee on the railways in 1918 reported in favour of unification of the railway system to utilize economies of co-ordination which war-time operation had demonstrated. Nationalization was one means of achieving this end, they noted.

26 D. Burn, *The Economic History of Steelmaking 1867-1939: A Study in Competition* (1940); K. Warren, 'Iron and Steel' in *British Industry Between the Wars: Instability and Industrial Development*, eds. N. K. Buxton and D. H. Aldcroft (1979).

27 S. Glaister and C. Mulley, *Public Control of the British Bus Industry* (1983) chs. 3 and 4.

28 J. Foreman-Peck and M. Waterson, 'The Comparative Efficiency of Public and Private Enterprise in Britain: Electricity Generation Between the World Wars' (1985) 95 *Economic J.* supplement, p. 83; L. Hannah, *Electricity Before Nationalization* (1979).

29 A. Briggs, *The BBC: The First Fifty Years* (1985). In 1922 the Postmaster General told the House of Commons: 'It would be impossible to have a large number of firms broadcasting. It would result only in the sort of chaos, only in a much more aggravated form than that which arises in the United States.' (id., p. 20).

30 E. Harcourt, *Taming the Tyrant: The First 100 Years of Australia's International Telecommunications Services* (1987) 219-38.

31 C. Barnett, *The Audit of War* (1986).

32 Sir N. Chester, *The Nationalization of British Industry 1945-51* (1975).

33 R. Kelf-Cohen, *Nationalization in Britain: The End of a Dogma* (1958) *vi*.

34 The term 'Morrisonian' and the description is from J. Vickers and G. Yarrow, *Privatization: An Economic Analysis* (1988).

35 National Economic Development Office, *A Study of Nationalized Industries* (1976) Appendix C; H. Clegg, 'The Nationalized Industries' in *The British Economy 1945-50*, eds. G. D. N. Worswick and D. H. Adys (1952).

36 K. Jones, 'Policy Towards the Nationalized Industries' in *British Economic Policy 1960-1974*, ed. F. T. Blackaby (1978).

37 R. Boyson (ed.), *Goodbye to Nationalization* (1971).

38 National Economic Development Office, *A Study of UK Nationalized Industries: Their Role in the Economy and Control in the Future* (1976).

39 Conservative Party, *The Right Approach* (1976), *The Conservative Party Manifesto 1979* (1979) 15, and *Our First Eight Years: The Conservative Manifesto 1983* (1983) 15.

40 Department of the Environment, *Privatization of Water Authorities in England and Wales* (1986; Cmnd. 9734).

41 M. Desai, *Testing Monetarism* (1981) 9.

42 Chick makes the point that this information problem has been a continuing influence upon policy for more than half a century: M. Chick, 'Privatization: The Triumph of Past Practice Over Current Requirements' (1987) 29 *Business History* 104.

43 Labour Party, *Social Ownership: Statement to the Labour Party Conference 1986* (1986).

44 C. Veljanovski, *Selling the State* (1987). On the economics of regulation see M. Waterson, *Regulation of the Firm and Natural Monopoly* (1988).

45 D. Heald, 'United Kingdom: The End of Nationalization, and Afterwards?' (1987; conference paper for the Politics of Privatization conference, Oxford, November 1987).

46 M. Friedman, *Capitalism and Freedom* (1962) ch. 8.

47 A regulator's response to these complaints is Office of Telecommunications, *Quality of Telecommunications Services* (1987).

48 'Crash on the Final Straight' *The Economist*, 16 July 1988; *Independent*, 15 July 1988.

49 Between 1979-80 and 1987 British Steel's productivity doubled; the Post Office reduced real unit costs by eleven per cent between 1981-2 and 1986-7; and productivity of the nationalized industry sector as a whole after 1979-80 exceeded that of the manufacturing sector. (See H. M. Treasury, *The Government's Expenditure Plans 1988-9 to 1990-1* (1988; Cm. 288))

50 S. Brittan, 'Privatization – A Comment: An Examination the Government Did Not Sit' (1986) 96 *Economic J.* 33.

51 Admittedly the 1987 stock market crash changed the rules of the game. In October the Government was obliged to introduce a scheme so that small buyers of BP shares did not make losses. The flotation of British Steel in December 1988 was dogged by poor trade figures on top of a sluggish stock market. The possibility of public speculative gains was therefore very small, and in fact the issue price was almost exactly right.